The Nottingham China Policy Institute Series

Series Editors
Shujie Yao
School of Contemporary Chinese Studies
University of Nottingham
Nottingham, UK

and

Chongqing University
Chongqing, China

Steve Tsang
School of Contemporary Chinese Studies
University of Nottingham
Nottingham, UK

"This is a comprehensive text on the evolution of Chinese banking industry with robust supportive empirical evidence on important issues, such as bank efficiency and competition, over nearly four decades. It also provides detailed elaboration on new developments in the post-crisis era such as shadow banking and internet finance. It is an excellent text for researchers, policy makers, and practitioners to gain insights into the largest banking system in the world".

—Iftekhar Hasan, *Professor of Finance and Corrigan Chair in International Business and Finance, Fordham University, US*

"I heartily endorse this text, which provides a comprehensive insight into developments in Chinese banking. The text includes chapters on banking sector performance, shadow banking, competition, Internet finance, in addition to key other issues. The text is a must for students and scholars wishing to obtain a contemporaneous insight into developments in Chinese banking".

—Philip Molyneux, *Professor of Banking and Finance, University of Sharjah, UAE*

The Nottingham China Policy Institute series brings cutting edge scholarship, policy relevance and accessibility together. It includes works on the economics, society, culture, politics, international relations, national security and history of the Chinese mainland, Taiwan and Hong Kong in the twentieth and twenty-first centuries. Books in this series are written in an accessible style though they are based on meticulous research. They put forward exciting ideas and research findings that specialist academics need to take note of while policy makers and opinion leaders will find inspiring. They represent innovative multidisciplinary scholarship at its best in the study of contemporary China.

More information about this series at
http://www.springer.com/series/14423

Chunxia Jiang · Shujie Yao

Chinese Banking Reform

From the Pre-WTO Period to the Financial Crisis and Beyond

palgrave
macmillan

Chunxia Jiang
Middlesex University
London, UK

Shujie Yao
University of Nottingham
Nottingham, UK

and

Chongqing University
Chongqing, China

The Nottingham China Policy Institute Series
ISBN 978-3-319-63924-6 ISBN 978-3-319-63925-3 (eBook)
https://doi.org/10.1007/978-3-319-63925-3

Library of Congress Control Number: 2017949207

Cover credit: robertharding/Alamy Stock Photo

Printed on acid-free paper

This Palgrave Macmillan imprint is published by Springer Nature
The registered company is Springer International Publishing AG
The registered company address is: Gewerbestrasse 11, 6330 Cham, Switzerland

Contents

List of Figures

List of Tables

1
Introduction

Preamble

China, one of the fastest-growing countries in transition, is leaping from its socialist past to its current market-oriented environment, making an economic miracle in history with an average annual growth rate of about 9% over nearly four decades (1978–2016). In 2010, China overtook Japan and became the second largest economy in the world. However, much of this near double-digit-type growth experience in China was achieved without a modern financial sector in place. Banking reform was regarded as a failure when mounting non-performing loans (NPLs) came to surface in 1999, and starting only in 2005, the largest Chinese banks entered the capital markets shattering the previous market capitalization records for financial intermediaries in the initial offering markets. While China's economy surpassed the European Union's economic bloc in 2011, its banking system overtook the Eurozone

---

Authors of the book are Chunxia Jiang and Shujie Yao, unless otherwise indicated in individual chapters. This book is financially supported by the National Natural Science Foundation of China (No. 71363014; No. 71673033) and the Chinese Ministry of Education Social Science Foundation (16YJA790058; 2017CDJSK).

C. Jiang and S. Yao, *Chinese Banking Reform*, The Nottingham China Policy Institute Series, DOI 10.1007/978-3-319-63925-3_1

and became the world's largest banking sector in terms of total assets five years later in 2016. As of the end of 2016, China's banking assets reached $33 trillion, which is higher than that of $31 trillion for the Eurozone, more than double that of $16 trillion for the United States, and more than four times that of $7 trillion for Japan (www.ft.com).
The banking sector in China dominates the financial sector and plays a major role in financial intermediation, accounting for 63% of capital in the economy as of the end 2016, declining from 80% in 2003. Bank credits to the non-financial sector accounted for 157% of GDP in 2016, rising by 31 percentage points from 126% in 2003. The stock market and bond market are still underdeveloped despite extensive progress over the past decade. The stock market and bond market financed 27.5 and 9.5%, respectively, of the country's capital in the economy as of the end of 2016, while their corresponding figures were only 19.7% and less than 1% in 2003.

The Chinese banking sector had been largely neglected until it started to attract worldwide attention from academics a few years ago. Early research focuses on the performance impact of ownership (Berger et al. 2009; Jiang et al. 2009; Fu and Heffernan 2009), China's entry into the World Trade Organization (WTO) (Yao et al. 2007), and deregulation (Chen et al. 2005), while later studies extended to a wider range of issues, including prudential behaviours of banks (Jia 2009), bank risk taking (Zhang et al. 2013), privatization (Jiang et al. 2013), and the impact of law enforcement (Zhang et al. 2012).

Despite the recent burgeoning literature on Chinese banking that has enriched our knowledge, few studies provide a comprehensive review of banking development and a systematic examination of the effects of banking reforms with detailed discussions on methodological issues and modelling. Against this backdrop, we developed this book to fill in the gap. We have conducted a series of research on Chinese banking since the early 2000s and have covered a range of important issues from the impact of reform measures to implications of the latest developments in the financial sector, such as shadow banking and internet finance. This book summarizes main findings of our research on the Chinese banking sector over the past 15 years and provides some useful policy recommendations.

It needs to be stressed that Chinese banking reform has its own unique features, which are distinctively different from other transitional economies. Although the Chinese authority is fully aware of the shortcomings of state ownership, it is equally keen not to totally privatize the country's industrial sector, let alone the banking sector. As a result, the reform process has been gradual in the sense that the authority has been trying to balance efficiency improvement and ownership diversification. If partial privatization can produce expected efficiency outcome, the authority would not be willing to adopt total privatization. However, if total state ownership is the main obstacle to efficiency improvement, then the authority would be more prepared to increase the level of privatization.

The reform in the state-owned banks has been gradual in the sense that core ownership is still state owned, but after the initial public offering (IPO), the ownership structure has changed as individuals and foreigners, including foreign banks, are allowed to buy shares of the listed state-owned banks. IPOs and share-holding subject the banks to market forces and hard budget constraints. Before the IPO, the reform was unrelated to ownership changes; it was all about how to improve the management structure and the separation of policy lending from commercial lending so that the performance of state-owned banks could become transparent.

Apart from the gradual reform in the state-owned banks, the Chinese government encourages other kinds of banks, mainly city commercial banks, joint-stock banks, rural financial cooperatives, unban credit unions, and foreign banks to compete with the state banking sector.

Up to now, China has built up a comprehensive and large banking sector that is still dominated by a few large state-owned banks although their market share has declined over time. Whether this is the ultimate market structure is not clear. Further reform and market transformation may be necessary and inevitable as the liberalization of interest rates, the globalization of China's currency (the renminbi or RMB), capital account liberalization, foreign exchange rate liberalization, internet finance, and technological changes will pose huge challenges to the banking industry, forcing them to face more competition and may even result in further ownership structure reform.

This introductory chapter provides an overview of this book and is organized as follows: Sect. 1.1 outlines the research questions and book map to introduce our main research questions; Sect. 1.2 provides chapter synopses to elaborate how these research questions have been addressed; and Sect. 1.3 concludes.

1.1 Research Questions and Research Objectives

Since the market-oriented banking reform started shortly after the Chinese authorities initiated economic reform in the late 1970s, the Chinese banking system has experienced far-reaching structural changes with significant impacts on a wide range of issues such as bank performance, competition, risk taking, and financial stability. The process of banking reform has faced a number of challenges. In the 1990s, due to the difficulty in structural reform in the real sectors—particularly the state-owned enterprises (SOEs) reform, and over-heating of the economy from the mid-1990s, the banking sector continued its policy lending, acting as government agents to support the transition of the real economy. This inevitably led to the failure of banking reform by the end of the 1990s with mounting non-performing assets cumulated in the large state-owned commercial banks.

The Asian financial crisis in 1998 demonstrated the importance of banking stability and the detrimental impact of crisis on economic growth. This awakened the Chinese authorities to remove the obstacles in transforming the banking industry to a market-oriented system. This was shortly reinforced by China's accession to the WTO in 2001. With the WTO obligations, China agreed to open up the banking sector to foreign institutions after a grace period of five years. Facing incoming threats from international financial giants, the Chinese government accelerated banking reform in the early 2000s through radical ownership reforms of the large state-owned banks that were dominant market players in the country's financial industry. A three-phase banking modernization programme was sequentially applied to the four largest state-owned banks. Financial restructuring and recapitalization of state banks was followed by partial privatization via attracting foreign investors and finally going public via IPOs to become listed banks on the stock exchanges.

The banking modernization reform was disrupted by the global financial crisis in 2008 triggered by the failure of the US investment banking giant Lehman Brothers in September 2008. The crisis resulted in the most severe economic recession since the Great Depression in the 1930s and it hit the developed world the worst. During the crisis, most developed countries such as the United States and the European Union experienced negative growth and clustered bank failures. This crisis, once again, highlighted the severity of financial instability and triggered policy reforms to resolve the crisis and prevent a repetition of these events. For example, worldwide regulatory reforms on capital requirement—Basel III was introduced and China adopted this capital regulatory framework.

Ironically, the global financial crisis became the catalyst for China to catch up with the major industrialized economies. The latest banking modernization programme has achieved impressive progress. By 2010, all the four large state-owned banks were successfully restructured and listed on the stock markets. Since then, the Chinese banking system has become increasingly important in the international financial market. In 2004, the China Construction Bank was the most profitable bank in the world with return on equity of 24%. In July 2007, the Industrial and Commercial Bank of China (ICBC) became the largest bank in the world after its IPO with a market capitalization of $246 billion. In July 2010, the Agricultural Bank of China (ABC) became the world's largest IPO by raising $22.1 billion, making China home to four of the world's 10 biggest banks by market capitalization. In 2016, the Chinese banking system became the largest banking sector in the world in terms of total assets, overtaking the Eurozone.

In the post-crisis era, the Chinese banking sector has faced a number of new challenges, leading to new developments in the banking sector. Internet finance prospered and shadow banking exploded with activities involving both the formal banking sector (via off-balance-sheet activities) and informal banking sector, posing a real threat to systemic financial stability. The flow of credits reached a new record in 2016 (156% of GDP) and the economy became overly dependent on bank-financed investment, which induces inefficient resource allocation and enormous credit risks. This new development requires immediate response to contain potential risks.

The reform and development experience of the Chinese banking sector has given rise to a number of important research questions. This book, in particular, addresses the following key issues. How has the banking sector evolved and developed over the past few decades? What are the theoretical underpinnings of banking reform in China? How have banking reform measures affected bank performance and competition? How well have Chinese banks performed relative to the banks in other emerging economies, in particular, Brazil, Russia, and India (known as BRIC including China)? Have China's WTO entry and global financial crisis had any impact on bank performance and competition? How have internet finance and shadow banking prospered and developed in the post-crisis era? As part of the shadow banking sector, how has the pawnbroking industry developed and what is its role in the financial sector in China?

This book attempts to provide answers to those questions thereby providing useful information for policy makers regarding further reform of the Chinese banking system. It should be noted that China has adopted a gradual reform approach, which is different from the banking reforms in other transition economies in Central and Eastern Europe where foreign banks played a vital role and in the former Soviet Union bloc where new banking systems were established via a "sudden death" approach. Experiences and lessons from China are of particular interest to policy makers in other developing countries, for example, Vietnam, Cambodia, Bolivia, Angola and to some extent Malawi; countries that have similarities to the "Chinese Model" when implementing new economic and financial reforms in recent decades.

This book is beneficial to bankers and practitioners by helping them identify the sources of inefficiencies against the industrial best practice and better understand the relationship between key variables such as risk taking, bank efficiency, and competition. Comprehensive discussion on internet finance and shadow banking help bankers and practitioners better understand the new developments, new trends, and associated risks in the banking industry and facilitate them to make better decisions. Moreover, this book also benefits researchers by providing detailed explanations and discussions on methodological issues. It introduces and illustrates different concepts, models, and estimation techniques and compares results from different methodologies, which help researchers to select appropriate methods to obtain more accurate results and derive more reliable findings.

1.2 Book Map and Chapter Synopses

This book starts from an introduction and unfolds seven main chapters that address research questions set out in the previous section, followed by conclusions and policy discussions.

Figure 1.1 shows the book map. Following the introduction in this chapter, Part 1 focuses on banking evolution and examines the impacts of banking reforms on banking performance and competition. Chapter 2 introduces the evolutionary process of banking since its establishment when the People's Republic of China was founded in 1949. Prior to economic reform commenced in the late 1970s, the banking system was the soviet-style monobank system acting as governmental agents to serve the centrally planned economy. The subsequent reform period can be divided into five phases: initial institutional restructuring (1979–1984), specialized state-owned banking (1985–1994), banking commercialization (1995–2002), banking modernization (2003–2010), and banking development in the post-crisis era (from 2011 onwards). Chapter 2 discusses reform measures and critically assesses their effectiveness. The theoretical rationale of banking reform in China is also explored in this chapter. Finally this chapter examines how bank performance (in terms of profitability, capital adequacy, asset quality, and liquidity) has been changed over the period 1995–2015 using traditional ratio analysis.

Chapter 3 introduces a variety of efficiency concepts, including technical efficiency, allocative efficiency, cost efficiency, revenue efficiency, and profit efficiency, as well as different estimation techniques, with

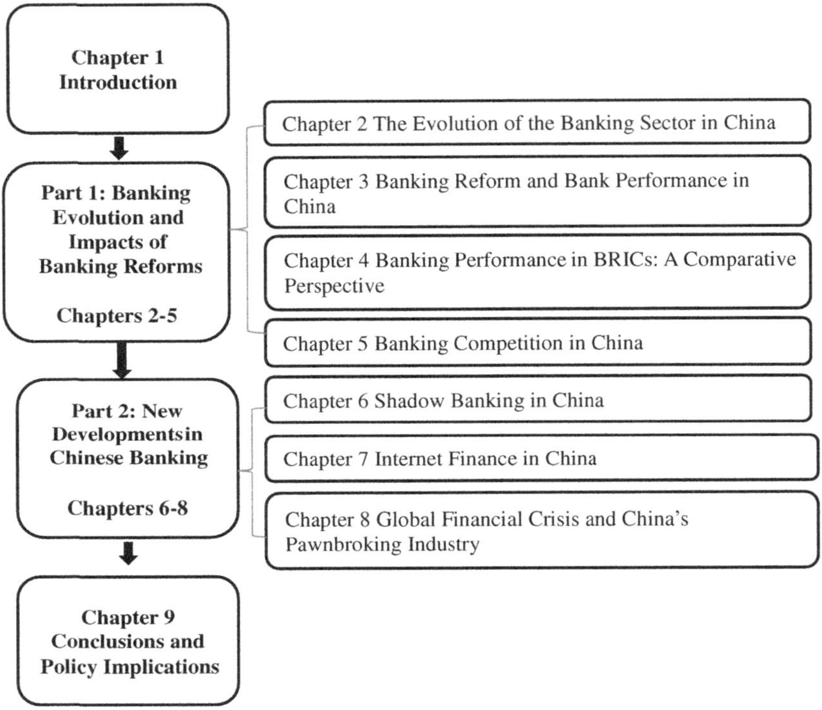

Fig. 1.1 Book map

detailed explanations of the preferred one-step parametric stochastic frontier analysis. This is particularly useful for researchers, especially young researchers, to gain a thorough understanding of these basic concepts and estimation methods. The chapter proceeds with empirical analysis: to rationalize the theoretical foundations of banking reform strategies by testing whether banking reform has been grounded on the agency theory and/or the budgetary constraints theory; to gauge how China's WTO entry affects bank efficiency as Chinese banks becoming real players in an open market competing with foreign banks; and to examine the impact of banking privatization on bank cost efficiency and profit efficiency. The results support two hypotheses confirming that ownership reform and changes in budgetary constraints are the right banking reform strategies. Results also indicate that banking performance has improved after privatization. WTO entry has a positive impact on technical efficiency but a negative impact on cost efficiency, while the latter is largely due to higher costs from more prudential practice after WTO entry, that is, the authority tightened regulatory requirements on loan loss provision.

Chinese banking reform has achieved staged progresses, leading to improved performance and rising status in the international financial markets. It is important to understand the resilience of Chinese banks compared with their peers in BRIC. Chapter 4 places Chinese banks in an international context, in particular, the context of emerging economies. Banking systems in BRIC have evolved from rather different paths, while all have served their countries' fast economic growth. For instance, both undergoing transition from a centrally planned banking system to a market-oriented one, Russian banking was newly established through a "sudden death" approach in the early 1990s, while the Chinese banking system adopted a gradual reform approach. This chapter first introduces BRICS' economies and provides a brief history of their banking systems. After reviewing existing research on these economies, this chapter compares bank performance across BRIC and investigates the impacts of bank risk taking, banking concentration, and the 2008 global financial crisis on bank efficiency. We find that on average Chinese and Brazilian banks outperform Indian and Russian ones, and BRIC's banking sectors were all negatively affected by the 2007–2008 global financial crisis with China and Russia being the least and most affected, respectively. Evidence also suggests a negative association between market concentration and performance, supporting the "quiet life" hypothesis, and indicates that banks taking a lower level of risks perform better, in favor of prudential practices.

The last chapter of Part 1 focuses on the issue of banking competition. One of the main goals of market-oriented economic transition is to increase market competition, which in turn is expected to improve performance, lower prices, stimulate innovation, and so on. There is extensive literature on banking competition but mainly for the developed countries, such as the United States and the EU member states. Banking competition in the emerging and transition economies is under researched. Moreover, it is also of particular interest to examine the changes in the degree of competition in the Chinese banking sector after nearly four decades of reforms. Chapter 5 starts by introducing a wide range of frequently employed competition measures in the literature under both structural and non-structural approaches. After a comprehensive literature review, it discusses in detail how to derive/estimate different competition measures, providing researchers hands-on help. As the literature has no consensus on which competition measure is superior over the others, multiple measures are used to assess the competition condition as well as its evolution in the Chinese banking sector over the period 1995–2015. Despite different measures disagreeing on the trend of banking competition before 2000, they are more consistent from 2000 onwards and suggest a steadily rising trend of competition in the Chinese banking industry.

Part 2 of this book unveils the new developments in the Chinese banking sector in the post-crisis era. Chapter 6 elaborates why and how the shadow banking sector has grown explosively in China in recent years. Shadow banking activities prospered worldwide after the 2008 global financial crisis, driven by regulatory arbitrage, financial innovation, technological advancement, and demand-side drivers. In addition to these general factors, in China the preferential lending to the state sector by the formal banking sector creates shortage of funding among the more productive private sector (especially small- and medium-sized firms), and this effect has become much stronger after the crisis. The cumulated strong demand for funding from the private sector forced them to turn to the informal lending channels, leading to a rapid growth of the shadow banking market in China. According to the Financial Stability Board's estimate, as of the end of 2014, entrusted loans amounted to RMB 9.3 trillion (15% of GDP), assets managed by trust companies reached RMB 14 trillion (22% of GDP), and as of the end of June 2014, bank wealth management products (WMPs) were RMB 12.7 trillion (around 20% of GDP). The explosive growth and massive deals have raised concerns over the systemic risk as shadow banking is largely unregulated. Subsequently, the authorities tightened up regulations after 2014. This chapter provides a detailed account of the development and evolution of shadow banking in China from its emergence to the status quo, from the definition to the intertwined relationship between shadow banking and the formal banking systems, and from risk implications to prudential regulations.

At the same time as shadow banking prospering, internet finance has also experienced explosive expansion, which is explored in Chap. 7. The development of internet finance in China is largely driven by government endorsement and the resultant open and friendly regulatory environment in order to promote finance inclusion, which is technically supported by the advancement of information and internet technologies and practically stimulated by the distortion and inefficiency of the financial sector. Internet finance is a new development of financial services, involving financial institutions, internet technologies firms, and e-commerce platforms with no clear boundaries. This complexity leads to regulations lagging behind the rapid development. While internet finance performs the core function of financial intermediation, its unique characteristics have significant implications on financial stability, which may impose huge negative externalities to the real sector. Chapter 7 enables readers to gain a comprehensive understanding of the current state of internet finance in China and how the sector has rapidly expanded. It also helps readers to gain insights into the theoretical framework, regulation and supervision, and challenges ahead.

Chapter 8 is the last chapter of Part 2 that explores one particular type of shadow banking—pawnbroking—as a typical case study of informal finance in China. Unlike most countries where pawnbroking is a financial instrument that helps private households or individuals to meet urgent short-term funding needs, pawnbroking in China has been used as a supplementary financing source for small and medium-sized enterprises (SMEs) and private entrepreneurs. This situation is caused by two main reasons: (1) financial market imperfection and institutional discrimination of the formal financial sector that limits SMEs' access to bank credits or other formal financing sources; and (2) the historically negative image of pawnbroking in the Chinese culture and restrictions on pawn objects that distance low-income individuals away from using the services. After the financial crisis, many companies experienced an acute shortage of cash, while liquidity was squeezed and banks were reluctant to lend. This led to increased funding demand from SMEs and the pawnbroking industry expanded along with the prosperity of shadow banking and internet finance. Chapter 8 introduces the history and development of the pawnbroking industry and identifies its main features. A theoretical model is developed to illustrate pawnbroking as a credible substitute for formal bank financing for the SMEs in the Chinese context.

The last chapter of the book, Chap. 9, wraps up our 15 years of research on the Chinese banking sector and summarizes main findings. In this chapter, we identify challenges and problems ahead and discuss policy implications on China's banking sector development, financial deepening and liberalization, and their potential impacts on the real economic sector. Finally, this chapter provides policy recommendations, which would help to build a sound financial sector that promotes sustainable economic growth in the long run.

1.3 Conclusion

In this chapter we outline the structure of this book. Our discussion in this chapter is very much a starting point in understanding the Chinese banking sector. The book map and chapter synopses enable readers to gain a preliminary understanding of the Chinese banking sector in terms of the evolutionary process over the past several decades, the latest development in the post-crisis era, challenges ahead, and the direction for future research. Experiences and lessons from the Chinese banking reform are of particular interest to policy makers not only in China but also in other emerging markets and developing countries that have features similar to those in China, including an important state sector, increasing foreign bank presence, rapid growth, and being in a phase of major economic and financial changes. This book provides some insights into the banking sector in China, which we believe will be beneficial on a broader scale.

References

Berger, A.N., I. Hasan, and M. Zhou. 2009. Bank Ownership and Efficiency in China: What Will Happen in the World's Largest Nation? *Journal of Banking & Finance* 33: 113–130.

Chen, X., M. Skuly, and K. Brown. 2005. Banking Efficiency in China: Application of DEA to Pre- and Post-Deregulation Eras: 1993–2000. *China Economic Review* 16: 229–245.

Fu, X., and S. Heffernan. 2009. The Effects of Reform on China's Bank Structure and Performance. *Journal of Banking & Finance* 33 (1): 39–52.

Jia, C. 2009. The Effect of Ownership on the Prudential Behavior of Banks—The Case of China. *Journal of Banking & Finance* 33: 77–87.

Jiang, C., S. Yao, and G. Feng. 2013. Bank Ownership, Privatization, and Performance: Evidence from a Transition Country. *Journal of Banking & Finance* 37: 3364–3372.

Jiang, C., S. Yao, and Z. Zhang. 2009. The Effects of Governance Changes on Bank Efficiency in China: A Stochastic Distance Function Approach. *China Economic Review* 20: 717–731.

Yao, S., C. Jiang, G. Feng, and D. Willenbockel. 2007. On the Efficiency of Chinese Banks and WTO Challenges. *Applied Economics* 39: 629–643.

Zhang, J., C. Jiang, B. Qu, and P. Wang. 2013. Market Concentration, Risk-Taking, and Bank Performance: Evidence from Emerging Economies. *International Review of Financial Analysis* 30: 149–157.

Zhang, J., B. Qu, and P. Wang. 2012. Bank Risk Taking, Efficiency, and Law Enforcement: Evidence from Chinese City Commercial Banks. *China Economic Review* 23 (2): 284–295.

2

The Evolution of the Banking Sector in China

Preamble

This chapter provides a systematic review of the evolution of the Chinese banking sector in Sect. 2.1, beginning from its establishment in 1949 through to early institutional reforms in the 1980s, commercialization reforms in the mid-1990s, modernization reforms in the early twenty-first century, and modern banking development in the post-crisis era from 2011 onwards. Section 2.2 discusses the theoretical underpinnings that motivate and guide the banking reform in China. Finally, Sect. 2.3 analyzes the banking sector's overall performance in terms of capital adequacy, asset quality, profitability, and liquidity for the period 1995–2015 based on a conventional financial ratio analysis using key macro-prudential indicators proposed by the International Monetary Fund (IMF).

C. Jiang and S. Yao, *Chinese Banking Reform*, The Nottingham China Policy Institute Series, DOI 10.1007/978-3-319-63925-3_2

2.1 A Brief History of Banking Reform

The new China's banking system was established in 1949, when the People's Republic of China (hereafter China) was founded. Over half a century, the banking system has gone through two distinctive evolutionary periods: a monobanking period (1949–1978) and a reforming period (1979–present). The mono-banking system was a highly centrally planned, unitary banking system dominated by the People's Bank of China (PBOC), the only bank in the country, in charge of nearly all financial functions, including the formulation and implementation of monetary policy and foreign exchange policy, foreign reserve management, deposit taking, commercial lending, and investment. The PBOC essentially combined the roles of the central bank and the commercial banks and its operation was subject to strict cash and credit plans set in accordance with the production plans projected by the State Planning Commission.

A few banks were established during this period without challenging the dominant status of the PBOC. The People's Construction Bank of China was founded in 1954 as a subsidiary of the Ministry of Finance. Bank of China (BOC), which was founded in 1912, became a subsidiary of the PBOC exclusively dealing with foreign currency transactions since the 1950s. The Agricultural Bank of China (ABC) was established in 1951, but lately ceased to operate. These banks were wholly state owned and passively collected household savings and channeled funds to serve the state's centrally planned production projects. Their operations were driven by government goals and resultant needs rather than profit maximization, and as a result, normal commercial banking skills such as risk management and project selection were largely ignored. During this period, the banking system played only a limited role in promoting economic growth (Yang 2002).

This centrally controlled mono-banking system lasted until 1978 when Deng Xiaoping started the economic reform and opening up policy in China. Since then, the banking system has entered into a gradual reform period that can be divided into five sub-periods: (1) initial institutional restructuring during 1979–1984; (2) specialized state-owned banking system during 1985–1994; (3) banking commercialization during 1995–2002; (4) banking modernization during 2003–2010; and (5) banking development in the post-crisis era.

2.1.1 Initial Institutional Restructuring During 1979–1984

Since the economic reform started in 1979, the centrally planned banking system was no longer fit for the need of economic development, urging institutional reforms to separate commercial banking operations from the regulatory and supervisory body of PBOC. Institutional reform was kicked off in 1979 by the introduction of a two-tier banking system—the first milestone in transforming the mono-banking system into a modern one. The government removed the monopolistic position of PBOC, which was broken up into two arms—the central bank and the commercial operations. Since then, PBOC became the central bank with the primary objective of maintaining price stability, enforcing strict supervision over financial institutions, conducting clearance, and issuing bank notes. The headquarters was also in charge of designing and implementing monetary policy and formulating a credit plan in accordance with the national economic plan.

The commercial operations of PBOC were stripped off and assigned to four specialized state-owned banks: ABC, which reopened in 1979, took over PBOC's rural banking business and responsibilities for supervising a network of rural credit cooperatives (RCCs) that had been providing small-scale rural banking services; the People's Construction Bank of China, renamed as China Construction Bank in 1996 and then as China Construction Bank Corporation (CCBC) in late 2004, specialized in dealing with fixed assets investment of the government and focused on urban large construction projects in the 1980s; BOC specialized in foreign currency transactions in 1979; and the Industrial and Commercial Bank of China (ICBC) was established in 1984, taking over commercial banking activities in urban areas from PBOC. These four state-owned banks operated as well-encapsulated monopolistic institutions within their own serving niches, with no responsibilities and incentives to penetrate or compete across regions and sectors, effectively ruling out free competition. They provided services to a designated sector of the economy and they were the official source of financing for state-owned enterprises (SOEs) within each assigned serving realm.

There was no stock and corporate bond market, leaving the entire role of financial intermediation to these four state-owned specialized banks.

2.1.2 Further Institutional Restructuring During 1985–1994

From 1985, the Chinese government advanced institutional restructuring to increase competition and create a competitive banking market. New banking institutions, such as joint-stock commercial banks (JSCBs) and foreign banks were allowed to enter into the banking market and restrictions on state-owned banks were gradually relaxed. From the mid-1980s to the 1990s, the majority of JSCBs were launched with a shareholding ownership structure, which was an institutional breakthrough in the Chinese banking industry.[1] JSCBs operate as commercial banks with the main objective of profit maximization and they have more freedom to develop their business scopes and geographical expansion. It is arguable to distinguish JSCBs from state-owned specialized banks since the key shareholders of most JSCBs are still local governments and/or the state-owned/controlled enterprises. However, JSCBs are more competitive, profit-oriented, and performance conscious due to a lower degree of government intervention, flexible personnel management, and overall better corporate governance structure.

Meanwhile, restrictions on the business scopes of state-owned specialized banks were removed in 1985 and four state-owned specialized banks were institutionally released and permitted to enlarge their business scopes to compete with each other and with JSCBs. In the 1980s, more RCCs and urban credit cooperatives (UCCs) were set up to diversify the banking system and to channel funds to projects in areas where resources were scarce. The main business of RCCs and UCCs was to finance small and medium-sized rural or urban enterprises and individuals. Their lending policies were governed by the local authorities rather than the central bank. Thousands of RCCs played an important role in

[1]These JSCBs include CITIC Industrial Bank, China Merchants Bank, Shenzhen Development Bank Co., Ltd, Industrial Bank Co. Ltd, Guangdong Development Bank, China Everbright Bank, Huaxia Bank, and Shanghai Pudong Development Bank.

mobilizing rural household savings, channeling funds to town and village enterprises, agricultural activities, and other development projects in rural areas. These financial institutions were an important supplement to the banking system.

In 1994, in recognizing that the policy lending practice of state-owned banks was detrimental to the health of the whole banking system, the Chinese government created three policy banks to take over policy lending activities from state banks, namely, China Development Bank, the Import-Export Bank of China, and the Agricultural Development Bank of China. China Development Bank dealt with long- and medium-term lending to finance construction projects in infrastructure and in strategic industries. The Import-Export Bank of China was responsible for providing loans to import and export companies. The Agricultural Development Bank of China was in charge of lending to the agricultural sector with specific policy focus.

By 1994, the institutional restructuring of the Chinese banking system was completed. The two-tier banking system took shape, dominated by state-owned specialized banks, along with JSCBs and a large number of UCCs and RCCs, as well as newly established state-owned policy banks.

However, banking reform in this period failed to transform a policy-driven banking system to a market-oriented system—competition was increased but insufficient, the banking system remained as policy-driven, and the role of state-owned specialized banks became rather vague and contradictory. State-owned banks were officially expected to be profit-driven institutions to compete with each other, while banks' operations were frequently intervened on by the central and local governments. These banks, as before, were governmental agencies to help implement production plans projected by the state and regional planning commissions. This policy-driven banking system extended loans to SOEs on the basis of fulfilling the national and regional production plans and to maintain employment, regardless of profitability. About two-thirds of SOEs were loss makers during this economic transition period, and the banking sector accumulated a huge amount of non-performing loans (NPLs). These NPLs and losses were regarded as the costs of institutional transition of the economy and the state was expected to clean up. Thus, state-owned specialized banks were implicitly guaranteed by the government and enjoyed a soft budget constraint when SOEs were increasingly subject to hardened budget constraints. Commercial banking practices and skills, such as risk management, were hardly developed due to the prevalence of policy lending practice.

2.1.3 Banking Commercialization During 1995–2002

From the mid-1990s, the government initiated the second wave of comprehensive reform to commercialize the banking sector; the necessity and urgency for banking reforms were further reinforced in 1999 in the wake of the 1997–1998 Asian financial crisis. Concrete reforming measures addressed legal and institutional restructuring, financial liberalization and opening up, and strengthening prudential regulation.

In 1995, the four state-owned specialized banks were legally defined as wholly state-owned commercial banks (SOCBs) when the Law of the People's Republic of China on Commercial Banks was enacted. They were expected to operate under the principles of profitability, safety, and liquidity and were responsible for their own profits and losses. They were supposed to be operationally independent and have the freedom to choose the clientele on a purely commercial basis. Although efforts were made on releasing SOCBs from the role as government agents, they still played a significant role in policy lending to support the economic development and to maintain social stability. The roles of the commercial bank and the policy bank were well defined in legal term but not in practice. Because of the lack of a branch network and capital, policy banks had insufficient serving and lending capacity and hence were unable to meet the need for policy lending previously provided by the four state-owned specialized banks. Consequently, SOCBs were often under pressures from both the central and regional authorities to make loans to their preferred sectors and enterprises.

Also in 1995, the PBOC was legally confirmed as the central bank by the Law of the PBOC. However, the central bank itself was not an independent regulatory body. It was ultimately overseen by the State Council (the cabinet)—the central government. Local governments also had the right to appoint senior managers for the local branches of the PBOC (as well as SOCBs). As such, governments had the power to force banks to lend in accordance with their preference, and government intervention in SOCBs' operations was common practice at that time. In order to eliminate government intervention, the central bank was reorganized at the end of 1998. Provincial-level branches were merged into nine large regional branches, located in Shenyang, Tianjin, Jinan, Nanjing, Shanghai, Guangzhou, Wuhan, Chengdu, and Xi'an. This reorganization reduced local governments' influences on SOCBs' lending decisions and commercial banks were released (Wong and Wong 2001).

Since the mid-1990s, City Commercial Banks (CCBs) were created by a way of restructuring and consolidating UCCs. CCBs served mainly the small and medium-sized enterprises and collectives as well as local residents within their geographical localities. CCBs adopted a shareholding ownership structure and capitals were provided by urban enterprises and local governments. In the meantime, RCCs were restructured as independent financial institutions. By then, the second layer of the banking system included two parts: (1) commercial banks and other banking institutions that were subject to prudential regulations and the PBOC's supervision, including JSCBs, CCBs, SOCBs, foreign banks, and RCCs and UCCs; and (2) three state-owned policy banks governed by individual charters, not subject to the commercial bank law.

Despite considerable efforts on banking reform, SOCBs became financially insolvent because of a stubbornly high level of accumulated NPLs by the end of the twentieth century, partially caused by the overheating of the Chinese economy and transitional reform of SOEs in the 1990s. By 1999, the total amount of NPLs in SOCBs was estimated as RMB 3.3 trillion under the four-category loan-classification system, accounting for 41% of GDP for the year. Low capitalization and massive NPLs posed a direct threat to the Chinese banking system. A financial crisis could tremendously damage the economy and wipe out years of economic achievements, as clearly demonstrated by the Asian financial crisis in 1997–1998. Perhaps alerted by the Asian financial crisis, the central government, as expected, commenced the first round of SOCBs bailout. In 1998, RMB 270 billion was injected into four SOCBs through issuing long-term treasury bonds. In 1999, the government offloaded NPLs worth RMB 1.4 trillion at book value (about 15.6% of the combined total of outstanding loans) from SOCBs to four newly established state asset-management companies, namely Cinda Asset Management Company, China Great Wall Asset Management Company, Oriental Asset Management Company, and China Huarong Asset Management Corporation. Financial restructuring of SOCBs improved the soundness and stability of the banking system. Immediately, the total amount of NPLs of SOCBs decreased to RMB 1.9 trillion, accounting for 22% of GDP in 2000.

Financial liberalization and opening up were also underway. In 1998, the credit plan for both working capital loans and fixed investment loans was replaced by an indicative non-binding target as a reference for commercial banks to plan their business—another milestone of the Chinese banking reform. SOCBs were granted more responsibility and autonomy in making lending decisions and government intervention in commercial lending activities was explicitly forbidden. Moreover, from 1996, interest rate liberalization started from the wholesale markets in which Interbank Offered Rate and repurchasing and trading interest rates of treasuries, for example, were allowed to be determined in accordance with the market conditions. In 1998, floating ranges on lending interest rates were raised to 20% for financial institutions and 50% for RCCs, giving more room for varying lending rates charged on different clients (Berger et al. 2009). The central government also lowered the reserve requirement for commercial banks from 20 to 6%. The most crucial milestone of financial liberalization was China's accession to the WTO in 2001 and the Chinese government committed to fully open up the banking market to foreign banks after a five-year grace period.

While liberalizing the financial market, the Chinese government also tightened prudential regulation and supervision that had long been behind international standards. Capital adequacy requirement was first introduced in 1995 in Shenzhen and the central bank started internal monitoring in accordance with the Basel Capital Accord from 1998. In 1995, the newly enacted commercial bank law prohibited commercial banks from engaging in investment banking business, such as securities trading and underwriting, investment in non-bank financial enterprises and productive enterprises, and investment in trust business, to reduce risk taking and protect depositors. In 1998, to better control asset quality, the authorities introduced an internationally accepted five-category loan-classification system by a trial application in Guangdong province. Although it was applied to all commercial banks nationwide since 2002, few banks followed this prudential norm and the authorities had to reinforce all banks to fully comply with it by the end of 2005.

The banking commercialization reform did not bring the Chinese banking sector into a modern era. The favorable outcomes of the financial restructuring and capital injection into SOCBs were short-lived and the total amount of NPLs rebounded to RMB 2.3 trillion in 2001 under the newly adopted five-category loan-classification system.[2] Capital adequacy ratio of SOCBs and JSCBs dropped. Banks, especially SOCBs and CCBs, were unable to raise sufficient capital to meet minimum requirements, making capital regulation unenforceable. The main reason was that reforms did not address the deep-rooted causes of the problems. SOCBs still played a significant role in policy lending to support the economic development and to maintain social stability. SOCBs' major clients were still SOEs, of which the majority remained inefficient and unprofitable. Moreover, this round of bailout seemed to send out a message that the government was the last resort of help once banks were in distress and the soft budget constraint invited moral hazard problems and inefficiency.

By 2002, the banking sector was still characterized by poor asset quality, high level of NPLs, deteriorated solvency ratios, low profitability, the lack of risk management skills, and so on. The reform was far from complete and the tough nut of reform remained to be cracked, while incoming WTO challenges were real. Under the opening-up schedule of the WTO accession in December 2001, the banking market was to be gradually opened up to foreign banks in a five-year grace period and foreign banks started to enjoy national treatment without

---

[2]The increase of NPLs was partially due to the change from the four-category classification system before 2001 to the five-category loan classification system afterward. The former was estimated to underestimate NPLs by 14% suggested by a PBC internal study since it provides leeway to retain NPLs unreported.

any restrictions by the end of 2006. This represents significant challenges to the Chinese banking system that were real and imminent, threatening domestic banks, both state-owned and non-state-owned in many aspects. On the other hand, the WTO accession presents an unprecedented opportunity for building up of a modern and internationally viable banking system. In the face of the increasing challenges, the Chinese authorities set the reform of SOCBs at the top of the agenda of financial reform at the second National Financial Work Conference in 2002 and outlined concrete strategies for next steps.

2.1.4 Banking Modernization During 2003–2010

Since 2003, the Chinese government has implemented more radical SOCBs reform measures. The SOCBs reform followed a three-phase roadmap sequentially: the first phase is to recapitalize SOCBs and resolve the NPLs burden through the second round of bailout and financial restructuring; the second phase is to transform SOCBs into modern financial enterprises with joint-stock ownership structure to optimize corporate governance; and the third phase is to list them on capital markets, subjecting their operations to market discipline.

The government initiated the second round of capitalization in 2003, and this long-awaited bailout was in the form of capital investment by Central Huijin Investment Company Limited, a government vehicle company. The government injected $45 billion into BOC and CCBC in 2003 (each received $22.5 billion), $15 billion into ICBC in 2005, and $19 billion into ABC in 2009. As part of financial restructuring, the government conducted the second round of NPLs divestment from SOCBs. NPLs were offloaded from BOC and CCBC by $57.4 billion (RMB 475 billion) in 2004, ICBC by $87.4 billion (RMB 705 billion) in 2005, and ABC by $133 billion (RMB 816 billion) in 2008. After financial restructuring, the assets quality of SOCBs improved significantly and balance sheets were strengthened. For instance, the NPL ratio of SOCBs dropped to 10% in 2005 from 20% in 2003 and the total amount of NPLs shrunk to RMB 1 trillion, accounting for 6% of GDP in 2005 from RMB 1.9 trillion, 17% of GDP in 2003.

After the divestment of historical burden of NPLs and recapitalization, SOCBs reform proceeded with the second phase of joint-stock ownership reform and SOCBs were encouraged to attract foreign investors, which was welcomed by foreign investors. Three newly financially restructured SOCBs successfully attracted international financial giants as foreign strategic investors. For example, CCBC teamed up with Bank of America, BOC with the Royal Bank of Scotland, and ICBC with Goldman Sachs. Following the path, all banks were encouraged to attract foreign investors for much-needed capital and modern banking skills to improve their capital level in line with minimum requirements set by the Basel Accords. Foreign investors reacted positively to this policy and acquired minority stakes in all types of banks, including SOCBs, JSCBs, and CCBs.[3]

Subsequently, SOCBs were restructured into joint-stock entities and organizationally transformed into modern enterprises aimed at forging ahead for going public. This was the boldest and toughest decision of the government—to convert SOCBs into truly commercial institutions. The main purpose is to improve corporate governance, risk management, internal control, and the management of finance, debt, and human resources. As planned, shortly after joint-stock restructuring, SOCBs reform proceeded to the third phase—going public. The going public strategy was motivated by the diversified ownership, better corporate governance structure, hardened budgetary constraints, and the role of market discipline, all of which help better solve the agent-principal problem and improve performance. The capital market investors reacted to SOCBs' initial public offerings (IPOs) positively. CCBC and BOC were successfully listed on the Hong Kong Stock Exchange in 2005 and 2006 when they raised USD $8 billion and $9.7 billion through IPOs, respectively. ICBC was simultaneously listed on both the Shanghai Stock Exchange and the Hong Kong Stock Exchange on 27 October 2006. The market reactions were unexpectedly positive and by July 2007, ICBC became the largest bank in the world after less than a year as a public company, overtaking Citigroup by market capitalization of $246 billion. ICBC raised about USD $21.9 billion in Hong

[3]See Sect. 1.6 for more details.

Kong (H-shares) and Shanghai (A-shares) and it was the world's largest IPO until ABC set the new world record by raising $22.1 billion in 2010. Successful IPOs and their subsequent extraordinary performance in stock markets provided a sound cornerstone for the overall success of China's further banking reform. By 2010, the overhaul of SOCBs was complete and all SOCBs had been transformed into public banks with a diversified shareholding structure.

Banking reform extended to policy banks starting with the establishment of China Development Bank Corporation in 2008, cofounded by the Ministry of Finance and Central Huijin Investment Company (the central government's vehicle company). China Development Bank became an ordinary commercial bank subject to normal banking regulation and supervision. However, the State Council officially defined the bank as a development finance institution in 2015. The reform of two other policy banks—the Export-Import Bank of China (EIBC) and the Agricultural Development Bank of China (ADBC)—has been to strengthen their policy service capacity with no intention to change their nature as policy banks.

Synchronously, the reform of the RCCs was carried out since 2004 and by the end of 2006, reforms have been rolled out across 30 provincial units across the country. The RCCs reform addressed areas such as the management system reform and ownership reform, which improved their earning ability to make profit. The reform also extended to China's Postal Savings. On 31 December 2006, the Postal Savings Bank of China (PSBC) was established as a wholly owned subsidiary of the China Postal Group, a historical step of commercialization of China's postal savings. CCBs also undertook a comprehensive reform program focusing on ownership reform and standardizing information disclosure. In 2006, CCBs were allowed to consolidate and set up cross-regional branches, becoming regional commercial banks.

During this period, the government also strengthened the regulatory and supervisory framework. In April 2003, the China Banking Regulatory Commission (CBRC) was established as a regulatory and supervisory body, taking over the responsibility and functions from the central bank to regulate and supervise all the banking institutions.

CBRC became in charge of the banking sector reform to strengthen the banking sector and improve banking capitalization. The PBOC started to be responsible for monetary policy and liquidity of the financial sector by managing the interest rates on loans and deposits and reserve requirement along with other monetary policy instruments. This separation showed the government's resolution to promote safe, sound, and efficient operations of the banking industry through strengthened supervision and risk control capacity (www.cbrc.gov.cn).

The authority understood that listing SOCBs on stock exchanges to raise fresh capital was not the end of the reform but a short-run goal. The long-run goal is to transform SOCBs into modern banks with good corporate governance in place and to create a sound and internationally competitive banking system. Building up a well-functioning corporate governance is the key to the success of Chinese banking reform, which ensures sustainable improvement in performance in the long term. For monitoring the ongoing bank reform, CBRC strengthened prudential regulation and supervision and set out 10 requirements for good corporate governance and seven performance indicators since 2004. These measures have been benchmarked to the top 100 largest banks globally, focusing on improving risk management and corporate governance. Against these benchmarks, CBRC monitors the pace of SOCBs moving toward modern enterprises and their performance. Ten requirements cover corporate governance structure, diversified ownership, goal of profit maximization, prudent accounting practices, market-oriented human resource management, and so on. In 2006, the CBRC issued the Guideline on the Corporate Governance Reforms and Supervision of State-owned Commercial Banks to further improve SOCBs' corporate governance and enhance their internal restructuring. It sets up seven quantitative benchmarks, covering operational performance, asset quality, and prudent operations. Operational performance parameters include net return on total assets, net return on equity, and expense-to-revenue ratio. Asset quality parameters refer to NPL ratio and prudent operations parameters include capital adequacy ratio, large exposure concentration, and coverage ratio of loan loss provisions.

2.1.5 Banking Development in the Post-Crisis Era from 2011 Onwards

After the major overhaul of SOCBs, the Chinese authorities focused on the sound development of the newly modernized banking sector in the post-crisis era by deepening banking reform, advancing regulation and supervision, improving risk-management skills, and promoting inclusive finance. In 2010, the authority initiated some pilot programs on universal banking, which were unfolded from 2011. The programs explore the models for commercial banks to extend operations into other financial segments, such as insurance and trust, to meet the increasingly diversified financial demands. The participating banks are mainly large commercial banks and some selected small- and medium-sized banks and they either establish or invest in companies in fund management, insurance, financial leasing, trust, and consumer finance.

Banking reform was deepened. The PSBC, incorporated in 2007, was the first move to commercialize China's postal savings. In 2012, the PSBC was transformed into a joint-stock limited company and subsequently listed on the Hong Kong Stock Exchange on 30 September 2016 after attracting 10 domestic and international strategic investors.[4] PSBC has the largest financial network bridging the rural and urban economies and societies and it aims to provide basic financial services to town and village communities and rural residents to finance the development of the new rural society.

Another focus of banking reform during this period is small- and medium-sized banking institutions, including CCBs, RCBs, UCCs, and RCCs, to enhance financial stability and promote financial inclusion. The reform of management system and ownership was accelerated to strengthen their corporate governance, risk management, and sustainable development capability. Under the "new normal" in the post-crisis era, small- and medium-sized banking institutions face challenges from

[4]Ten strategic investors include six globally well-known financial institutions: United Bank of Switzerland, J. P. Morgan Chase, Development Bank of Singapore, CPP Investment Board, Temasek, and International Finance Corporation; two large state-owned enterprises: China Life Insurance and China Telecom; and two internet enterprises: Ant Financial and Tencent.

interest rate liberalization, disintermediation, internet finance, and the like. In response, they have accelerated strategic transition to improve market competitiveness through innovations and operational expansion. These institutions have targeted niche markets, such as micro and small enterprises (MSEs) and other disadvantaged groups usually overlooked by large state-controlled banks and joint-stock banks. UCCs and RCCs have made good progress in equity restructuring, corporate governance, operational efficiency, and business performance.[5] Some have been restructured as CCBs or RCBs, while others are either being transformed into rural cooperative banks or exiting from the market. By the end of 2011, altogether 800 UCCs completed restructuring and reform. Some 2667 existing rural cooperative financial institutions, including 212 RCBs and 190 rural cooperative banks, cover 76% of the townships or villages that were previously not reached by any financial institutions or services. New-type rural financial institutions have also been established, such as village and township banks, lending companies, and rural mutual cooperatives. As of the end of 2015, there were 1377 village and township banks.

In the process of banking ownership reform, the biggest challenge is the shortage of capital. Unlike SOCBs and JSCBs that have been able to raise capital from a variety of sources, such as central/local governments and foreign investors, small- and medium-sized financial institutions generally lack capital sources. Private capitals have been gradually allowed to enter into the banking sector. Remarkably, the authorities launched a pilot project to establish five entirely privately funded banks in 2014. By March 2015, the five pilot private banks had all opened for business serving the real economy. The KinCheng Bank of Tianjin (KCB) focused on differentiated services to serve small- and medium-sized enterprises with loans and deposits from corporate units. Shanghai Huarui Bank positions itself as an asset management bank and

[5]Since their establishment in 1951, RCCs have been providing financial services to farmers, the agricultural industry, and rural development. RCCs are also the main channel for disbursing national subsidies to farming households via the most widely distributed outlets in rural areas, playing a crucial role in supporting rural areas in China. RCCs were first managed by ABC, subsequently became independent cooperatives overseen by the Central Bank, and currently are under management by respective provincial governments.

adopts new technologies to serve micro- and small enterprises (MSEs), technology and innovative start-ups, and free trade zone reforms. Zhejiang MYbank focuses on the development of "micro credit" to serve MSEs and rural markets. Wenzhou Minshang Bank also serves MSEs via a mass marketing mode and offers distinctive financial products such as "business flourishing loan," "businessman loan," and so on. Shenzhen Qianhai WeBank operates an open and inclusive financing platform based on big data technology to serve the general public, MSEs, and start-ups. It offers three main lines of internet finance products—retail credit "Weilidai," online wealth management platform "WeBank APP," and "Platform Finance." One important feature of these five privately funded banks is the deep integration of innovations and information technology into banking business, which substantially reduces the transaction costs and asymmetric information problems, which in turn enables high quality, more efficient financial services available to a large number of individuals and MSEs. As of the end 2015, the total assets of these five banks reached RMB 79.432 billion and outstanding loans and deposits were at RMB 23.604 billion and RMB 19.943 billion, respectively. Private capital not only provides capital support but also helps improve corporate governance thereby building a sound and viable banking sector to better serve the economy and society. These institutions have embraced internet finance to expand service channels and explore business innovations while lowering costs. Private capital has become a significant part of the equity of banking institutions, especially for the small- and medium-sized commercial banks/rural financial institutions. As of the end of 2015, the share of private capital in CCBs, rural cooperative financial institutions, and village and township banks was around 53%, 90%, and more than 72%, respectively (CBRC).

After the global crisis, internet finance and shadow banking expanded prosperously and have become an important integrated part of the financial sector in China. New business models are introduced, such as setting up electronic business platforms that offer e-commerce services and financial support to merchants and consumers, undertaking intermediation and clearing function for direct loan settlement among individuals, and setting up platforms for online sales of financial products. These developments are accompanied by financial innovations and numerous high value-added innovative products have emerged. These new developments will be discussed in more detail in later chapters.

In short, taking the 2008 global financial crisis as an opportunity, the Chinese authorities have advanced banking reform towards a sound, comprehensive, and competitive banking sector to serve the real economy. These staged impressive achievements have paved the way for future development of the financial system in China.

2.1.6 Foreign Banks in China

Foreign banks have grown at a snail's pace in the Chinese banking market although the Chinese economy was growing at about 10% per year. In the early 1980s, the Chinese government opened just a crack of the financial market to foreign financial institutions. Foreign banks first were allowed to open representative offices and subsequently permitted to open operational braches in Special Economic Zones. This geographical restriction was extended to 23 coastal cities during the first half of the 1990s and foreign banks were allowed to open branches across China in 1996. In the past, entry barriers and business restrictions for foreign banks were high. Foreign banks' operations were restricted within some designated geographical zones and they must have launched and operated a representative office for two years in order to apply for establishing branches. Foreign banks were also restricted to serve foreign companies and residents and conduct foreign currency business. Foreign banks with about 2% share of the banking total assets played a limited role in China.

China's entry into the WTO implied a faster removal of the barriers and restrictions blocking foreign bank entry. To honour WTO commitments, the CBRC has been continuously speeding up the opening up of the banking system in an attempt to create a level playing field for both domestic and foreign banks. Since 2003, CBRC has gradually loosened geographical restrictions on customers and business. Foreign banks have been given greater access to the local market by: (1) allowing them to conduct local currency business with local companies from 1 December 2003; (2) lowering the minimum capital requirement to RMB 500 million for foreign financial institutions to set up a full-service branch; and (3) expanding to 18 cities that have been fully opened to foreign banks for local currency business.

Foreign banks prospered in the Chinese banking market, attracted by the rapidly growing financial services markets and the promising prospective of the economy. By the end of 2015, there were 37 wholly foreign-owned banks with 306 branches, 2 joint-venture banks with 4 branches, 114 branches of 69 banks, and 174 representative offices of 153 banks in China. Foreign banks operate in 69 cities of 27 provinces with the total operating outlets amounted to 1044. Total assets of foreign banks were RMB 2.68 trillion in 2015, increased five times from RMB 0.42 trillion in 2003. However, the share in the total banking asset was 1.38% in 2015, which has been declining largely due to the faster growth of the total banking assets (CBRC 2015).

In contrary to opening wholly owned operations, most foreign investors have chosen to acquire equity stake in domestic banks. Prior to 2004, only a few foreign institutions acquired shares in domestic banks due to high entry barriers and business restrictions. In 1996, the Asian Development Bank acquired 1.9% share in China Everbright Bank, which made the latter the first domestic bank with foreign minority ownership. A few other foreign institutions, such as International Finance Corporation (IFC), Hong Kong and Shanghai Banking Corporation (HSBC), and Citigroup, followed the practice and acquired equity stakes in carefully selected JSCBs and CCBs. Motivated by the desire to attract foreign strategic investors for domestic banks, the authorities have relaxed the provisions relating to business cooperation and equity links between the domestic and foreign banks. At the end of 2003, the maximum equity share of total overseas investment in any Chinese financial institution was increased to 25%, of which the maximum equity share of a single overseas investor was 20% (www.cbrc.gov.cn).

Acquiring equity stakes in domestic banks became a popular move among foreign banks, which give investors immediate access to well-developed distribution networks and help them to position a strategic seat before fully opening up the banking market. Although foreign banks and institutions would be granted a full range of banking services and financial products to domestic customers in 2007, most of them

Table 2.1 Foreign direct investment in domestic banks

Chinese Bank	Date	Share %	Foreign strategic investor
China Everbright Bank	Dec-96	1.9	Asian Development Bank
	Jun-97	21.2	China Everbright Limited (HK)
Bank of Shanghai	1999, 2001	7.0	IFC
	Dec-01	8.0	HSBC
Bank of Nanjing	Nov-01	15.0	IFC
	Jan-06	19.2	BNP Paribas
Shanghai Pudong Development Bank	Dec-02	5.0	CITI Group (increased to 19.9 in 2005)
Industrial Bank	Dec-03	15.98	Hang Seng Bank
	Dec-03	4.0	IFC
	Dec-03	5.0	GIC Special Investments
Shenzhen Development Bank	May-04	17.9	Newbridge Capital
Bank of Communications	Aug-04	19.9	HSBC
Minsheng Bank	Oct-04	4.6	Temasek
Ji'nan City Commercial Bank	Nov-04	11.0	Commonwealth Bank of Australia
Xi'an City Commercial Bank	Nov-04	5.0	IFC and Bank of Nova Sctia
Bank of Beijing	Mar-05	19.9	ING group
Bank of Hangzhou	Apr-05	19.9	Commonwealth Bank of Australia
	Jun-06	5.0	Asian Development Bank
China Construction Bank Corporation	Jun-05	9.0	Bank of America
	Jul-05	5.1	Temasek
Nanchong City Commercial Bank	Jul-05	10.0	DEG
	Jul-05	3.0	SIDT & SBFIC
Bank of China	Aug-05	10.0	Royal Bank of Scotland & co-investors
	Aug-05	10.0	Temasek
China Bohai Bank	Sep-05	19.9	Britain's Standard Chartered
ICBC	2006	4.93	Goldman Sachs
	2006	1.93	DRESDNER BANK LUXEMBOURG S.A.
Huaxia Bank	Oct-05	14.0	Deutsche Bank AG
Bank of Ningbo	May 2006	12.2	Oversea-Chinese Banking
China Guangfa Bank	Nov 2006	20	CITI Group
	Nov 2006	4.74	IBM Credit LLC
Bank of Chengdu	2007	19.99	Hong Leong Bank Berhad

(continued)

Table 2.1 (continued)

Chinese Bank	Date	Share %	Foreign strategic investor
Shanghai Rural Commercial Bank	Sep 2007	19.9	Australia and New Zealand Banking Group
Bank of Yingkou	Mar 2008	19.99	Commerce International Merchant Bank
Ximen Bank	2008	19.99	Fubon bank
Hengfeng Bank	2008	15.38	United Overseas Bank
Bank of Jilin	2010	18.27	South Korean Hana Bank

Source banks' website, official press, etc. Information is correct to our best knowledge on the date of producing this table in April 2017

chose to acquire equity stakes in domestic banks as a means of entering this emerging and attractive market. By doing so, foreign investors avoid potential low efficiency associated with foreign-owned banks in developing and transitional countries and avoid significant investment in establishing a branch network to serve their customers. The combination of these factors resulted in a surge of foreign direct investment in domestic banks in 2004 and the following years. For instance, British-based HSBC bought 19.9% of the Bank of Communications for $1.74 billion and Newbridge Capital became the biggest shareholder of Shenzhen Development Bank in 2004. In 2005, total foreign investment in Chinese banks reached $24 billion (including $8 billion and $1.9 billion raised by CCBC and the Bank of Communications in their IPOs on the Hong Kong Stock Exchange). International financial giants also embraced SOCBs and invested a significant amount of capital to acquire minority stakes of SOCBs after their radical joint-stock restructuring. Table 2.1 provides a list of domestic banks that have teamed up with foreign strategic investors. Foreign strategic investors come from more than 20 countries around the world, targeting all types of Chinese domestic commercial banks. They are also trying to participate in the management of the partner bank and exert influence on the business development. Chinese banks, on the other hand, benefited by obtaining much-needed capital, advanced technology, management skills, operational expertise, good corporate governance structure, and so on. The opening up policy achieved a "win-win" situation between the Chinese and foreign banks.

2.2 The Theoretical Underpinnings of Banking Reform and Development

The importance of a well-functioning banking system for economic growth has been well appreciated by governments in developing and transitional economies (La Porta et al. 2002). As a result, the reform of the banking system has become a high priority on the policy agenda of these countries in recent years. The market-oriented banking reform in China has been to improve domestic banks' performance, strengthen risk management, enhance competitiveness, and ultimately to build a sound and viable banking system in the long run that better serves economic development. The banking reform strategies have been formulated in accordance with economic theories from three perspectives.

The first theoretical perspective guiding banking reform in China is related to industrial organization theories. These theories indicate that competition, as in other industries, promotes production efficiency, improves product quality, widens product range, and stimulates innovation thereby maximizing social welfare. Any constraints, like regulations in resources allocation, increase the costs of production and induce inefficient resource allocation because of the lack of competition. In the past, government protective policies and financial depression prevailed in developing and transition economies. A monopolistic banking market induces moral hazard problems as these banks are well aware of the arguments of "too-big-to-fail" or "too important to fail." Such a market lacks competition and undermines the access of firms and households to financial services, which affect overall economic growth. Accordingly, banking reform commonly began with financial deregulation aiming at creating a competitive and flexible environment in which banks have more freedom over their operations. The unleashed competitive pressure forces banks to be more efficient by altering their input and output mix, upgrading technologies, and basing their operational decisions on market principles. Chinese banking reform at an early stage focused on deregulation. For example, institutional restructuring allowed more banks to enter into the market and the removal of business restrictions on SOCBs freed them to compete with their peers.

The second theoretical perspective guiding banking reform in China is related to the budgetary constraints theory that was first introduced by Kornai (1979). When a firm can expect to get financial subsidies in the future in case of financial distress and economic failure, it is considered to face a soft budget constraint. One argument for the existence of a soft budget constraint is that government bailout appears necessary and cheaper when the political and/or social price of the bankruptcy of firms is high due to unemployment that could lead to social unrest. The argument becomes especially stronger for sectors, like the financial sector, that are of strategic importance for the stability of the economy. However, literature has generally suggested that the adverse effects of a soft budget constraint outweigh its benefits. A soft budget constraint was common practice in banking. Typically, state-owned banks are faced with a soft budget constraint and largely capitalized by state funds. In transition economies, governments are under various pressures during the transformation of the economy from a centrally planned to a market-oriented one. Government bailout appears necessary to the financial sector for maintaining employment and social stability. The expected bailouts inevitably lead to a moral hazard problem and low performance.

A hard budget constraint implies that a firm has no access to government financial subsidies. The determination of a firm's continuation or bankruptcy should be purely based on market disciplines and considerations on performance, re-allocating capital to more productive firms in the best interests of shareholders as well as the economy as a whole. The theory suggests that the state needs to abandon the role of being the last resort for state-owned banks. The hope is that banking commercialization will harden budget constraints and the state will never have to bail banks out in the future. Banks have to rely more and more on raising capital from shareholders, rendering them responsible for shareholders' interests rather than the state's. The competitiveness of these banks will depend on their ability to earn profits and paying dividends to shareholders. In the short run, the state has a responsibility to remove all or much of the NPLs and let them have a fresh capital structure similar to that of a truly commercial bank so that they can compete with the incoming foreign competitors on a level playing field. In the long term, the state banks will have to be entirely responsible for their own profits and losses without any political or administrative interference.

The third theoretical perspective guiding the banking reform in China is related to the agency theory (Jensen and Meckling 1976; Jensen 1986). The principal-agent problem arises in an agency relationship where one party (the agent) acts on behalf of another party (the principal) under the principal's delegation. When there is a separation between owners and management, owners (principals) delegate the responsibility and related authorities of daily management and even strategic management to senior managers (agents). There is a danger that the agent may not act in the best interests of the owners (shareholders), for example, they may not work as efficiently as they could. They may also pursue their own interests at the expense of the shareholders' interests. This is because of the information asymmetry problem that the agents are involved in daily operations and possess more information than the principals. The central dilemma of the principal-agent theory is how to ensure the agent (the manager or employee) acts in the best interests of the principal (the shareholder or employer), given the agent has more information on the business than the principal and different, possibly conflicting, interests from the principal. The principal has to exercise due care in running the business and monitoring the management. The principal needs to assess the management performance exceptionally and periodically through mechanisms such as external auditing and a board of directors. The principal also needs to ensure these governance mechanisms are in place and well functioning. However, the corroboration of agents' behaviours and the evaluation of actual performance could be difficult or costly.

Firms with different ownership types have different corporate governance mechanisms to solve the agent-principal problem, resulting in variations in performance (Williams and Nguyen 2005). The principal-agent problem becomes more prominent in the case of state ownership of banks. Being the only influential representative of principals, the state pursues multiple and maybe conflicting commercial and social goals. Its role is ambiguously defined being both the owner and regulator. This rather complex situation makes the agents (the bank managers) unclear regarding what the principal exactly expects from them. In the past, the Chinese banking system was dominated by the wholly state-owned banks and these banks historically acted as government agents to finance the country's economic development plan. Whatever these state banks did, the principal (the state) had to bail them out if the banks ran into difficulty, as they always did. The agents (the banks), knowing that the principal was the last resort for help, lent relentlessly to whatever clients they considered to be trustworthy, resulting in mounting NPLs in the late 1990s that could never be recovered. In other words, the huge volume of NPLs was partially the result of moral hazard problems. The solution is to provide appropriate incentives so that agents are more likely to act in the best interest of the principal. Ownership reform that changes the state banks into joint-stock companies with multi-ownership aims at enhancing corporate governance and improving incentive structure, which is expected to address more effectively the agent-principal problem.

2.3 A Snapshot of the Chinese Banking System

2.3.1 The Status Quo of the Chinese Banking Sector

China's unremitting efforts on banking reform have resulted in a comprehensive and multi-layered banking system, providing a full range of banking products and services to the economy. The structure of the present banking system is illustrated in Fig. 2.1. The top tier includes two regulatory bodies—the PBOC and CBRC. The mainstay of the second tier is domestic commercial banks, including central government-controlled large banks, JSCBs, CCBs, and RCBs. Policy banks, foreign banks, rural credit cooperatives, postal savings banks, and other banking institutions (such as financing companies, new-type rural financial institutions of village or township banks, and consumer financing companies) are important complements, playing significant roles in serving the economy with wide coverage. According to CBRC, as of the end of 2015, the number of incorporated banking institutions

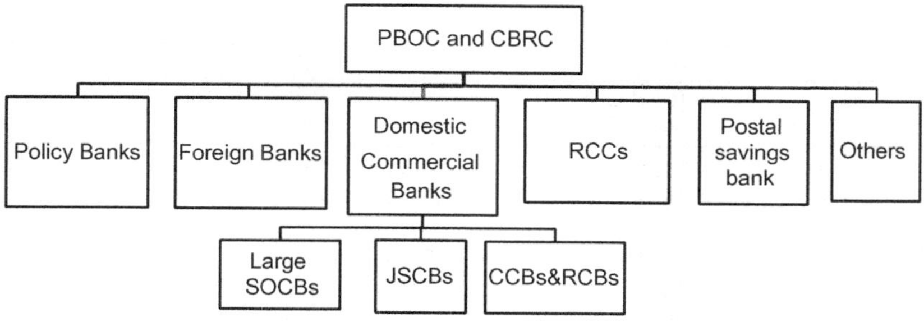

Fig. 2.1 Structure of the Chinese banking system. *Notes* PBOC = People's Bank of China, CBRC = China Banking Regulatory Commission, RCC = rural (and urban) credit cooperatives, SOCB = large state-controlled commercial bank, JSCB = joint-stock commercial bank, CCB = city commercial bank, RCB = rural commercial bank

was 4262 with 3.8 million employees. In particular, there were 3 policy banks,[6] 5 large commercial banks, 12 JSCBs, 133 CCBs, 5 private banks (under the pilot program of establishing entirely private-funded banks in 2015), 1 postal savings bank, 4 asset management companies,[7] 40 locally incorporated foreign banking institutions, 859 RCBs, 1311 village or township banks, and more than 1800 other banking institutions.

Table 2.2 gives an overview of the market structure of the Chinese banking system. Five large commercial banks, JSCBs, and CCBs together control about 70% of total banking assets. Five large central government-controlled banks (four former SOCBs plus the Bank of Communication) are the key players in the Chinese financial sector even though their market share in total banking assets declined by nearly one-third from 58% in 2003 to 39% in 2015. Over the same period, the market share of JSCBs and CCBs increased by about 8 and 6 percentage points, respectively. RCBs' market share increased by

[6]China Development Bank Corporation was incorporated in December 2008 as a commercial bank, while the State Council officially defined it as a development finance institution in March 2015. Thus it is essentially still a policy bank.

[7]Four assets management companies are Cinda Asset Management Company, China Great Wall Asset Management Company, Oriental Asset Management Company, and China Huarong Asset Management Corporation.

Table 2.2 The share of banking assets by institution types

	2003		2015	
	Total assets (RMB billion)	Share %	Total assets (RMB billion)	Share %
SOPBs	2125	7.68	19,285	9.67
SOCBs (Large banks)	16051	58.03	78,163	39.21
JSCB	2960	10.70	36,988	18.55
CCBs	1462	5.29	22,680	11.38
RCBs	39	0.14	15,234	7.64
RCCs	2651	9.58	8,654	4.34
New-type rural FIs & Postal savings bank	898	3.25	8,302	4.16
Others	1473	5.32	10,039	5.04
Total	27,658	100.00	1,99,345	100.00

Notes SOPB = state-owned policy banks, SOCBs = state-owned commercial banks (including Bank of Communication according to regulators classification), JSCB = joint-stock commercial bank, CCB = city commercial bank, RCB = rural commercial bank; RCC = rural credit cooperatives, FIs = financial institutions.
Source www.cbrc.gov.cn

7.5 percentage points, partially due to the restructuring of RCCs whose share declined from 9.58 to 4.34%. Meanwhile, policy banks have played a more active role with an increase in market share in total assets by 2 percentage points from 2003 to 2015.

2.3.2 An Assessment of Major Commercial Banks' Soundness and Performance

To probe how the Chinese banking system's soundness and performance have evolved over the past two decades, this section analyses a set of core financial soundness indicators developed by the IMF. The IMF finalized a core set and an encouraged set of financial soundness indicators in the Compilation Guide on Financial Soundness Indicators (2004). Core financial soundness indicators for deposit-taking institutions include regulatory capital to risk-weighted assets, regulatory Tier 1 capital to risk-weighted assets, nonperforming loans net of provisions to capital, nonperforming loans to total gross loans, sectoral distribution of loans to total loans, return on assets, return on equity, interest margin to gross income, noninterest expenses to gross income, liquid assets to total assets, liquid assets to short-term liabilities, and net open position in foreign exchange to capital (www.imf.org). These financial soundness indicators cover the main development in income statements, balance sheet conditions, capital adequacy, and asset quality, providing insights into the financial health and soundness of a country's financial institutions.

Ratio analysis is widely applied to financial institutions because of its clarity and simplicity. Its potential limitation is that it assumes that all other factors are held constant when considering a particular ratio. To overcome this limitation, a wide range of financial soundness indicators are selected to evaluate banks from different dimensions (profitability, capital adequacy, asset quality, and liquidity) and over a longer period 1995–2015.

2.3.2.1 Capital Adequacy

Banking is a highly leveraged industry. According to regulatory minimal capital requirements, shareholders' equity capital only accounts for about 8% of total assets with the remaining 92% financed by depositors and other creditors. Such a small portion of equity capital plays a fundamental role in the banking business and it is vital to the survival and growth of banks in the long run. Bank capital functions as a source of funds, a cushion to absorb unexpected operating losses, and the final safeguard against bank insolvency. When losses exceed bank capital in the extreme, banks become insolvent and face closure. It is important for banks to have adequate capital. The IMF has introduced four financial soundness indicators for capital adequacy, including two core indicators—regulatory capital to risk-weighted assets and regulatory Tier 1 capital (core capital) to risk-weighted assets—and two additional indicators—equity capital to total asset ratio (E/A ratio) and large exposures to capital. We focus on the first three indicators due to the lack of data on the last indicator. Regulatory capital adequacy ratios measure the capacity of the financial sector to absorb losses and indicate bank solvency and are regulated in most countries for the purposes of maintaining a sound banking system and protecting depositors. The E/A ratio reflects the proportion of total assets financed by equity capital.

Tier 1 capital is common in all countries and it is the most important capital because of its greatest ability to absorb losses. It is related to bank profitability and competitiveness and has become an informative basis for interested parties to judge a bank's capital adequacy. The Basel Capital Accord sets minimum capital requirements for banks: 8% for total regulatory capital ratio and 4% for Tier 1 core capital ratio (Basel III sets Tier1 capital ratio at 6%). Generally, the higher the ratio, the safer the bank is. Adequate banking capitalization is crucial for a sound banking sector, while over-capitalization may also imply economic inefficiency, waste, and opportunity cost for both shareholders and society (Cade 1997).

In China, authorities have internally monitored banks' capital adequacy in accordance with the Basel Capital Accord since 1998. The CRBC issued the *Regulation Governing Capital Adequacy of Commercial Banks* in 2004; it came into effect on 1 March. Commercial banks had a transition period up to 1 January 2007 with a feasible phase-in plan to meet the minimum capital requirements. The disclosure of capital adequacy ratios is not an official requirement for banks before 2004. After the crisis, authorities have focused on prudential regulations and risk control, and committed to global regulatory reform. Chinese embraced the Basel III framework and issued the *Capital Rules for Commercial Banks* in 2012 that came into force on 1 January 2013 with full implementation by March 2019.

Low capitalization has been one of the major plights haunting the Chinese banking system. In order to increase banks' capital adequacy, the government had made considerable efforts since 1998, including two rounds of capitalization and two rounds of NPLs off-loading. After a capital injection of RMB 270 billion in 1998, SOCBs met minimum requirement of 8%, while by 2003 all commercial banks in China were under-capitalized according to Basel standards. Under the challenges from WTO accession, the government initiated banking modernization reform. To boost banking capital, the government adopted a variety of measures, including injecting capital into the banking sector using state funds, attracting foreign strategic investors, raising capital in the capital market, and allowing private capital to enter into the banking sector.

In 2004, nearly half of commercial banks (47.5%) met minimum capital requirement, and by 2009 all banks held capital well above regulatory minimum requirements. As of the end of 2015, the average Tier 1 capital ratio and total regulatory capital ratio of commercial banks were 11.3 and 13.5%, respectively.

Figure 2.2 plots Tier 1 capital ratio and total capital ratio of SOCBs over the period 2003–2015. In 2003, all SOCBs had total capital adequacy ratio below the minimum requirement of 8%, while their Tier 1 capital ratio was above the minimum requirement of 4%. To make SOCBs ready for the opening up of the banking sector in 2006 under the WTO agreement, Chinese authorities sped up the SOCBs reform and as a result, all SOCBs increased capital rapidly, except for ABC whose reform lagged behind and started in 2008. From 2004, both Tier 1 capital and total capital ratio of SOCBs were well above regulatory requirements and increased further to a higher level of 11.2 and 13.25% (on average), respectively in 2006. Affected by the global financial crisis, capital ratios declined slightly in 2009 and then increased steadily until 2012, which is partially due to the government stimulus package and partially due to the continuous rapid expansion of the economy at a GDP growth rate of 10% in 2010, 9.5% in 2011, and 7.8% in 2012. In the last two years of the sample period, SOCBs' capital adequacy ratios gained momentum and increased at a faster speed. On average, CCBC and ICBC have slightly higher risk-weighted regulatory capital ratios than BOC, while ABC holds the lowest regulatory capital ratios.

E/A ratio is a risk-unweighted measure since total assets (not adjusted for risks) and equity (including capital and reserves) are taken from banks' balance sheets directly. Although less risk-sensitive than regulatory capital ratios, the changes in E/A ratio reveal shifts in bank balance sheet structure and shifts in bank risk taking. Figure 2.3 plots the E/A ratio of SOCBs over the period 1997–2015. In general, the movement of E/A ratio is consistent with that of risk-adjusted regulatory capital ratios. In the first half of the sample period, SOCBs were wholly state-owned and the government implemented the first round of banking recapitalization in 1998 that lifted their E/A ratio. Afterwards, SOCBs' capital level diverged. While BOC managed a steady increase in E/A ratio, the E/A ratio of CCBC and ICBC declined slightly and that of

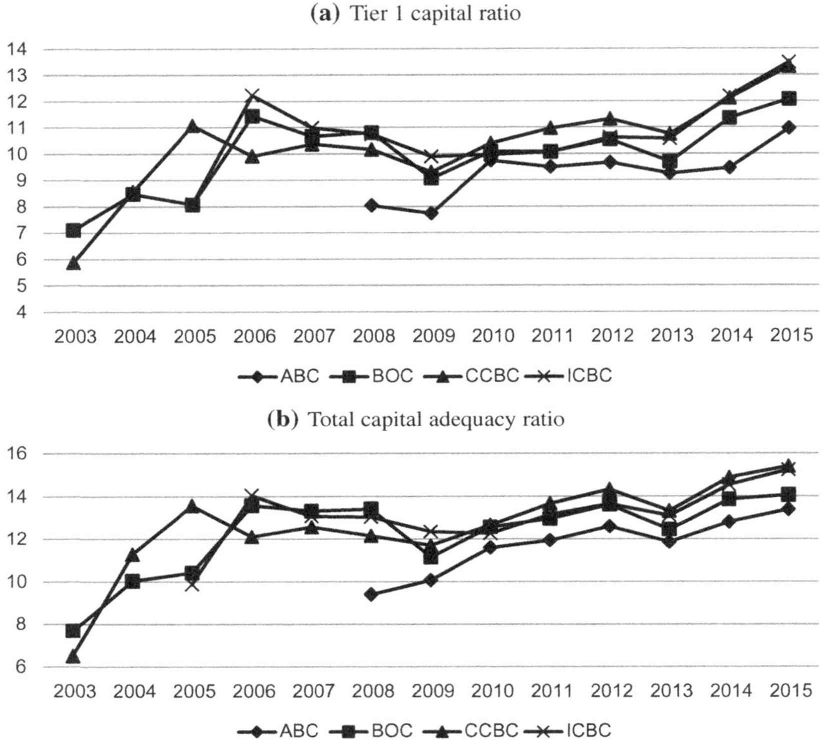

Fig. 2.2 Tier1 capital ratio and total capital ratio of SOCBs (2003–2015). *Notes* ABC = Agricultural Bank of China, BOC = Bank of China, CCBC = China Construction Bank Corporation, ICBC = Industrial and Commercial Bank of China. *Sources* CBRC, the Banker, Almanac of China's Finance and Banking, and press release

ABC deteriorated further to a level below 2%. By the end of 2006, BOC had the highest E/A ratio at 7.75%, which is nearly five times that of ABC (1.67%). In the second half of the period, the E/A ratio of SOCBs was lifted by the second round of banking recapitalization and then followed a consistent movement pattern—a steady increasing trend, especially after the reform of ABC in 2008.

2.3.2.2 Asset Quality and Non-Performing Loans

The quality of a bank's loan portfolio is of fundamental importance to profitability and long-run viability. A commonly used asset quality indicator is NPL ratio—the ratio of loans that are non-performing to gross loans. It is a backward-looking measure based on historical information on bank loan portfolio. A higher ratio indicates lower asset quality.

Detailed NPL information had been unavailable until 2000 when the central bank required other banks to disclose NPL ratios in accordance with the newly adopted internationally accepted, five-category loan-classification system. Since 2002, all banks were officially required to disclose NPL figures in their annual reports. In 1998, for the first time, the government disclosed SOCBs' NPL ratio of less than 30%. However, based on officially released information, our estimate was much higher (as shown in Table 2.3) and consistent with those of 35–50% by international agencies (such as Standard & Poor's and Moody's).

Unlike bank NPLs in other countries that are caused by losses from managerial and operational failure, much of SOCBs' NPLs occurred in the process of economic transition in China and were caused by a

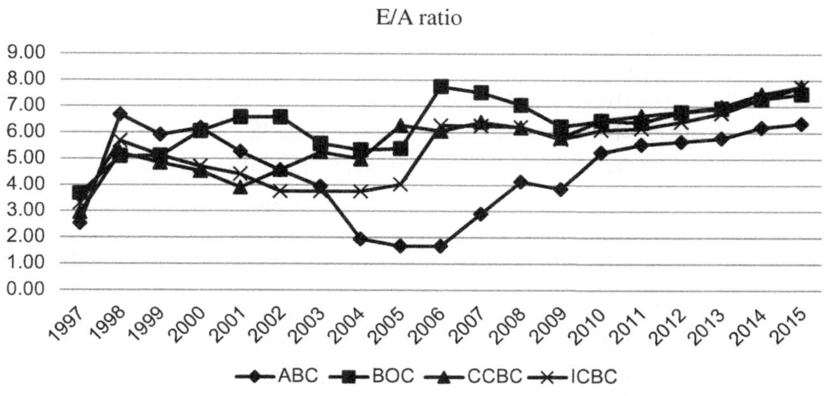

Fig. 2.3 Equity to total asset ratio of SOCBs (1997–2015). *Notes* ABC = Agricultural Bank of China, BOC = Bank of China, CCBC = China Construction Bank Corporation, ICBC = Industrial and Commercial Bank of China. *Source* BankScope, banks' annual reports

number of factors. Such factors include government intervention to support loss-making SOEs, excessive credit expansion to finance the overheated economy during the economic bubble in the early 1990s, the lack of commercial banking experiences in a market-oriented environment, a weak supervisory and regulatory system, and the underdeveloped legal and accounting framework. SOCBs' NPLs were the costs of the transition from a planned economy to a market-oriented one for maintaining social stability and sustaining high economic growth. SOCBs were the main contributor of massive NPLs in the Chinese banking system. The NPL problem was the key issue for banking reform in China and the central government made considerable efforts to solve it. As shown in Table 2.3, in 1999, the total amount of NPLs in SOCBs reached RMB 3.35 trillion and the NPL ratio was 43% under the four-category loan-classification system, accounting for about 40% of the country's GDP in that year. This figure would be higher if NPLs had been identified under the five-category loan-classification system. After the first round of NPL divestment by RMB 1.4 trillion in 1999, the total amount of NPLs rebounded to RMB 2.29 trillion and the NPL ratio of the banking sector was 31% in 2001 under the newly adopted five-category loan-classification system. After 2001, NPLs declined dramatically.

Figure 2.4 plots NPL ratio of different types of banks over the period 2001–2015. Prior to the 2008 global financial crisis, SOCBs had the highest NPL ratio, followed by CCBs, RCBs, JSCBs, and foreign banks. From 2006, commercial banks' NPL ratio entered into a single-figure era, and dropped further down to 2.8% in 2008. The rapid decline in SOCB's NPL ratio in the crisis time was partially attributable to the government's RMB 4 trillion stimulus package. This stimulus package was implemented mainly through the banking system via SOCBs, which, however, have raised concerns regarding asset quality and NPL problems in the future. From 2010 onwards, NPL ratio has been around 1% without much variation among different types of banks, lower than the internationally widely accepted level of 2%. Overall, foreign banks had the lowest NPL ratio over the sample period. JSBCs had the lowest NPL ratio among domestic banks, indicating better asset

Table 2.3 NPLs of four state-owned commercial banks

	Four-category system			Five-category system		
	Ratio (%)	Balance (RMB trillion)	Share of GDP (%)	Ratio (%)	Balance (RMB trillion)	Share of GDP (%)
1999	42.83	3.35	40.76			
2000	29.18	1.95	21.82			
2001	25.37	1.88	19.29	31.02	2.29	23.49
2002				26.10	2.21	20.99
2003				19.74	1.96	16.75
2004				15.57	1.58	11.54
2005				10.49	1.07	5.88

Note NPL = non-performing loan. *Sources* CBRC, Almanac of China's Finance and Banking, China Statistical Year book and author's calculation

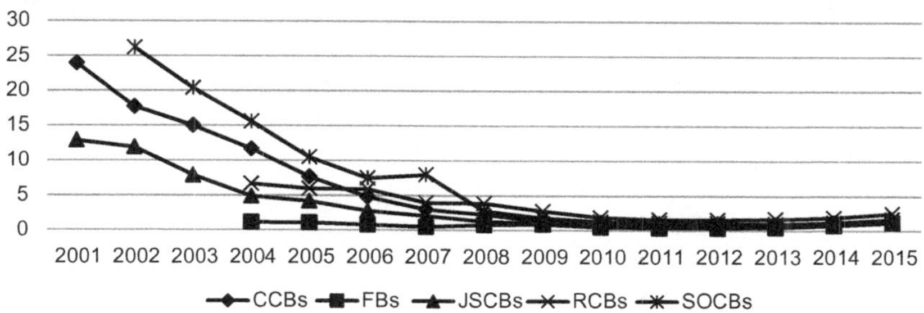

Fig. 2.4 NPL ratio of different types of bank 2001–2015. *Notes* CCB = city commercial bank, FB = foreign bank, JSCB = joint-stock commercial bank, RCB = rural commercial bank; SOCBs = large state-owned commercial banks. *Source* www.cbrc.gov.cn

quality control and risk management practice compared with SOCBs and CCBs.

Figure 2.5 plots SOCBs' NPL ratio over the period 2001–2015, which is consistent with the main trend in Fig. 2.4. Under a sequential SOCBs reform program, all SOCBs have dramatically reduced their

NPLs ratio from a sky-high level of 17–37% in 2002 to 5% or lower in 2005, except for ABC that was restructured and achieved this target in 2008. In the second half of the sample period, all SOCBs had low NPL ratios with trivial differences. The remarkable decline in the NPL ratio and year-end NPLs volume is largely due to the massive disposal of bad assets. Following the first round of NPLs divestment in 1999, the second round of NPLs divestment was implemented in 2003 and 2005 totaling RMB 1.18 trillion and in 2008 by RMB 815 billion. These divestments reduced absolute value of NPLs in SOCBs, significantly improving their asset quality. Moreover, the decline in SOCBs' NPLs is also attributable to the favourable economic environment and the rapid expansion of the credit market. Total loans extended by SOCBs increased one-third from RMB 6.4 trillion in 1999 to RMB 10 trillion in 2005, then increased four times in 10 years—reaching 40.46 trillion in 2015. The expansion helped reduce the NPLs ratio in the short run irrespective of the quality of new loans. Furthermore, the significant improvement in NPLs condition is the result of the ongoing bank reform that enhances internal control, risk management, the decision-making mechanism of credit expansion, disclosure requirements, and quality control for new loans.

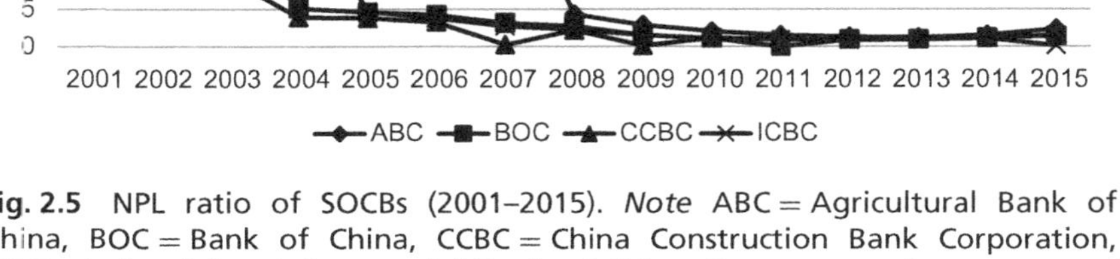

Fig. 2.5 NPL ratio of SOCBs (2001–2015). *Note* ABC = Agricultural Bank of China, BOC = Bank of China, CCBC = China Construction Bank Corporation, ICBC = Industrial and Commercial Bank of China. *Source* www.cbrc.gov.cn and others such as press release

2.3.2.3 Profitability

Bank profitability is evaluated by two frequently used performance measures—return on assets (ROA) and return on equity (ROE). ROA (ROE) is defined as the ratio of net income to average total assets (equity), measuring how well banks use their assets (capital) to generate profit. ROE needs to be interpreted in connection with indicators of capital adequacy, as it contains information on both profit and capital adequacy. A high ROE could result from high profitability and/or low capitalization.

Figure 2.6(a,b) plots the average ROA and ROE of different types of commercial banks in China. All banks' profitability experienced a systematic shock in 1997—the adverse effect of the Asian financial crisis, which lasted until 1999 when the Chinese government had to implement the first round of bailouts to SOCBs to stabilize the banking sector. CCBs and JSCBs outperformed SOCBs by both ROA and ROE during the first half of the period and slightly underperformed SOCBs and newly restructured RCBs during the second half of the period. The outstanding performance of CCBs in the early years is mainly due to sample bias, as only a few CCBs are included in the sample for the first five years. These CCBs are under better governance structure and better management and they operate in well-developed economic regions, such as Shanghai, Beijing, Tianjin, Shenzhen, and Xiamen. During the second half of the sample period, with the inclusion of more CCBs, their performance becomes in line with the industry average. JSCBs were established during the late 1980s and the early 1990s as profit-oriented commercial banks and these banks are under less government intervention and hence bear less political burden compared with SOCBs. SOCBs were the least profitable banks in China until 2004 and the subsequent SOCBs reform improved their performance significantly, making them the most profitable banks in terms of both ROA and ROE since 2005. Foreign banks' profitability has been stable over the whole sample period. They were the best performers in terms of ROA in the first few years and from 2005 became the least profitable banks in the Chinese banking market in terms of both ROA and ROE. One reason could be their smaller assets size and a higher level

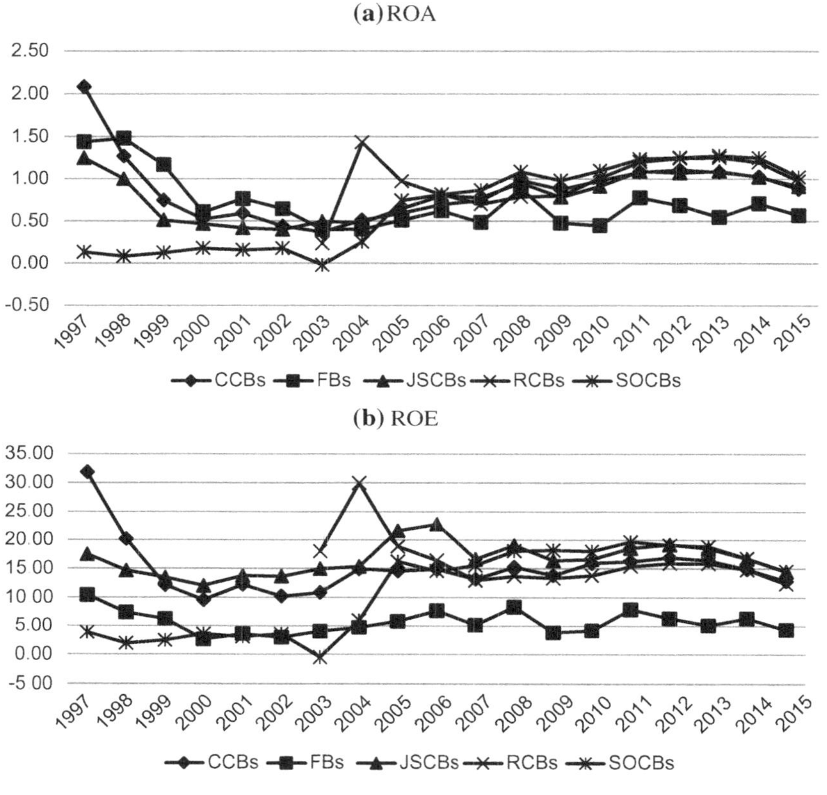

Fig. 2.6 ROA and ROE of different types of bank (1997–2015). *Source* BankScope and banks' annual reports. *Notes* ROA = return on assets, ROE = return on equity, CCB = city commercial bank, FB = foreign bank, JSCB = joint-stock commercial bank, RCB = rural commercial banks, SOCB = state-owned commercial bank

of capitalization, relative to their domestic counterparts. Overall, the banking modernization reform started in 2003 has led to significant improvement in banking profitability, which has been stable.

The four SOCBs are at pivot of the Chinese banking system and were at the forefront of the banking reform. After sequential successful reforms started in 2004, they are now the top four largest banks in the world by total assets. Figure 2.7(a,b) plots SOCBs' ROA and ROE over the period 1997–2015.[8] The 1997 Asian financial crisis hit ABC and BOC the hardest and their ROA and ROE decreased by half in 1998. The first round of SOCBs recapitalization in 1998 stabilized these banks' profitability up to 2002 and their ROA and ROE rose sharply during 2003–2008. Unexpectedly, all SOCBs achieved further improvement in profitability during the crisis time and remained highly profitable for the rest of the period. In 2004, CCBC was the most profitable bank in the world with ROE of 25.4%.

2.3.2.4 Liquidity

Liquidity represents the extent to which bank funds are available to meet the most important cash demand for deposit withdrawals, loans, and profitable investment opportunities. The banking system is a highly leveraged industry, and it is important for banks to maintain a prudent level of liquid assets. Serious problems in banking liquidity could cause financial losses, bankruptcy of an individual bank, and bank run due to contagion effect. It could even trigger a financial crisis in a country, or a region, or internationally in an extreme case as witnessed in 2008. As a result, banking liquidity has been closely monitored by the authorities.

There exists a trade-off between asset liquidity and profitability—highly liquid assets are associated with lower profitability. It is necessary to maintain a certain level of liquid assets to meet cash demand in daily operations, while excessive liquid assets have an adverse impact on profitability. Lower level of liquid assets to total assets may result in the risk of being unable to meet cash demand from depositors or more profitable investment opportunities. Financial losses might occur when banks have to liquidate assets or raise more expensive funds to meet cash demand in case of depositors' withdrawals to avoid adverse publicity and maintain reputation. Therefore, liquidity management is important for smoothing banks' daily operations, controlling systemic risk, and thus the well-being of the economy.

---

[8]The ROE of ABC in 2006 and 2007 reported in annual reports is not under normal business conditions due to financial restructuring and ownership reform. To avoid abnormal trends, we use an interpolation method to obtain ROE in 2006 and 2007 based on ROE in 2005 and 2008, assuming a constant growth rate.

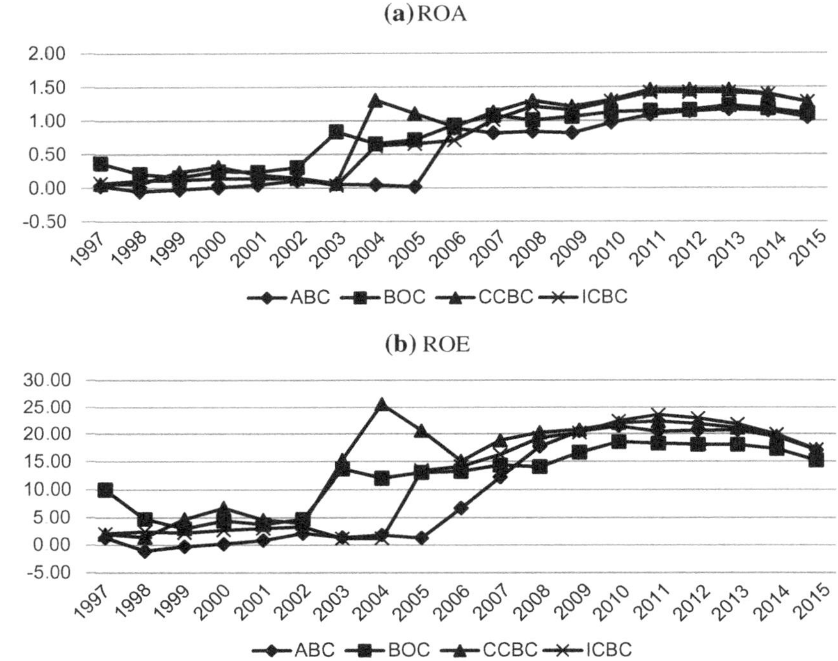

Fig. 2.7 ROA and ROE of large commercial banks (1997–2015). *Source* BankScope and banks' annual reports. *Notes* ROA = return on assets, ROE = return on equity, ABC = Agricultural Bank of China, BOC = Bank of China, CCBC = China Construction Bank Corporation, ICBC = Industrial and Commercial Bank of China

Liquid assets are those that can be readily converted into cash without significant loss under normal business conditions. It is difficult to measure and assess liquidity because of the involvement of subjective judgment when identifying liquid assets. There is no exact benchmark specifying the extent to which liquid assets holding is adequate. The IMF suggests two liquidity indicators—the ratio of liquid assets to total assets (liquidity ratio) and the ratio of liquid assets to short-term liabilities. Liquidity ratio indicates the proportion of liquid assets held by banks for meeting expected and/or unexpected demand for cash. The higher the ratio, the lower the liquidity risk a bank faces. In 1995, on average, 43% of banking assets were liquid assets, ranging from the highest of 48% (SOCBs) to the lowest of 39% (JSCBs). In the following few years, banking liquidity deteriorated. By the end of 2003, the banking liquidity ratio decreased to 13% and SOCBs were the worst bank group holding liquid assets less than 10%. Following the banking modernization reform, bank liquidity improved. The average liquidity ratio of commercial banks was 45% and fluctuated between 38% and 49% during the period 2010–2015.

Figure 2.8 plots SOCBs' liquidity ratio over the period 1997–2015. All SOCBs experienced a rapid decline in liquidity ratio in the first few years and decreased to less than 10% by the end of 2000. BOC made the first move to improve liquidity and its liquidity ratio increased by more than 15 percentage points in one year from 6.6% in 2000 to 22.3% in 2001. CCBC boosted liquidity dramatically in 2002 and ICBC made significant improvement since 2003. As the last reformed SOCB, ABC lagged behind but started catching up in liquidity ratio from 2006. In the post-crisis era, all SOCBs held 40–50% of their total as liquid assets and ABC was the most liquid bank.

The ratio of liquid assets to short-term liabilities captures the liquidity mismatch of assets and liabilities. It reflects a bank's ability to meet short-term liabilities without serious liquidity problems. As shown in Fig. 2.9, the trend of the liquid asset to short-term liabilities ratios of SOCBs

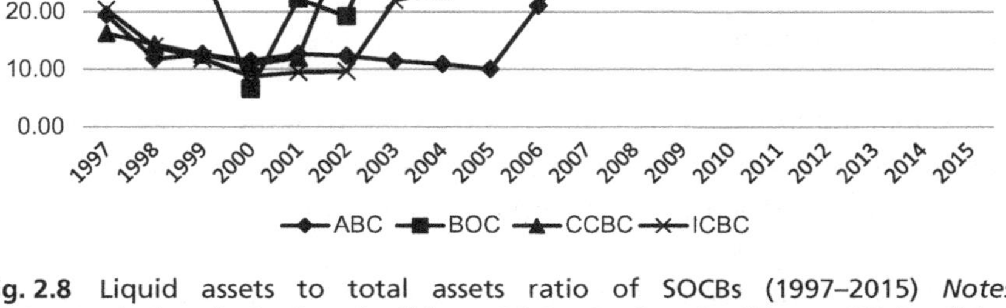

Fig. 2.8 Liquid assets to total assets ratio of SOCBs (1997–2015) *Notes* ABC = Agricultural Bank of China, BOC = Bank of China, CCBC = China Construction Bank Corporation, ICBC = Industrial and Commercial Bank of China. *Source* BankScope, banks' annual reports

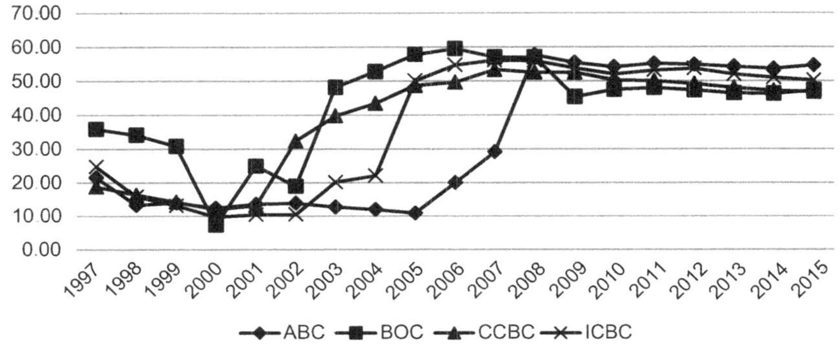

Fig. 2.9 Liquid assets to short-term liabilities ratio of SOCBs (1997–2015). *Source* BankScope. *Notes* ABC = Agricultural Bank of China, BOC = Bank of China, CCBC = China Construction Bank Corporation, ICBC = Industrial and Commercial Bank of China. Source: BankScope, banks' annual reports

mirrors that shown in Fig. 2.8; declined at the beginning, improved significantly during the radical banking reforming period 2003–2007, and remained stable at about 50% from 2008 onwards. Two liquidity indicators are consistent. In the past, SOCBs were able to operate at a low liquidity level without facing serious liquidity problems. These banks were wholly state-owned and domestic depositors believed they were guaranteed by the state. Bank run was highly unlikely even though SOCBs were technically insolvent. After ownership reform, these banks have become profit-oriented commercial banks and operated according to industry norms—maintaining a stable and relatively high level of liquidity.

2.4 Conclusion

Since its establishment in 1949, the Chinese banking system has experienced significant changes, from acting as government agents to serve the centrally planned economy prior to the economic reform to undergoing radical market-oriented reforms to perform commercial banking practices. The banking reform has been motivated and guided by a number of theoretical considerations, including the industrial organization theory, budget constraint theory, and agency theory. The goal is to transform the banking system to a market-oriented one that is viable in the long run thereby better serving the economic development of the country. When the 2008 global financial crisis seriously hit major advanced economies and their banking sectors, the Chinese authorities took up with the challenge and turned it into an opportunity for catching up. Both the banking sector as a whole and major commercial banks individually have made impressive progress in improving performance and soundness. In the post-crisis era, the Chinese banking sector has been stable and sound based on a systemic assessment using IMF's key financial soundness indicators. The assessment covers four dimensions: profitability captured by ROA and ROE; asset quality proxied by NPL ratio; capital adequacy measured by regulatory total capital ratio, Tier1 capital ratio and risk-unweighted equity to capital ratio; and liquidity indicated by liquid assets to total assets ratio and liquidity asset to short-term liabilities. Now the Chinese banking system has become a multi-layered system with more than 4000 banking institutions providing a full range of banking products and services to serve the economy. It also plays an increasingly important role in the world financial arena—it is home to the four largest banks in the world in terms of market capitalization.

References

Berger, A.N., I. Hasan, and M. Zhou. 2009. Bank Ownership and Efficiency in China: What Will Happen in the World's Largest Nation? *Journal of Banking & Finance* 33: 113–130.

Cade, E. 1997. *Managing Banking Risks*. Cambridge: Gresham.

CBRC. 2003–2015. *Annual Reports*. China Banking Regulatory Commission, China.

Jensen, M., and M. Meckling. 1976. Theory of the Firm: Managerial Behavior, Agency Costs and Ownership Structure. *Journal of Financial Economics* 3: 305–360.

Jensen, M. 1986. Agency Costs of Free Cash Flow, Corporate Finance, and Takeovers. *American Economic Review* 76: 323–339.

Kornai, J. 1979. Resource-Constrained Versus Demand-Constrained Systems. *Econometrica* 47 (4): 801–819.

La Porta, R., F. Lopez-De-Silanes, and A. Shleifer. 2002. Government Ownership of Banks. *Journal of Finance* 57: 265–302.

Williams, J., and N. Nguyen. 2005. Financial Liberalization, Crisis, and Restructuring: A Comparative Study of Bank Performance and Bank Governance in South East Asia. *Journal Banking and Finance* 29: 2119–2154.

Wong, Y.C.R., and M.L.S. Wong. 2001. Competition in China's Domestic Banking Industry. *Cato Journal* 21 (1): 19–41.

Yang, X. 2002. *General Financial History of China (In Chinese)*. Beijing: China Finance Publishing House.

3
Banking Reform and Bank Performance in China

Preamble

One main objective of banking reform in China is to improve bank performance so that the banking sector could allocate capital more efficiently. While three decades of reform give rise to a number of important research questions, this chapter addresses the following three issues: Has the banking reform been motivated by the agency theory and the budget constraint theory? Has the banking sector become more efficient? What impact has the privatization strategy had on bank efficiency? This chapter starts with an introduction of the efficiency concept and a brief literature review on bank efficiency in Sect. 3.1. After outlining research methodology in Sect. 3.2, this chapter empirically tests for whether banking reform strategies have been motivated by the agency theory and/or the budgetary constraint theory in Sect. 3.3. The privatization of state banks has been the focus of banking reform to alleviate the agency problem and to harden budget constraints aiming at improving bank efficiency. Partial privatization has led to significant changes in banking, and this chapter examines how concrete privatization strategies affect bank cost and profit efficiency in the short run and in the long run in Sect. 3.4. Section 3.5 concludes.

C. Jiang and S. Yao, *Chinese Banking Reform*, The Nottingham China Policy Institute Series, DOI 10.1007/978-3-319-63925-3_3

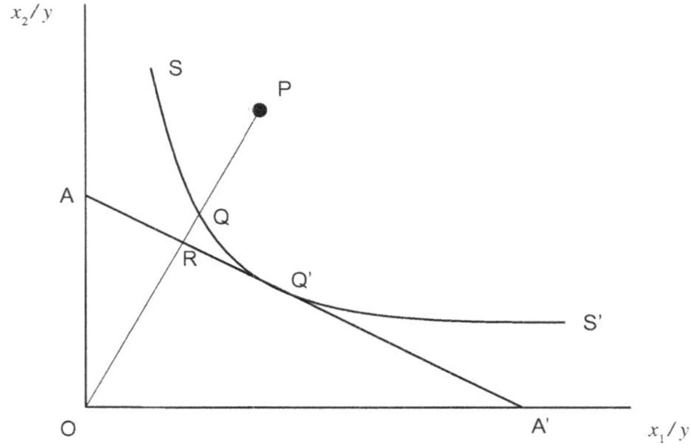

Fig. 3.1 Farrell efficiency (Coelli et al. 1998)

3.1 Efficiency Concept and Bank Efficiency Literature

3.1.1 Efficiency Concept

Farrell (1957) proposes a path-breaking way of measuring operational efficiency (economic efficiency) of a firm, defined as the product of technical efficiency and allocative efficiency. Technical efficiency refers to the ability of optimal utilization of available resources either by producing maximum output given an input level or by using minimum inputs given an output level, while allocative efficiency reflects the ability to achieve the optimal combination of inputs and outputs for a given level of prices (Lovell 1993). In Farrell's simple example, firms produce a single output (y) using two inputs (x_1 and x_2), assuming constant returns to scale. The technical inefficiency of a firm that uses inputs to produce a unit of output at point P can be expressed by the distance QP shown in Fig. 3.1. All inputs could be proportionally reduced by the distance QP without affecting the output level. The technical efficiency of a firm is defined as the distance to a production frontier that provides the upper boundary of production possibilities. In particular, technical efficiency is measured by the ratio OQ/OP that is less than 1. The isoquant SS' represents fully efficient firms and is used as a benchmark to measure technical efficiency of other less efficient firms. When information on input prices is available, the allocative efficiency of the firm located at point P is represented by the ratio OR/OQ, capturing inefficiencies due to a sub-optimal input combination picked by the firm for given input prices. Allocative efficiency requires the use of a right input mix in producing the correct output mix in the light of their respective prevailing prices (Coelli et al. 1998). Technical efficiency can be estimated from either an input-orientated model focusing on input conservation without changing the output quantities produced, or an output-orientated model aiming at output augmentation without altering the input quantities employed. Both models estimate exactly the same frontier and identify the same set of best-practice firms, but the efficiency measures of inefficient firms may differ (Coelli et al. 1998). The selection of the orientation depends on over which quantities the managers have most control.

When information on input and output prices is available and a behavioural assumption is appropriate, economic efficiency measures—cost efficiency, revenue efficiency, and profit efficiency—can be derived against cost, revenue, and profit frontiers, respectively. Economic efficiency is defined as the distance to an economic frontier. Assuming that SS' represents a cost frontier in Fig. 3.1, cost efficiency is measured by the ratio OR/OP, suggesting a theoretical possible cost reduction by the amount of RP (Coelli et al. 1998). Economic efficiency requires both technical efficiency and allocative efficiency. Technically efficient firms could economically inefficient and vice versa, due to the differences in managers' ability to use best technology and their abilities to respond to market price conditions (Bauer et al. 1998). X-efficiency, first introduced by Leibenstein (1966), is attributed to overall objective determinants, such as improvement in management and application of technologies. Within a dataset, the best-practice frontier or the worst-practice frontier can be estimated and the difference between the best-practice frontier and the practice of a particular firm measure is its x-inefficiency.

Producers may be a cost minimizer or a profit maximizer, or both, which lead to deviations of actual performance from the best practice.

Cost efficiency is defined as the ratio of minimum feasible costs to observed actual costs, bounded between zero and unity, reflecting the proportion of costs or resources is used efficiently. Cost efficiency is the most commonly used measure in efficiency research. Cost efficiency is derived by estimating a cost function where total costs is a dependent variable and explanatory variables are exogenously given variables, including output quantities, input prices, netput quantities (fixed inputs or fixed outputs), environmental factors, and a composite error term that consist of bank managerial inefficiency and random errors. When assuming that producers face output prices and seek to maximize revenue for a given level of input, revenue efficiency can be measured against the revenue frontier, defined as the ratio of actual revenue of a firm to maximum revenue that could be raised if the firm is fully efficient. It is bounded between unity and zero. Revenue efficiency is rarely used alone in practice but incorporated into profit efficiency.

Profit maximization requires both costs minimization and revenue maximization. Profit efficiency is defined as a ratio of actual profit to maximum attainable profit, which cannot be greater than unity, but can be below zero because of possible negative actual profit. A firm's profit efficiency reflects the proportion of maximum profit the firm has earned (Kumbhakar and Lovell 2000) and to maximize profit, a firm needs to be technically efficient, allocative efficient, and scale efficient (Berger and Mester 1997). Subject to varying exogenous business conditions, profit efficiency has two variants, namely standard profit efficiency and alternative profit efficiency. Standard profit efficiency measures the extent to which a firm produces the maximum possible profit for a given level of input and output prices, assuming that producers face exogenously determined input and output prices in competitive factor markets and make decisions on the mixture of inputs to use and the mixture of outputs to produce.

Alternative profit efficiency measures the extent to which a firm earns maximum profits when facing exogenously determined input prices and output quantities. Output prices are no longer taken as given and firms are assumed to have some degree of pricing power over their output markets. Both output prices and quantities are to be determined under the market demand conditions and only input prices are part of external conditions (Kumbhakar and Lovell 2000). Alternative profit efficiency is derived from a profit function that is identical to the standard profit function except for output prices replaced by output quantities (Berger and Mester 1997). The alternative profit function approach is generally preferred to the standard profit function approach in bank efficiency study (Berger and Mester 1997; DeYoung and Hasan 1998) for a number of reasons. First, it enables the estimation of profit efficiency when the prices of certain outputs, such as transaction services and fee-based transactions, are unavailable or hard to measure reliably. Second, the variation in output quantities is likely to be more variable across banks than the variation in output prices. Third, the unmeasured differences in the quality of services provided by banks could be better controlled in the alternative profit function. The extra costs spent on improving output quality are offset against extra corresponding revenue in the alternative profit function, while these costs are accounted as inefficiencies in a cost function. Finally, alternative profit efficiency better controls for the heterogeneity in bank size by including output quantities rather than output prices. Alternative profit efficiency reflects the bank's ability to generate profits at the same output levels for different-sized banks. This approach could reduce possible scale bias in profit efficiency estimation when optimal output levels cannot be reached by small banks.

3.1.2 Bank Efficiency Literature

There are a wealth of literature on bank efficiency but mainly in the US and European countries.[1] In developed countries, efficiency research has been concerned about the impacts on performance of market structure and concentration, deregulation, mergers and acquisitions, foreign bank entry, risk-taking, and regulation. The association between market concentration and the bank performance has been examined extensively by testing four hypotheses: (1) the structure-conduct-performance

[1]Berger and Humphrey (1997) provide a valuable survey on financial institutions efficiency studies.

hypothesis, (2) the relative-market power hypothesis, (3) X-efficient structure hypothesis, and (4) scale efficient structure hypothesis, while empirical research shows mixed results (Berger 1995; Kapopoulos and Siokis 2005; Evanoff and Fortier 1998). Deregulation is one of the key trends in the banking sector across the world. In developed countries, empirical studies find a positive impact on bank efficiency in some countries such as Australia (Sturm and Williams 2004) and Spain (Kumbhakar and Lozano-Vivas 2005) but little effect in the United States in the early 1980s (Bauer et al. 1993). Disagreements in findings are likely due to the industry conditions prior to deregulation and the deregulation measures being implemented (Berger and Humphrey 1997). Following deregulation, bank mergers and acquisitions become popular practices in developed countries. Despite a widely claimed positive effect on efficiency, the extant literature has not yet reached such a consensus. Empirical studies show evidence for improved profit efficiency but not cost efficiency, while improvement in profit efficiency is argued to be attributable mainly to the proper shifting of portfolio that generates more revenues (Berger et al. 1999; Hughes et al. 1999; Avkiran 1999; Berger and Mester 2003). More recent studies investigate the nexus between efficiency, risk, and regulation. Fiordelisi et al. (2011) find that lower bank efficiency Granger-causes higher bank risk and more efficient banks become better capitalized, which in turn tend to improve efficiency, while Delis et al. (2016) show a negative risk-efficiency nexus with causality running both ways. Based on a large dataset of banks from 72 countries over the period 1999–2007, Barth et al. (2013) find tighter restrictions on bank activities negatively affect bank efficiency, while more stringent capital regulation has a positive effect on bank efficiency.

During the last two decades, bank efficiency research has been extended to developing and transitional economies. Banking systems in these countries are different from those of developed countries and banking efficiency studies have focused on different issues, such as ownership structure and privatization, in addition to common issues such as deregulation. Most of these economies underwent market-oriented reform, and banking reform commonly started from financial deregulation in order to increase competition and improve performance. Studies generally find significant improvement in bank performance after deregulation (Isik and Hassan 2003; Gilbert and Wilson 1998; Chen et al. 2005).

In previous centrally planned economies, financial sectors were usually dominated by the banking sector with pervasive state ownership in banking. It is believed that governments could channel funds to sectors (projects) with low financial returns but high social benefits. Governments could act "benevolently" when there is a desire to promote industrialization and development but lack of sufficient private (venture) capital to finance growth. State ownership is arguably economically efficient by balancing social and economic objectives (Megginson 2005). However, state ownership is inherently inefficient according to some political and economic theories. Firstly, the agent-principal problem becomes more prominent under state ownership. When there is a separation between ownership and management controls, managers (agents) may pursue their own interests rather than acting in the best interest of owners (principals) (Bearle and Means 1932), which may adversely affect performance. The incentives for state bank managers to efficiently allocate resources might differ for those under other ownership arrangements (Laeven 1999). On the one hand, state bank managers have no incentive and no pressure to improve efficiency and therefore are less diligent in maximizing revenues and minimizing costs. They are more likely to pursue "a quiet life" or their own interests at the expense of owner interests. There also exists a collective action problem in state-owned banks, resulting in the lack of means for punishing managers when they act in the best interest of sub-part's performance (Megginson 2005). In fact, managers of state banks are rarely punished individually for poor performance, whereas the managers will be replaced by shareholders or a hostile takeover for poor performance in a private bank. In the absence of proper capability to monitor the activity of management and appropriate methods of disciplining managers in state-owned banks, agency problems become serious.

Secondly, state ownership in banks facilitates governments to provide funds to financially inefficient but politically desirable projects (La Porta et al. 2002). It is common practice that state-owned banks act as government agents to fulfil national development plans with much less concern for profitability and efficiency. Under the control of state ownership, state banks finance state-owned enterprises (SOEs) to pursue non-economic goals of maintaining social stability and patronage employment as well as economic growth goals by supporting infrastructure investments and exports. These goals are in conflict with the commercial goal of profit maximization and the latter commonly gives way to other goals, resulting in poor performance. Moreover, government acts as both the owner and the regulator who might also have somewhat conflicting interests (Megginson 2005).

The third argument for low efficiency of state banks is soft budget constraint faced by state-owned banks. Soft-budget constraints faced by state banks invite moral hazard problems leading to poor performance. State-owned banks are normally large banks in size and play a crucial role in the economy. The fear of too-big-to-fail or too-important-to-fail permits the survival of inefficient state banks. The government is unlikely to make or let poorly performing state-owned banks become bankrupt by subsidizing insolvent state-owned banks in pursuit of its multiple objectives. Managers of poorly performing state-owned banks develop a dependency on the government for funding when their banks go into financial difficulties. When state banks are in difficulties, they expect help from governments and managers have little incentive to improve performance. Managers of private banks do not have such a dependency and their clear understanding is that banks facing financial distress may be bankrupt. Managers of state banks are under weak capital markets discipline and less threat of financial distress than those of private banks. Finally, the free-rider problem becomes more common. State ownership theoretically means that all citizens are co-owners who in practice have no power and incentive to influence and monitor the management of state banks, leaving governments as the only effective representative goals (Huibers 2005). However, government essentially uses state banks as a mechanism to help accomplish their multiple, often conflicting, goals, which would lead to inefficiency.

Empirical research generally points to a negative impact of state ownership on bank efficiency with a few exceptions. La Porta et al. (2002) find that financial performance of publicly owned banks is inferior to that of private banks using a dataset of large banks in 92 countries. Hao et al. (2001) report a negative association between bank cost efficiency and the share of government ownership in Korean banks. In transition economies, state-owned banks are found to be significantly less efficient then their private counterparties (Bonin et al. 2005b; Fries and Taci 2005). Nevertheless, Spong et al. (1995) argue that no single organizational structure appears to be a guarantee of efficiency. Little evidence from Altunbas et al. (2001) suggests superior efficiency of privately owned banks, while Shanmugam and Das (2004) find state banks outperform other types of banks in India.

Over the last two decades, bank privatization has been prioritized on the policy agenda in developing countries and transitional economies, involving more than 250 commercial banks in 59 countries in developed, developing, and transition economies (Megginson 2005). It is seen as the ultimate way to improve bank performance by constructing good governance structure to solve agent-principal problems more efficiently. Privatized banks face a hardened budget constraint and bank managers are under pressure to improve efficiency. Shareholders are expected to exercise due diligence to monitor management performance in order to safeguard their investments. Empirical evidence shows clear performance improvements after privatization (e.g., Berger et al. 2005; Williams and Nguyen 2005).

In the process of privatization, most governments welcome foreign investors who are expected to bring in capital as well as advanced technology and know-how, modern banking techniques, and superior managerial skills in financial intermediation. Foreign investors also benefit from ownership participation in domestic banks to share local partners' soft information and extensive network. Empirical studies suggest that banks with foreign ownership are significantly more efficient (e.g., Hasan and Marton 2003; Fries and Taci 2005) and therefore strategic foreign investors are desirable during banking privatization (e.g., Bonin et al. 2005b). Going public is another major step of privatization, which subject banks to market discipline and encourage managers to improve efficiency to remain in the market. Empirical evidence shows that publicly traded firms are more efficient in the United States (e.g., Berger and Mester 1997).

The Chinese banking sector had been largely neglected until it started to attract worldwide attention from academics a decade ago. Extant literature generally suggests that the four largest state-owned commercial banks (SOCBs) underperform other types of banks in the early reform period and banking reform improved bank efficiency (e.g., Berger et al. 2009; Yao et al. 2007; Jiang et al. 2009, 2013). Two exceptions are Fu et al. (2007) that reports banks efficiency declined during 1993–2002 compared with 1985–1993, and Chen et al. (2005) that finds SOCBs were more efficient than JSCBs. Berger et al. (2009) suggests that banks with minority foreign ownership experienced significant improvement in efficiency for the period 1994–2003.

3.2 Research Methodology

3.2.1 Estimating Best Practice Frontier and Efficiency

There are two main approaches to estimating efficiency, namely the parametric approach and non-parametric approach with five different methods (Berger and Humphrey, 1997). Overall, two approaches give similar average efficiency estimates, while they disagree on inefficiency rankings of individual firms. On average, there is about 20% cost inefficiency and about half of profit inefficiency in the United States. Non-parametric techniques yield lower average efficiency estimates and greater dispersion compared with parametric techniques. The parametric approach includes three main approaches of determining the best practice frontier: (1) the stochastic frontier analysis (SFA), which is developed by Aigner et al. (1977) and Meeusen and van den Broeck (1977), independently (see more details in Sect. 3.2.2); (2) the distribution free approach (DFA) assumes that efficiency differences are stable over time and the estimated efficiency of each firm is the difference between its mean residual and industrial mean residual on the frontier; and (3) the thick frontier approach (TFA) has no restriction of distributional assumption and TFA estimates provide an overall level of efficiency rather than point efficiency estimates for individual firm. The non-parametric approach includes data envelop analysis (DEA) and free disposal hull (FDH). DEA is a linear programming method used for estimating efficiency of decision-making units (DMUs). DEA creates a production frontier directly based on a particular data set of firms and the distance from the best practice frontier reflects a firm's inefficiency (Charnes, et al. 1978). FDH is a special case of DEA by releasing the hypothesis of convexity.

There is no consensus on whether the parametric or non-parametric approach is superior over the other and they are roughly equally adopted in efficacy research. The parametric method has been criticized for using a predetermined frontier functional form, which may be misspecified as well as the pre-assumed distributional assumptions with respect to the random error terms and inefficiencies. However, a parametric method has its virtues. First, a major advantage is the allowance for random errors. Deviations of actual performance from best practice are represented by composite errors that are theoretically decomposable into inefficiencies and random shocks. The separation of random errors and inefficiencies tends to provide more accurate estimated technical efficiency. Second, although distributional assumption on inefficiencies induces the suspicion of the estimated efficiency level, SFA always rank the firm efficiency in the same order as their cost function residuals. Third, parametric methods appear to be more consistent with the competitive conditions in the banking market and more consistent with non-frontier measures of bank performance such as return on assets Bauer et al. (1998). A non-parametric approach does not specify a functional form for the frontier, and requires no prior assumption of the distribution of inefficiency across observations while allowing efficiency to vary over time. Using a linear programming technique, the best practice frontier is formed as the piecewise linear combinations. However, its important drawback is the assumption of no random errors influencing bank performance. Ignoring the existence of potential errors, the effects of omitted errors may be composed into efficiency estimates (Berger and Humphrey 1997).

3.2.2 Stochastic Frontier Analysis (SFA)

This chapter employs a parametric method of SFA—one of the widely applied methods of investigating efficiency in the literature (e.g., Ferrier and Lovell 1990; DeYoung and Hasan 1998; Hasan and Marton 2003; Fu and

Heffernan 2007; Berger et al. 2009; Jiang et al. 2013; Delis et al. 2016). SFA specifies a functional form for the cost, profit, or production function, which allows inefficiencies to be included in the error term. The error terms are separated based on two distributional assumptions that the inefficiencies (μ) follow an asymmetric half-normal distribution based on the logic that inefficiencies only increase costs above frontier levels, and random errors (v) follow a symmetric standard normal distribution because random fluctuations can either increase or reduce costs. The estimated inefficiencies of any firm is taken as the conditional mean or mode of the distribution of the efficiency term, μ, given the observations of the composed error term, ε (Bauer et al. 1993). Later studies argue that alternative distributions for inefficiencies, such as truncated-normal distribution, may be more appropriate than the half-normal and exponential distributions.

Efficiency studies employing SFA, frequently adopt a two-stage estimation procedure. The first stage specifies and estimates a stochastic frontier to derive inefficiencies for individual companies, assuming these inefficiencies are distributed identically. The second stage regresses these estimated inefficiencies on a set of firm specific characteristics, such as managerial experience, ownership, location, and the like, to explain differences in estimated inefficiencies. This two-stage procedure suffers from serious econometric problems, due to its contradictory assumptions regarding the independence of the inefficiency effect in two stages (Battese and Coelli 1995; Kumbhakar and Lovell 2000). Using the two-stage procedure, the elements of z_i must be assumed to be uncorrelated with the elements of input vector (x_i) in order to assure that maximum likelihood estimates of the first stage stochastic frontier model are unbiased. Moreover, the predicted inefficiencies are assumed to be identically and independently distributed in the first stage, but they are assumed to have a functional relationship with z_i in the second stage. This contradiction between two stages makes the two-stage procedure the so-called schizophrenic approach. Addressing the issues, researchers have developed one-stage models that simultaneously estimate inefficiencies and the potential relationship between the firm specific variables and estimated inefficiencies (Huang and Liu 1994; Battese and Coelli 1995). Wang and Schmidt (2002) explore theoretical insights into reasons why the two-stage procedure is biased and provide extensive Monte Carlo evidence that shows the severity of the bias. Their results are in favour of one-stage models.

As such, this chapter adopts a one-stage model proposed by Battese and Coelli (1995) (hereinafter the BC95 model). It assumes that non-negative technical inefficiencies are a function of company-specific and environmental variables, independently distributed as truncations of normal distribution with a constant variance, but with means that are a linear function of observable variables. The BC95 model is flexible by allowing the estimation of both technical change in the stochastic frontier and time-varying technical inefficiencies in the technical inefficiency effects. Productivity changes are decomposed into the shift in the frontier and the movement towards or away from the theoretically predicted production frontier. Greater efficiency can be gained through either technological innovations or improvement of efficiency in general caused by learning-by-doing effects or dissemination of the best practice.

When estimating efficiency, how to measure banking outputs and inputs is controversial. Unlike manufacturing firms producing physical goods, banks produce unidentifiable intermediary services and multi-products. The production approach treats banks as firms producing different deposit and loan accounts and the number and type of transactions and documents are considered to be the best measure of bank output. As such, detailed data are generally unavailable; in practice the number of deposit and loan accounts is usually employed as the measure of bank output. The intermediation approach (Sealey and Lindley 1977) treats banks as financial intermediaries channeling funds between depositors and creditors. This approach differs from the production approach by adding deposits to inputs and considering both operating cost and interest cost (Goddard et al. 2001). Neither the production approach nor the intermediation approach is perfect; they are complementary (Berger and Humphrey 1997). The production approach is appropriate for studying the cost efficiency of banks addressing banks' operation costs, while the intermediation approach is appropriate for studying the economic differentiation of banks by controlling the overall costs of banking (Ferrier and Lovell 1990). This chapter adopts the intermediation approach when defining inputs and outputs.

Another methodological issue is whether to estimate an industry "best practice" frontier or to estimate separate frontiers for different types of banks. The former is a commonly used approach based on the argument that all firms in the marketplace face the same external macroeconomic environment and they are subject to similar market conditions regardless of bank types. Efficiency estimates are comparable since they are derived against the same industry "best practice" frontier. The latter approach argues that different types of firms may adopt different production technology and therefore using pooled industry frontier could confound inefficiencies and the effects of technology choice (Mester 1993). This more rigorous approach limits cross-firm comparison to the same type, not possible for comparison across different types of firms. Thus, it is of limited usefulness when concerning bank liberalization and privatization (Altunbas et al. 2001). This chapter adopts a single frontier approach that allows the comparison of efficiencies among banks with different ownership types.

3.3 Theoretical Foundations of Banking Reform Strategy

3.3.1 Hypothesis

To investigate whether reform strategies are based on the agency theory and/or the budgetary constraints theory, as discussed in Chap. 2, we test for two hypotheses. The agent-principal problem and the soft budgetary constraint problem simultaneously become prominent in state banks. The role of state banks and the role of government are ambiguously defined and it is hard for the agent (managers) to understand what the principal (government) exactly expects from them. The solution is to provide appropriate incentives so that agents are more likely to act in the best interest of the principal by better solving the agent-principal problem. A joint-stock ownership structure more clearly defines managers' responsibilities and incentives, which helps solve agency problems and hence JSCBs are expected to outperform wholly state-owned banks. As such, the first hypothesis is as follows: *Non-state joint-stock commercial banks are more efficient than the state-owned commercial banks (Hypothesis 1).* If this hypothesis holds, we conclude that the ownership reform by turning the state-owned banks into joint-stock enterprises is motivated by the agency theory. Ownership reform leads to multi-ownership in state banks, which will enhance corporate governance and improve efficiency.

State banks are capitalized by the state fund and face a soft budget constraint. Managers have little incentive to improve performance as they expect help from the state when they are facing difficulties. Banks subject to a harder budget constraint have to raise capital from shareholders. Managers are under pressure to satisfy existing shareholders and attract potential investors and hence have strong incentive to improve performance. As such, the second hypothesis is as follows: *Banks that are subject to a harder budget constraint are more efficient than banks that are subject to a softer budget constraint (Hypothesis 2).* If this hypothesis holds, we conclude that joint-stock ownership reform is also consistent with the budget constraint theory. The retreat of state ownership in banks hardens budgetary constraints and banks have to rely more and more on raising capital from various shareholders. Turning state-owned banks into joint-stock companies will change the incentive structure, which is expected to improve bank efficiency.

3.3.2 Model and Data

Two empirical models are specified to test the aforementioned two hypotheses. Technical efficiency is obtained from estimating a traditional Cobb–Douglas production function using the one-stage BC95 model. The Cobb–Douglas functional form is criticized because of its inability to accommodate multiple outputs, while it has the virtue of self-duality, simplicity, and the economic interpretability of the coefficients on output, input, and control variables. The profit model is shown in Eq. (3.1) and (3.2), where a time trend is included in both the frontier model and the technical inefficiency effects model. The loan model is identical to this profit model, except for the dependent variable being replaced with total loans.

$$\ln(profit_{it}) = \beta_0 + \beta_1 t + \beta_2 \ln(Fixedasset_{it}) + \beta_3 \ln(Deposit_{it}) + \beta_4 \ln(Equity_{it}) + \beta_5 \ln(Overhead) + \beta_6 WTO + v_{it} - u_{it} \quad (3.1)$$

$$|U_{it}| = \delta_0 + \delta_1 t + \delta_2 Ownership + \delta_3 E/A + w_{it} \quad (3.2)$$

where subscripts *i* and *t* respectively denote banks and time; *ln* denotes natural logarithm.

In the production frontier model (Eq. 3.1), the output is defined as the book value of the profit and loans in two specifications, respectively. Profit is measured before tax to avoid any potential taxation effects. The value of loans includes shortterm, medium, and long-term, and other loans, net of loan loss reserves. Bank inputs are defined as fixed assets, deposits, equity, and labour. Fixed assets are net of depreciation reflecting the bank's physical capital capacity to provide service to its customers. The value of deposit includes short-term customer deposits and long-term deposits, while equity is capital input including share capital and retained profits. Labour cost is proxied by overhead as an approximation. A dummy variable is included in the production frontier estimation for testing the effect of WTO accession, which is assumed to influence bank efficiency via affecting the structure of banking production technology, rather than a direct effect on the efficiency. The dummy has a value of 0 until WTO accession in 2001 and 1 since 2002. This variable is expected to have a positive sign as under the incoming competition and challenges, Chinese banks are expected to improve performance.

In the technical inefficiency effect model (Eq. 3.2), two variables are employed to statistically ascertain the economic rationale of ongoing bank reform in China. An ownership dummy takes a value of 1 for JSCBs and 0 for SOCBs, expecting a negative sign, which is for testing *Hypothesis 1.* A capitalization ratio—equity to total assets ratio (E/A ratio) reflects the extent to which banks are subject to a hard budget, which is for testing *Hypothesis 2.* Banks with a high E/A ratio are better capitalized and more likely subject to a softer budget constraint, while banks with a lower E/A ratio are subject to a harder budget constraint.

When a bank faces a hard budget constraint and raises capital from shareholders, it needs to maintain high profitability in order to satisfy existing shareholders and attract potential investors. Such banks have no incentives to raise more capital than needed as higher equity lowers return to equity, holding other things constant. If a bank is capitalized and supported by the state, equity consists of relatively abundant state capital. Governments have resources and incentives to bail out failing banks especially in post-socialism nations, giving rise to a soft budget constraint for state banks. Unlike private shareholders, government as a shareholder concerns less profitability and usually, the state will support the state-owned banks with capital injection and increase E/A ratio. As a soft budget constrain induces moral hazard problem and inefficiencies, the E/A ratio is expected to have a positive sign.

The sample is restricted to JSCBs and SOCBs for the period from 1995 when state banks were officially granted the status as commercial banks to 2005 when major SOCBs just completed joint-stock ownership restructuring (except for ABC).[2] During this period, SOCBs and JSCBs were the main players in the banking sector. Data are obtained from Bankscope for 22 commercial banks, of which 11 are JSCBs and 11 are SOCBs.[3] The sample is an unbalanced panel with 204 observations and Table 3.1 reports the summary statistics at 1995 price level.

3.3.3 Empirical Results and Analysis

Maximum-likelihood estimates of parameters from the profit model and the loan model are reported in Table 3.2. In Panel C, estimated variance parameters and LR test suggest that the one-stage SFA models have been well estimated. The variance ratio of gamma ($\gamma = \sigma_u^2/(\sigma_u^2 + \sigma_v^2)$) is 0.99

[2]SOCB ownership reform started in 2003 and was partially completed in 2005. The main reason for the sample period up to 2005 (instead of 2003) is to investigate the impact of WTO on the banking sector.

[3]The 11 SOCBs include ABC, BOC, CCBC, ICBC, and seven banks ultimately owned by one of the state banks or state council, namely Kincheng Banking Corporation, Kwangtung Provincial Bank (The), National Commercial Bank Ltd., Sin Hua Bank Limited, Yien Yieh Commercial Bank Ltd., China & South Sea Bank Ltd., and (The) China State Bank Ltd.

Table 3.1 Summary statistics of variables (mean over 1995–2005)

	Profit	Loans	Fixed assets	Deposits	Equity	Overheads	E/A ratio	Total assets
SOCBs	9.26	856.67	26.85	1335.99	67.32	16.14	7.33	1504
JSCBs	1.86	112.07	2.68	165.36	7.47	2.22	4.65	200

Sources Bankscope. *Note* (1) SOCB = wholly state-owned commercial bank, JSCB = joint-stock commercial bank, E/A ratio = equity to total assets ratio. (2) Data shown by ownership in RMB billion except for E/A ratio

Table 3.2 Empirical results (1995–2005)

Dependent variable	ln (profit)		ln (loan)	
	Coefficients	T-Value	Coefficients	T-Value
	(1)	(2)	(3)	(4)
A. Production frontier				
Time	-0.07***	−4.41	0.01	1.17
Fixed-asset	0.08*	1.73	0.02	0.96
Deposit	0.46***	4.48	0.80***	19.21
Equity	0.42***	7.85	0.08**	2.82
Labor	−0.21**	−2.40	0.14***	4.87
WTO entry	0.66***	4.85	0.13***	3.12
B. Inefficiency effect model				
Time	0.14**	2.65	0.05***	9.03
Ownership	−1.76**	−2.66	−0.15***	−4.50
Equity/Asset Ratio	0.20*	1.40	0.05***	7.06
C. parameters and other information				
Sigma-squared	4.98**	2.9	0.02***	10.5
Gamma	0.99***	236	0.11***	9.75
LR test	148		68	
Ln (likelihood)	−123		129	
Average technical efficiency	0.69		0.89	
Number of observations	204		204	
Number of years	11		11	
Number of cross-sections	22		22	

Notes (1) All the variables are in natural logarithms; (2) Negative sign in the inefficiency function indicates that the variable has a positive effect on technical efficiency and vice versa because the dependent variable is inefficiency; (3) *, **, *** indicate significance level at 10%, 5%, and 1% respectively

in column (1), indicating that half of the error terms is attributable to the inefficiency element u_{it}; while gamma in column (3) is 0.11, indicating that only a small part of the error terms is attributable to the inefficiency element of u_{it}. However, the presence of the one-sided error component is justified by the highly significant LR test in both the profit model and the loan model. These statistics demonstrate the significance of inefficiency effects, which suggests the frontier model better fits Chinese banking data compared with the classical production function. The average technical efficiency over the sample period is 69% in the profit model, indicating that the Chinese banking industry generates 31% less than the maximum possible level of profit. The most efficient bank is a JSCB—China Merchants Bank (82%)—while the least efficient bank is a SOCB—ABC (43%). In the loan model, the average technical efficiency is 89%. The most efficient bank is Guangdong Development Bank, closely followed by Shanghai Pudong Development Bank and Shenzhen Development Bank, all of them are JSCBs. The most inefficient banks are those small state-owned banks. The spread between best- and worst-performed banks is much smaller than that in the profit model.

In Panel A, the signs of the estimated coefficients for the stochastic frontier are as expected and consistent in two specifications in columns (1) and (3) and most coefficients are statistically significant. The negative coefficient on time trend in column (1) indicates that output decreases by 7% per annum and the best practice frontier has been downward moving over the sample period. The insignificant coefficient on time trend in column (3) suggests shift in loan production frontier is insignificant. The estimated coefficients on fixed-asset, deposit, equity, and labour are their elasticities with respect to bank outputs because the production frontier model is in a log-linear form. In column (1), the elasticity of fixed-asset is relatively small (0.08) but significant. Deposit and equity have a positive impact on output and a 1% increase in deposit or equity would result in an increase in profit by 0.46% and 0.42% respectively, holding all other things constant. Labour has an expected negative impact on outputs at 1% statistically significant level and a 1% rise in labor expense would lead to a reduction in profit by 0.2%. In column (3), the elasticity of fixed-asset is 0.02 and insignificant. Deposits have a strong influence on loans that a 1% increase in deposit would result in an increase in loans by 0.8%. The significant importance of deposits also helps explain the positive sign on labour. In China, deposits are mainly collected from a labour-intensive branch network. Extensive coverage of a branch network is important for attracting more deposits but requiring more manpower. The increase in labour cost by 1% would lead to an increase in loans by 0.14%. The elasticity of equity is significant but the economic magnitude is small. As shown in columns (1) and (3), the coefficient on the WTO dummy is positive and highly significant, highlighting a positive impact of WTO accession on the Chinese banking system. Facing more competition pressure from incoming foreign banks, the banking system as a whole has actively responded by upgrading production technology to improve efficiency. After WTO, profit and loans have increased by 0.66% and 0.13%, respectively, suggesting a stronger impact on generating profit.

Results from the technical inefficiency effect model, shown in Panel B of Table 3.2, are of particular interest. The coefficient on the time trend is positive and significant, indicating that technical efficiency decreases (technical inefficiency increases) by 5–14% per annum, depending on model specifications. The coefficient on ownership is negative and significant in both the profit model in column (1) and the loan model in column (3), indicating that ownership is an important variable in explaining the variations in bank inefficiencies. JSCBs are found to be more efficient than SOCBs, providing strong evidence supporting *Hypothesis 1.* On average, JSCBs outperform SOCBs by 2 percentage points in the profit model and by 14 percentage points in the loan model. Figure 3.2(a, b) plots the average estimates of technical

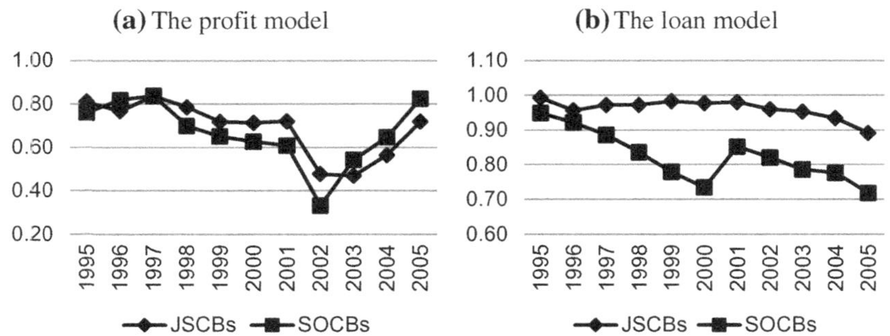

Fig. 3.2 Technical efficiency of JSCBs and SOCBs. *Notes* JSCB = joint-stock commercial bank, SOCB = state-owned commercial bank

efficiency for SOCBs and JSCBs, which shows a similar trend. In both the profit and loan model, the technical efficiency of SOCBs deteriorated at a faster speed than that of JSCBs before ownership reform started in 2003 and at a similar speed after SOCBs were restructured into joint-stock ownership. Evidence indicates that shareholding ownership structure solves the agent-principal problem better and supports Chinese authorities' banking reform strategies that partially privatize SOCBs to build up a good corporate governance structure.

In columns (1)–(3) of Table 3.2, the positive and significant coefficient on E/A ratio indicates that well-capitalized banks are consistently less efficient regardless of model specifications. Banks that are subject to a hard budget with lower capitalization are more efficient than those subject to a softer budget constraint and more capitalization. The results provide strong evidence supporting *Hypothesis 2*. The economic impact is substantial. The elasticity of E/A ratio is 0.20 in the profit model and 0.05 in the loan model, suggesting that for a 1% increase in the E/A ratio, bank technical efficiency will decrease by 0.2% in generating profit and by 0.05% in growing loans. The results support Chinese authorities' banking reform measure of hardening SOCBs budget constraint by diversifying their capital structure, listing them on the stock market, and implicitly indicating no more bailout in the future. These concrete measures aim to mitigate moral hazard problems and improve efficiency.

Overall, the empirical results support the hypotheses that joint-stock banks are more efficient than state-owned banks and banks facing a hard budget constraint outperform banks subject to a soft budget constraint. The results provide evidence for ownership reform and change in budgetary constraints that lead to greater efficiency gains. Therefore, it is rationalized that the economic foundations for bank reform have been the agency theory and the budgetary constraint theory. Moreover, evidence shows that Chinese authorities and banks, facing incoming threats from foreign banks, have positively responded by upgrading production technology in banking. WTO entry has a significant positive impact on bank performance by affecting production technology employed by the banking industry.

3.4 The Impact of Privatization on Bank Efficiency[4]

This section comprehensively examines how privatization affects bank performance in terms of cost and profit efficiency in China. To construct a good corporate governance structure and harden state banks' budget constraints, the Chinese government implemented two main privatization measures—foreign acquisitions (of minority interest in domestic banks) and IPOs. Privatization leads to significant changes in corporate governance and it is important to examine the short- and long-term influences of attracting foreign investors and IPOs by comparing bank efficiency before and after the implementation of these privatization strategies.

3.4.1 Model and Data

The dual approach to estimating a cost or profit function to derive cost and profit efficiency is more appropriate for industries producing multiple outputs when behavioural assumptions of cost minimization or profit maximization are appropriate (Kumbhakar and Lovell 2000). In China, SOCBs were legally granted the status as commercial banks in 1995 and subsequently partially privatized, and banks become more and more profit-oriented concerning both cost minimization and profit maximization. The empirical specification of the cost frontier in translog form is shown in Eq. (3.3). The standard restriction of linear homogeneity in input prices is imposed using the price of fund (w_2). Total costs, profits, output variables, and netputs are normalized by total assets to control for scale biases and heteroskedasticity. The alternative profit frontier is estimated by replacing total costs with total profit with adjustment to error terms in Eq. (3.3).

[4]This section is largely based on a published paper "Bank ownership, privatization, and performance: Evidence from a transition country" by Chunxia Jiang, Shujie Yao, and Genfu Feng, in *Journal of Banking and Finance* 2013, Vol. 37, 3364–3372.

$$\begin{aligned}
\ln(TC/w_2TA) =& \alpha + \sum_{i=1}^{3} \beta_i \ln(Y_i/TA) \\
&+ \sum_{k=1} \psi_k \ln(W_k/w_2) + \sum_{r=1} \varphi_r \ln(Z_r/TA) \\
&+ \rho_1 NPL + \tau_1 T \\
&+ \frac{1}{2}\sum_{i=1}^{3}\sum_{j=1}^{3} \beta_{ij} \ln(Y_i/TA)\ln(Y_j/TA) \\
&+ \frac{1}{2}\sum_{k=1}\sum_{m=1} \psi_{km} \ln(W_k/w_2)\ln(W_m/w_2) \\
&+ \frac{1}{2}\sum_{r=1}\sum_{s=1} {}_{rs} \ln(Z_r/TA)\ln(Z_s/TA) \\
&+ \sum_{i=1}^{3}\sum_{k=1} \varpi_{ik} \ln(Y_i/TA)\ln(W_k/w_2) \\
&+ \sum_{i=1}^{3}\sum_{r=1} \kappa_{ir} \ln(Y_i/TA)\ln(Z_r/TA) \\
&+ \sum_{k=1}\sum_{r=1} \sigma_{kr} \ln(W_k/w_2)\ln(Z_r/TA) + \rho_2 NPL^2 \\
&+ \tau_2 T^2 + \ln v_{it} + \ln u_{it}
\end{aligned} \tag{3.3}$$

where TC is the total costs of a bank in a given year; TA is the total assets of a bank in a given year; Y_i are outputs; W_k are input prices (w_1: labour and capital, $w_{2:}$ fund price); Z_r are netputs; NPL is the NPL ratio; T is a time trend; v_{it} are identical and independently distributed random errors, which are independent of u_{it}; u_{it} are non-negative inefficiencies; and $\alpha,\ \beta,\ \psi,\ \varphi,\ \tau, \varpi,\ \kappa,\ \sigma,\ \rho\ \eta,\ a,\ and\ b$ are parameters to be estimated.

The inefficiency effect model is shown in Eq. (3.4):

$$u_{it} = \delta_0 + \sum_{a=1}^{13} \delta_a X_{it} + \delta_{14} t + \varepsilon_{it} \tag{3.4}$$

where t is a time trend; X_{it} is a vector of variables.

In this section, the intermediation approach (Sealey and Lindley 1977) is modified by defining deposits as an output as in Bonin et al. (2005a, b). The cost function and alternative profit function contain identically defined input and output variables—three outputs (total loans, other earning assets, and deposits), two variable inputs (price of fund and price of labour), and one fixed netput (equity). To capture the neutral technical progress on efficiency, linear and quadratic time trend and its interaction terms are included. Equity capital is included in the model to control for varying risk preferences (Berger and Mester 1997) and take into account both the cost of debt and the cost of equity (Hughes and Mester 2010). Equity acts as a cushion to absorb losses and insolvent banks may face high costs due to factors such as a risk premium on funds. The inclusion of equity in a cost function is particularly important in China where the bank insolvency risk is high given a high level of NPLs. NPLs are treated as a control variable following Berger and Mester (1997) rather than an undesirable output as in Park and Weber (2006) because the main causes of NPLs in Chinese banking industry are considered to be exogenous to individual banks.

Both cost and profit functions assume that banks face exogenously determined input prices in competitive factor markets so that the behavioural assumptions of costs minimization and profit maximization become reasonable (Fare and Primont 1995). However, many studies calculate bank-specific inputs prices by dividing total costs attributable to a factor by the number of units employed, implicitly assuming that banks face imperfect factor markets. Labour prices and financial capital prices obtained in such a way might be misspecified (Mountain and Thomas 1999) and poor measurement of explanatory variables could substantially distort efficiency estimates (Greene 1993). Bos and Kool (2006) and Koetter (2006) show that different input prices matter to efficiency estimate and suggest the use of market input prices. Benchmarking to market average prices, excessive input prices taken by banks are treated as inefficiencies, not random errors. Furthermore, market average prices could average out some measurement errors of individual banks. Taking into account both theoretical rationale and the speciality of the Chinese banking industry, this analysis defines one single national fund market. The price of funds is defined as the ratio of total interest expenses to total interest-bearing funds and the market average price of fund is computed as the unweighted average price of other banks excluding the bank's own price. As to labour and physical capital factors, markets are defined by bank types, namely SOCBs, JSCBs, and CCBs. The price of labour and physical capital is defined as the ratio of non-interest expenses to total assets (Hasan and Marton 2003; Fries and Taci 2005; Patti and hardy 2005; Bonin et al. 2005a, b) and market average price of labour and physical capital is constructed as the unweighted average prices of other banks excluding the bank own price for each bank type.

The sample period is restricted to 1995–2010 as this section focuses on the impact of privatization on bank efficiency and SOCBs privatization completed in 2010. The sample of 481 observations covers major commercial banks in China. Data are mainly collected from Bankscope, complemented by data from the *Almanac of China's Finance and Banking* (1986–2010) and the *China Statistical Yearbook* (1995–2010). Table 3.3 provides summary statistics for input prices and outputs.

The inefficiency effect model examines various static ownership effects, the dynamic effect of privatization and macro-environmental effects. *CCB, JSCB, and SOCB* are employed to examine the variations

Table 3.3 Summary statistics of input prices and outputs (1995–2010)

	Mean	SD	Min	Max
Total costs	28,610	74,815	93	774,029
Pre-tax profit	8769	26,037	−231	236,910
Gross loans	425,848	962,197	1186	6790,506
The volume of NPLs	46,542	145,700	1	1,121,782
NPLs ratio	0.10	0.12	0.00	0.55
Other earning assets	330,543	854,272	1138	6,510,179
Total deposits	621,522	1,506,717	1940	11,145,557
Equity	39,450	104,576	−267*	821,657
Total assets	781,481	1,832,528	2516	13,458,622
Bank specific price of fund	0.02	0.02	0.01	0.28
Market price of fund	0.02	0.01	0.01	0.07
Bank specific price of labour	0.01	0.00	0.00	0.03
Market price of labour	0.01	0.00	0.01	0.02
Share of foreign ownership	4.16	7.66	0	24.99

Note All variables in RMB million except for input prices, NPLs ratio, and share of foreign ownership. All values have been deflated to 1995 price level. *The negative equity is due to the written off of SCOBs' NPLs before financial restructuring in 2003

in efficiency due to different types of bank, and *Foreign Minority* is for examining the effect of minority foreign ownership. *Listed Bank* is to see whether banks perform differently with dispersed ownership structure and subject to multiple monitoring. We expect a positive association between listing status of banks and efficiency. These dummy variables take a value of 1 for such a bank and 0 otherwise. *Share of foreign ownership* captures how the degree of foreign ownership involvement affects bank efficiency. Four dynamic effect indicators capture the short- and long-term influences of privatization strategies. Following Berger et al. (2005), two short-term dynamic variables—*Underwent Foreign Acquisition (ST)* and *Underwent IPOs (ST)*—are defined as dummies that take a value of 0 prior to foreign investors taking minority stakes or going public and one after. Two long-term dynamic variables—*Underwent Foreign Acquisition (LT)* and *Underwent IPOs (LT)*—are dummies that equal to 0 prior to foreign investors taking minority stakes or going public and equal to the number of years starting from one after the implementation of respective strategy. Two environmental variables—*WTO Entry* and *CBRC Launch*—are included to control for the potential effect of these events, taking a value of 1 after these events and 0 before. *GDP* growth representing the macroeconomic environment in which banks operate and a time trend *t* for capturing the catching-up effect of efficiency are included.

3.4.2 Empirical Results and Analysis

Table 3.4 reports estimation results from the cost frontier and the alternative profit frontier, using market average input prices. Frontier results in Panel A focus on estimated parameters as estimated coefficients for the frontier model using a translog functional form commonly provide no economic meanings because of the collinearity problem in the presence of second order and interaction terms. Estimated parameters of gamma and LR test indicate that all models are of good fit and a large part of the total composite error term attributable to inefficiencies. The mean cost efficiency is 76% and profit efficiency is 78%.

Figure 3.3 plots mean cost and profit efficiency of Chinese banks. Over the sample period 1995–2010, cost efficiency improved by 16

Table 3.4 Results of cost and alternative profit function

	Cost function	Alternative profit efficiency
Panel A: The frontier model		
Gamma ($\gamma \equiv \sigma_u^2 / \sigma_v^2 + \sigma_u^2$)	0.94***	0.95***
Sigma-squared ($\sigma^2 \equiv \sigma_v^2 + \sigma_u^2$)	0.16***	1.1***
Log likelihood function	118	−183
LR test of one-sided error	187	362
Mean cost efficiency	0.76	0.78
Panel B: The inefficiency effect model		
SOCBs	−0.2*	6.36***
JSCBs	−0.72***	3.8***
Foreign acquisition	0.09	−1.19***
Share of foreign ownership	−0.28**	0.84***
Listed banks	−0.44***	−1.36***
Foreign acquisition-ST	0.84**	1.06*
Foreign acquisition-LT	−0.1***	−0.1**
Underwent IPOs-ST	−1.36**	−2.0***
Underwent IPOs-LT	0.05**	−0.22***
WTO entry	0.41***	−0.44
CBRC Launch	0.11	−1.4**
GDP growth	−0.04	−2.6***
t	−0.11***	0.06

Notes a. JSCB = joint-stock commercial bank, SOCB = state-owned commercial bank, IPOs = initial public offerings; b. *, **, *** signifies significance level at 10%, 5% and 1% respectively; c. negative sign of the estimated coefficient indicates that the particular variable has a positive effect on cost or profit efficiency and vice versa; d. *CCBs* is excluded from the estimation for comparison purposes

percentage points from 75% in 1995 to 91% in 2010. The efficiency level remained relatively stable at close to 80% until experiencing a sudden drop by 9 percentage points in 2002. The drop is largely due to tightened regulatory requirement on loan loss provision. To reflect assets quality, loan loss provisions could be up to 100% of loans concerned, compared with the previous requirement of 1%, resulting in a substantial increase in costs for major banks. From 2003, cost efficiency increased steadily and peaked at 91% in 2010. Profit efficiency has improved by 10 percentage points from 75% in 1995 to 85% in 2010 and appears more sensitive to a financial crisis compared with cost efficiency. As shown in Fig. 3.3, profit efficiency encountered two significant shocks in 1998 and 2008, coinciding with the 1997–1998 Asian financial crisis and the 2008–2009 global financial crisis. While the turnaround in 1998 is attributable to the first round of SOCBs' bailout

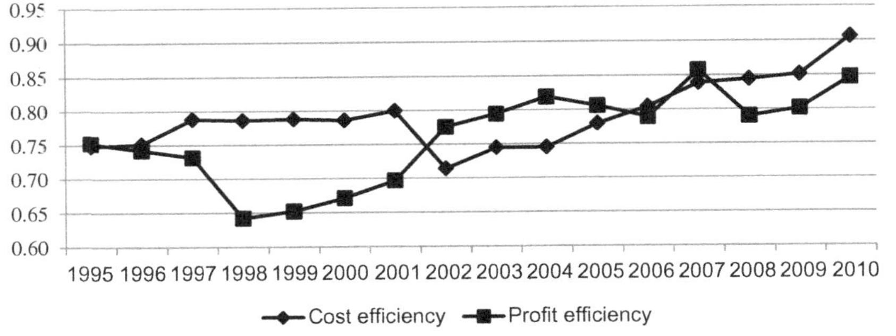

Fig. 3.3 Mean efficiency levels of Chinese banks (1995–2010)

in 1998–1999, the subsequent improvement is largely due to ongoing banking reform. After the 2008–2009 crisis, banks recovered rapidly and profit efficiency reached 85% in 2010, only 1 percentage point below the pre-crisis peak level.

Panel B of Table 3.4 reports results from the inefficiency effect model, which offers insights into the impacts of ownership and banking privatization on bank efficiency. In the cost frontier model, the coefficients of SOCBs and JSCBs are negative and significant, indicating that SOCBs and JSCBs are more efficient than the control group of CCBs. JSCBs are the most efficient banks at an average cost efficiency of 87%, followed by SOCBs at 84% and CCBs at 72%. As shown in Fig. 3.4a, the efficiency level of JSCBs was more stable relative to SOCBs and CCBs over the sample period. The cost efficiency of CCBs struggled at low level between 60–70% in the first half of the sample period and then steadily improved from 2002 onwards. Figure 3.4a also shows a converging trend in cost-efficiency levels across different types of banks.

In the profit efficiency model, the positive and significant coefficients on SOCBs and JSCBs suggest that these banks underperform CCBs. The average profit efficiency of CCBs is 85%, higher than that of JSCBs by 10 percentage points and that of SOCBs by 30 percentage points. Figure 3.4b shows relatively stable profit efficiency of JSCBs and CCBs but more dramatic changes of SOCBs. During the 1997 Asian financial crisis, the profit efficiency level of SOCBs declined sharply from 61% in 1997 to 23% in 1998, mainly caused by surfaced NPL problems. In

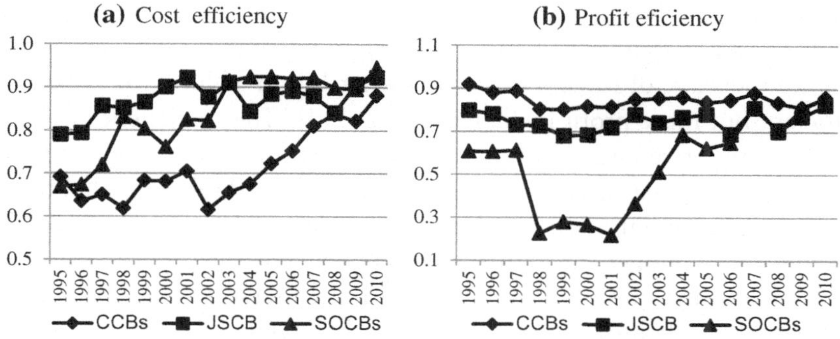

Fig. 3.4 Mean efficiency levels by bank types (1995–2010)

the 1990s, SOCBs were the main financier to SOEs, of which two-third were loss making and unable to pay interests on their borrowings. It was common practice that SOCBs rolled over existing loans and made new loans to SOEs that were taken back immediately as interest payments on those extended existing loans. On SOCBs' accounts, there were no overdue loans and interest payments were prompt. In 1997, the central bank tightened the terms of rolling over existing loans and making new loans to SOEs and it became very difficult for most loss-making SOEs to meet their borrowing obligations and the NPL problems came to surface. SOCBs' profit efficiency remained at a low level between 20–30% in the subsequent four years, despite government implementing the first round of SOCBs bailout to deal with NPL problems. The second round of SOCBs bailout and more radical ownership reform tripled SOCBs' profit efficiency from 22% in 2001 to 69% in 2004. Since then, the profit efficiency of SOCBs has improved with fluctuations. Overall, profit efficiency has been converging across different types of banks in the second half of the sample period.

On average, banks with foreign minority ownership are more profit efficient than bank without foreign investors as the coefficient on *Foreign acquisition* is negative and significant in the profit frontier model, the impact of foreign minority ownership on cost efficiency is insignificant. The share of minority foreign ownership is employed to investigate if the degree of foreign investors' involvement in domestic banks affects efficiency. The results suggest a positive association with cost efficiency but a negative association with profit efficiency. The higher the share of foreign minority ownership in a bank, the more cost efficient but more profit inefficient the bank is. The coefficient on *Listed banks* is negative and significant in both cost and profit frontier models, indicating that listed banks are more efficient. Publicly traded banks operating in capital markets subject to multiple monitoring and vetting, facing a hard budget constraint, are more efficient regardless of the types of bank and the finding is consistent with the literature (e.g., Berger and Mester 1997; Jiang et al. 2009). Since all foreign minority ownership acquisitions and IPOs took place during the sample period except for Shenzhen Development Bank that was listed prior to the sample period, the coefficients on *Foreign acquisition* and *Listed banks* can be alternatively interpreted as a selection effect. The results suggest a strong selection effect that better performing banks are selected by foreign investors or for going public.

As to the dynamic effect of privatization, the coefficient on *Foreign acquisition-ST* is positive but negative on *Foreign acquisition-LT*. The interpretation is that foreign minority ownership led to efficiency losses in the short term but gains in the long term for both cost and profit efficiency. It takes more time to benefit from the foreign owners' transfer of advanced technology and know-how in financial intermediation. This finding is consistent with recent literature in developing and transitional economies (e.g., Bonin et al. 2005b). The coefficient on *Underwent IPOs-ST* is negative in both cost efficiency model and profit efficiency model, which is evident for a positive impact on both cost efficiency and profit efficiency in the short term. In the long term, IPO strategy has led to higher profit efficiency but lower cost efficiency as the coefficient on *Underwent IPOs-LT* becomes positive in the cost-efficiency model. Overall, privatization via IPO has improved bank profit efficiency in both short and long terms, while the effect of attracting minority foreign ownership is more relevant and significant in the long term for both cost and profit efficiency.

Results from a set of control and environmental variables show China's WTO entry has a significant and negative impact on cost efficiency. One of the reasons for higher costs is more prudential practice after WTO entry, that is, the authority tightened regulatory requirements on loan loss provision. The launch of CBRC is found to have a positive impact on profit efficiency, while its impact on cost efficiency is insignificant. Banks are found to be more profit efficient in a favourable macroeconomic condition, consistent with expectations. The results show a strong catching up effect that cost efficiency improves with the passage of time, which is not observed for profit efficiency.

Overall, results clearly suggest that bank ownership matters and bank privatization has improved bank efficiency over the period 1995–2010. JSCBs are the most cost efficient banks, while SOCBs are the least profit efficient banks. CCBs are the most profit efficient banks, but they are the least cost efficient banks. Banks with minority foreign ownership are more profit efficient, while foreign minority ownership induces inefficiency in the short run and then leads to improvement in the long run. The positive impact of IPO strategy lasts longer for profit efficiency, but is short lived for cost efficiency.

3.5 Conclusion

Over the past three decades, the Chinese government adopted a gradual banking reform approach to reshape a market-oriented banking sector. As the dominance of the banking sector, SOCBs reform is the key to the success of banking reform. Employing a one-stage stochastic frontier approach (SFA), this chapter empirically tests for whether SOCBs reform strategies have been motivated by the agency theory and the budgetary constraints theory. The results support SOCBs reform strategy, and joint-stock ownership reform addresses both issues of agency problems and soft budget constraints. This chapter also comprehensively examines the static effect of ownership and the dynamic effect of privatization on bank efficiency over the period 1995–2010. We find that the privatization of banks has improved performance. Attracting foreign investors strategy has improved bank efficiency in the long run and IPOs strategy has delivered immediate efficiency gains but at a diminishing pace over the long term. Moreover, China's WTO entry has a direct negative impact on cost efficiency perhaps due to more prudent regulation, while changes in regulatory environment seem to have helped banks improve profitability.

References

Aigner, D., C.A.K. Lovell, and P. Schmidt. 1977. Formulation and Estimation of Stochastic Frontier Production Models. *Journal of Econometrics* 6: 21–37.

Altunbas, Y., L. Evans, and P. Molyneux. 2001. Bank Ownership and Efficiency. *Journal of Money, Credit, and Banking* 33: 926–954.

Avkiran, N.K. 1999. The Evidence on Efficiency Gains: The Role of Mergers and the Benefits to the Public. *Journal of Banking & Finance* 23: 991–1013.

Barth, J.R., C. Lin, Y. Ma, J. Seade, and F.M. Song. 2013. Do Bank Regulation, Supervision and Monitoring Enhance or Impede Bank Efficiency? *Journal of Banking and Finance* 37: 2879–2892.

Battese, G.E., and T.J. Coelli. 1995. A Model for Technical Inefficiency Effects in a Stochastic Frontier Production Function for Panel Data. *Empirical Economics* 20: 325–332.

Bauer, P.W., A.N. Berger, G.D. Ferrier, and D.B. Humphrey. 1998. Consistency Conditions for Regulatory Analysis of Financial Institutions: a Comparison of Frontier Efficiency Methods. *Journal of Economics and Business* 50 (2): 85–114.

Bauer, P.W., A.N. Berger, and D.B. Humphrey. 1993. Efficiency and Productive Growth in US Banking, in Fried, H. O., Lovell, C. A. K. and Schmidt, S. S. (eds), *The Measurement of Productive Efficiency: Techniques and Applications*, Oxford University Press, New York.

Bearle Jr., A.A., and G.C. Means. 1932. *The Modern Corporation and Private Property*. New York: Macmillan.

Berger. 1995. The Profit-Structure Relationship in Banking—Tests of Market-Power and Efficient-Structure Hypotheses, *Journal of Money, Credit, and Banking* 27: 404–431.

Berger, A.N., G.R.G. Clarke, R. Cull, L. Klapper, and G.F. Udell. 2005. Corporate Governance and Bank Performance: A Joint Analysis of the Static, Selection, and Dynamic Effects of Domestic, Foreign, and State Ownership. *Journal of Banking & Finance* 29: 2179–2221.

Berger, A.N., R.S. Demsetz, and P.E. Strahan. 1999. The Consolidation of the Financial Services Industry: Causes, Consequences, and Implications for the Future. *Journal of Banking & Finance* 23: 135–194.

Berger, A.N., I. Hasan, and M. Zhou. 2009. Bank Ownership and Efficiency in China: What Will Happen in the World's Largest Nation? *Journal of Banking & Finance* 33: 113–130.

Berger, A.N., and D.B. Humphrey. 1997. Efficiency of Financial Institutions: International Survey and Directions for Future Research. *European Journal of Operational Research* 98 (2): 175–212.

Berger, A.N., and L.J. Mester. 1997. Inside the Black Box: What Explains Differences in the Efficiencies of Financial Institutions? *Journal of Banking & Finance* 21: 895–947.

Berger, A.N., and L.J. Mester. 2003. Explaining the Dramatic Change in Performance of US banks: Technological Change, Deregulation, and Dynamic Changes in Competition. *Journal of Financial Intermediation* 12: 57–95.

Bonin, J.P., I. Hasan, and P. Wachtel. 2005a. Bank Performance, Efficiency and Ownership in Transition Countries. *Journal of Banking & Finance* 29: 31–53.

Bonin, J.P., I. Hasan, and P. Wachtel. 2005b. Privatization Matters: Bank Efficiency in Transition Countries. *Journal of Banking & Finance* 29: 2155–2178.

Bos, J., and C. Kool. 2006. Bank Efficiency: The Role of Bank Strategy and Local Market Conditions. *Journal of Banking & Finance* 30: 1953–1974.

Charnes, A., W.W. Cooper, and E. Rhodes. 1978. Measuring the Efficiency of Decision Making Units. *European Journal of Operational Research* 6: 429–444.

Chen, X., M. Skuly, and K. Brown. 2005. Banking Efficiency in China: Application of DEA to Pre-and Post-Deregulation Eras: 1993–2000. *China Economic Review* 16: 229–245.

Coelli, T., D.S. Prasada Rao, and G.E. Battese. 1998. *An Introduction to Efficiency and Productivity Analysis*. Boston: Kluwer Academic Publishers.

Delis, M., M. Iosifidi, and M.G. Tsionas. 2016. Endogenous Bank Risk and Efficiency. *European Journal of Operational Research* 260 (1): 376–387.

DeYoung, R., and I. Hasan. 1998. The Performance of de novo Commercial Banks: A Profit Efficiency Approach. *Journal of Banking & Finance* 22: 565–587.

Evanoff, D.D., and D.L. Fortier. 1988. Re-evaluation of the Structure–Conduct–Performance Paradigm in Banking. *Journal of Financial Services Research* 1: 277–294.

Fare, R., and D. Primont. 1995. *Multi-Output Production and Duality: Theory and Applications*. Boston: Kluwer Academic Publisher.
Farrell, M.J. 1957. The Measurement of Productive Efficiency. *Journal of Royal Statistical Society A* 120 (3): 253–281.
Ferrier, G.D., and C.A.K. Lovell. 1990. Measuring Cost Efficiency in Banking: Econometric and Linear Programming Evidence. *Journal of Econometrics* 46: 229–245.
Fiordelisi, F., D. Marques-Ibanez, and P. Molyneux. 2011. Efficiency and Risk in European Banking. *Journal of Banking & Finance* 35: 1315–1326.
Fries, S., and A. Taci. 2005. Cost Efficiency of Banks in Transition: Evidence from 289 Banks in 15 Post-Communist Countries. *Journal of Banking & Finance* 29: 55–81.
Fu, X., and S. Heffernan. 2007. Cost X-Efficiency in China's Banking Sector, *China Economic Review* 18: 35–53.
Gilbert, R.A., and P.W. Wilson. 1998. Effects of Deregulation on the Productivity of Korean Banks. *Journal of Economic and Business* 50: 133–166.
Goddard, J., P. Molyneux, and J. Wilson. 2001. *European Banking*. Wiley, Chichester, UK.
Green, W.H. 1993. *The Econometric Approach to Efficiency Analysis*. New York: Oxford University Press.
Hao, J., W.C. Hunter, W.K. Yang. 2001. Deregulation and Efficiency: The Case of Private Korean Banks, *Journal of Economics and Business* 53: 237–254.
Hasan, I., and K. Marton. 2003. Development and Efficiency of the Banking Sector in a Transitional Economy: Hungarian Experience. *Journal of Banking & Finance* 27: 2249–2271.
Hughes, J.P., W.W. Lang, L.J. Mester, and C. Moon. 1999. The Dollars and Sense of Bank Consolidation. *Journal of Banking & Finance* 23: 291–324.
Hughes, J.P., and L.J. Mester. 2010. Efficiency in Banking: Theory, Practice, and Evidence, Chapter 19. In *The Oxford Handbook of Banking*, ed. A.N. Berger, P. Molyneux, and J. Wilson. New York: Oxford University Press.
Huibers, F.E. 2005. Initial Public Offerings. In *The Future of State-Owned Financial Institutions*, ed. G. Caprio, J.L. Fiechter, R. Litan, and M. Pomerleano. Washington, DC: Brookings Institution Press.
Huang, C.J., and J.T. Liu. 1994. Estimation of a Non-Neutral Stochastic Frontier Production Function. *Journal of Productivity Analysis* 5: 171–180.

Isik, I., and M.K. Hassan. 2003. Financial Deregulation and Total Factor Productivity Change: An Empirical Study of Turkish Commercial Banks. *Journal of Banking & Finance* 27 (8): 1455–1485.

Jiang, C., S. Yao, and G. Feng. 2013. Bank Ownership, Privatization, and Performance: Evidence from a Transition Country, *Journal of Banking and Finance* 37: 3364–3372.

Jiang, C., S. Yao, and Z. Zhang. 2009. The Effects of Governance Changes on Bank Efficiency in China: A Stochastic Distance Function Approach. *China Economics Review* 20: 717–731.

Kapopoulos, P., and F. Siokis. 2005. Market Structure, Efficiency and Rising Consolidation of the Banking Industry in the Euro Area. *Bulletin of Economic Research* 57 (1): 67–91.

Koetter, M. 2006. Measurement Matters: Alternative Input Price Proxies for Bank Efficiency analyses. *Journal of Financial Services Research* 30: 199–227.

Kumbhakar, S.C., and C.A.K. Lovell. 2000. Stochastic Frontier Analysis. Cambridge University Press.

Kumbhakar, S.C., and A. Lozano-Vivas. 2005. Deregulation and Productivity: The Case of Spanish Banks. *Journal of Regulatory Economics* 27 (3): 331–351.

La Porta, R., F. Lopez-de-Silanes, and A. Shleifer. 2002. Government Ownership of Banks. *Journal of Finance* 57 (1): 256–301.

Laeven, L. 1999, Risk and Efficiency in East Asian Banks, World Bank Working Paper No. 2225.

Leibenstein, Harvey. 1966. Allocative Efficiency Versus 'X-Efficiency'. *American Economic Review* 56: 392–415.

Lovell, C.A.K. 1993. Production Frontiers and Productive Efficiency. In *The Measurement of Productive Efficiency: Techniques and Applications*, ed. H.O. Fried, C.A.K. Lovell, and S.S. Schmidt. New York: Oxford University Press.

Meeusen, W., and J. van den Broeck. 1977. Efficiency Estimation from Cobb-Douglas Production Functions with Composed Error. *International Economic Review* 18: 435–444.

Megginson, W.L. 2005. The Economics of Bank Privatization. *Journal of Banking & Finance* 29: 1931–1980.

Mester, L.J. 1993. Efficiency in the Savings and Loan Industry. *Journal of Banking & Finance* 17: 267–286.

Mountain, D.C., and H. Thomas. 1999. Factor Price Misspecification in Bank Cost Function Estimation. *Journal of International Financial Markets, Institutions and Money* 9: 163–182.

Park, K.H., and W.L. Weber. 2006. A Note on Efficiency and Productivity Growth in the Korean Banking Industry, 1992–2002. *Journal of Banking & Finance* 30: 2371–2386.

Patti, E.B., and D.C. Hardy. 2005. Financial Sector Liberalization, Bank Privatization, and Efficiency: Evidence from Pakistan. *Journal of Banking & Finance* 29: 2381–2406.

Sealey, C.W., and J.T. Lindley. 1977. Inputs, Outputs and a Theory of Production and Cost at Depository Financial Institutions. *Journal of Finance* 32: 1251–1266.

Shanmugam, K.R., and A. Das. 2004. Efficiency of Indian Commercial Banks During the Reform Period. *Applied financial Economics* 14: 681–686.

Spong, K., R. Sullivan, and R. DeYoung. 1995. *What makes a bank efficient?* Federal Reserve Bank of Kansas City Financial and Industry Perspectives: A Look at Financial Characteristics and Bank Management and Ownership Structure.

Sturm, J.E., and B. Williams. 2004. Foreign Bank Entry, Deregulation and Bank Efficiency: Lessons from the Australian Experience. *Journal of Banking & Finance* 28: 1775–1799.

Wang, H.J., and P. Schmidt. 2002. One-Step and Two-Step Estimation of the Effects of Exogenous Variables on Technical Efficiency Levels. *Journal of Productivity Analysis* 18: 129–144.

Williams, J., and N. Nguyen. 2005. Financial Liberalization, Crisis, and Restructuring: A Comparative Study of Bank Performance and Bank Governance in South East Asia. *Journal of Banking & Finance* 29: 2119–2154.

Yao, S., C. Jiang, G. Feng, and D. Willenbockel. 2007. On the Efficiency of Chinese Banks and WTO Challenges. *Applied Economics* 39: 629–643.

4

The Global Financial Crisis and Banks in BRIC Countries: A Comparative Perspective

The empirical analysis of this chapter is based on a paper by Jianghua Zhang, Chunxia Jiang, Baozhi Qu, and Peng Wang, published in *International Review of Financial Analysis* in 2013. We are grateful for all the authors and the journal for allowing us to include this paper in this book as we believe that this comparative analysis provides a useful addition for understanding the Chinese banking sector.

Preamble

Banks are the cornerstone of the financial system, especially in developing countries where capital markets are underdeveloped. The global financial crisis in 2007–2008 caused great turmoil in the banking sectors of the developed world with the clustered collapses of international financial giants in the advanced economies. However, there have been fewer bank failures in transitional and emerging economies and it is important to understand the role of the banking sector in developing countries and transitional and emerging economies. This chapter takes a comparative approach and puts Chinese banking into the context of the emerging economies. The importance of the banking systems in Brazil, Russia, India, China, and South Africa (hereinafter the BRIC refers to Brazil Russia, India, and China and the BRICS includes South Africa) has

C. Jiang and S. Yao, *Chinese Banking Reform*, The Nottingham China Policy Institute Series, DOI 10.1007/978-3-319-63925-3_4

been rising in the global banking marketplace, noticeably witnessed by the launch of the New Development Bank in 2015. Moreover, BRICS' banking sectors have withstood the storm wave of the 2008–2009 global financial crisis without major bank failures. This chapter, in particular, examines the impact of bank risk-taking and market concentration on bank performance from the perspective of emerging economies. The rest of this chapter unfolds as follows. Section. 4.1 reviews related literature on developing countries and transitional and emerging economies. Section 4.2 introduces the economies and the evolutionary background of the banking systems in BRICS. Section 4.3 outlines the research methodology—the output distance function approach—and describes data. Section 4.4 discusses empirical results, and Sect. 4.5 concludes.

4.1 Literature Review

4.1.1 Literature on Developing Countries and Transitional and Emerging Economies

In the past three decades, the banking sectors in the developing countries and transition economies have experienced drastic changes for different reasons. For instance, banking re-formations and reforms in Russia and the Eastern and Central European countries were caused by the significant political and economic changes in 1989. Banking reforms were a response to the financial crises in Southeast Asian and Latin American countries. In China and India, banking reforms were initiated by governments to improve bank performance thereby better serving the real sector development. The changing banking landscape has attracted great research interest in examining the performance effect of banking reform in terms of deregulation, ownership, corporate governance, privatization, foreign bank entry, and so forth, across developing countries, transitional economies, and emerging economies.

As a result, the banking sectors in these countries and economies have received great research attention. Existing literature has examined a wide range of issues, including bank capital buffers (Fonseca and Gonzalez 2010), bank distress and financial crisis (Mannasoo and

Mayes 2009; Bongini et al. 2000), banking problems in Asia and South America in the 1980s and 1990s (Arena 2005), and bank performance in individual countries (Berger et al. 2005; Jiang et al. 2009) or a group of countries (Fries and Taci 2005; Williams and Nguyen 2005).

Extensive literature examines the ownership impact on performance. The theoretical literature suggests that ownership has a significant influence on performance. The empirical literature generally agrees on a negative impact of state ownership on performance in developing countries and transitional (Bonin et al. 2005; Fries and Taci 2005) and emerging economies (Yao et al. 2007; Jiang et al. 2009). This effect is found to be more significant on profit efficiency than on cost efficiency (Berger et al. 2009; Jiang et al. 2013). Being aware of the poor performance of state banks, many governments privatized state banks, which has improved bank performance (Berger et al. 2005; Jiang et al. 2013), especially with the involvement of foreign strategic investors (Fries and Taci 2005; Hasan and Marton 2003). As a result of deregulation, globalization, and technological advancement, foreign banks have penetrated into developing countries. On average, the efficiency advantages of foreign-owned banks relative to domestically owned banks tend to outweigh the disadvantages in many developing and transitional countries (Berger 2007).

Research on banking in the BRICs mainly focuses on single country case studies. Brazilian and Russian banking sectors are largely unresearched relative to Indian and Chinese ones. Findings in general are consistent with the literature in developing countries and transition economies, except for evidence showing that state banks perform better than their private counterparties. In Brazil, research suggests that state banks outperform both foreign banks and private banks (Tecles and Tabak 2010; Staub et al. 2010); well-capitalized banks are more efficient (Tecles and Tabak 2010); and bank performance has improved for privatized banks but not for restructured banks (Beck et al. 2005). Tabak et al. (2015) find that the Brazilian banking industry is characterized as monopolistic competition and bank market power is negatively related to risk-taking. Banks that experience a decline in market power and a simultaneous increase in capital levels tend to take more risks. After crisis, state-owned banks behave more aggressively and undertake riskier activities to expand market shares.

One might not be surprised by the scarcity of banking literature in Russia given the short history of the banking system. Styrin (2005) reports that foreign banks are more efficient than domestic banks and Karas et al. (2010) suggests that public banks are more cost efficient than private banks, while the introduction of deposit insurance has no significant impact on narrowing down the efficiency gap between these two types of banks. Fungáčová et al. (2010) analyze bank competition over the period 2001–2006, reporting slightly improved bank competition and the most competitive banks being foreign banks at the beginning and state-owned banks at the end of the period. They also find evidence suggesting that market powers are enhanced for foreign-owned banks but reduced for state-controlled banks over the period under study.

In India, an earlier study (Bhattacharyya et al. 1997) suggests that public banks are the best performers benefiting from deregulation, while subsequent work of Kumbhakar and Sarkar (2003) finds that the performance effect of deregulation is insignificant. In the post-liberalization period, empirical research suggests that banking deregulation has led to performance improvement for state banks (Zhao et al. 2010) and state banks outperform private banks regardless of efficiency measures employed (Sensarma 2005; Das and Ghosh 2009; Sathye 2003; Ray and Das 2010). A more recent study (Sanyal and Shankar 2011) shows that private banks outperform both public banks and foreign banks.

In China, existing research generally concludes that bank performance has improved and joint-stock banks are more efficient than state banks (Yao et al. 2007; Ariff and Can 2008; Berger et al. 2009; Jiang et al. 2013). Although it may take a longer time to realize the benefits (Jiang et al. 2009), foreign minority ownership has a significant positive effect on performance (Berger et al. 2009; Jiang et al. 2013). Moreover, Zhang et al. (2012) find that a sound legal environment and stronger protection of intellectual property rights help regional city commercial banks improve performance. Jia (2009) shows that state-owned banks lend less prudently than joint-equity banks, consistent with the hypothesis that the accountability to shareholders and depositors provides joint-equity commercial banks incentives to conduct business more prudently. The finding also supports the hypothesis that the reform of the banking system has improved the incentive for state-owned banks to behave more prudently in lending.

The noticeable absence in literature is an empirical comparative study across the BRICS' banks. Although the BRICS' banks may exhibit a similar dynamic trend in performance when facing a big worldwide shock (i.e., the global financial crisis), the quantitative effect may vary across the BRICs due to differences in macroeconomic and institutional environment, industrial market conditions, and bank-specific characteristics. For instance, at the country level, stronger institutional and regulatory infrastructure may promote more prudential practice, which eases the impacts of unexpected shocks on banks. Moreover, existing literature on the relationship between market concentration, risk-taking, and performance have mainly focused on the US and European banking markets, leaving the issue unexamined in the emerging economies. This chapter fills in the gap in the literature by investigating the issue in the context of emerging economies.

4.1.2 Literature on Banking Concentration, Risk-Taking, and Performance

The relationship between market concentration and performance has long been subject to theoretical debates. The Structure–Conduct–Performance (SCP) hypothesis from traditional industrial organization literature suggests a positive relationship between market concentration and performance based on the conjecture that in a concentrated market large banks collude to earn higher profits (Bain 1956). Affirming this positive relationship, the efficient structure hypothesis, however, asserts a reverse causality that efficient banks are more profitable and gain market shares, resulting in a concentrated market (Demsetz 1973). In contrast, the "quiet life hypothesis" predicts a negative association between market concentration and performance arguing that firms with market power tend to operate inefficiently as managers may relax their efforts and enjoy the monopoly profit of a "quiet life" (Hicks 1935). Empirical literature has achieved no unanimity. In the European banking sector, the "quiet life" hypothesis is rejected in Maudos and Fernández de Guevara (2007) but accepted in Delis and Tsionas (2009). In the US market, an early study of Berger and Hannan (1998) finds strong evidence for the "quiet life" hypothesis. A recent study by Koetter et al. (2012) presents a more complex picture with a negative association between market power and profit efficiency but a positive association between market power and cost efficiency.

On the other hand, bank intermediation involves a variety of risks. Excessive risk-taking could lead to bank failures, which in turn may cause bank runs and even costly financial crises. Motivated by more frequently occurring financial crises with disastrous damages to the economy, a growing body of research addresses the macro stability of the banking/financial systems with two contrasting views emerged. The competition-fragility view believes that competition may encourage banks to take more risks for higher return and thus undermine financial stability, while monopoly rents increase a bank's charter value and discourage risk-taking behaviour (Allen and Gale 2004; Keeley 1990). The competition-stability view argues that monopoly allows banks to charge higher interest rates, which exaggerate the adverse selection effect and jeopardize banking/financial stability (Boyd and De Nicolo 2005; Allen et al. 2011; Schaeck et al. 2009).

Other researchers take a micro approach to gauging how risk-taking behaviour interacts with bank performance. The "bad luck" hypothesis argues that an increase in problem loans caused by precipitated external events induces credit risk and banks may become inefficient due to greater efforts and expenses on those problem loans (Berger and De Young 1997). Empirical studies have examined the relationship between performance and a wide range of risks, including credit risk, capital risk, liquidity risk, market risk, operational risk, and overall risk (Altunbas et al. 2007; Berger and De Young 1997; Brissimis et al. 2008; Fiordelisi et al. 2011). This strand of literature to date is primarily based on the US and European countries with, if any, fewer insights and discussions on the banking industry in emerging economies.

Literature on the relationship between bank performance and risk-taking is still in its infancy. In the US banking market, researchers observe a negative association between bank performance and risk-taking (Berger and De Young 1997; Kwan and Eisenbeis 1997). In the EU banking markets, empirical evidence is mixed. While Altunbas et al. (2007) find no such a negative association as in the US market, Fiordelisi et al. (2011) provide evidence that banks with a lower level of capital risk are more efficient. Brissimis et al. (2008) suggest that bank performance is negatively affected by capital risk and credit risk but positively influenced by liquidity risk.

Despite the rising status of the BRICS with 42% of the world's population, their banking sectors are under-researched. In fact, the 2007–2008 financial crisis has catalysed the catching up process for banks in the developing world, noticeably 4 Chinese banks have become the top 10 largest banks in the world after the crisis. Meanwhile, the 2007–2008 financial crisis has fuelled active public policy debates on issues such as bank performance, market concentration (market power), competition, risk-taking, financial stability, regulation, and so forth. The rapid recovery of the BRIC economies and banking sectors provide a natural experiment and rare opportunity to study these issues and compare bank performance across BRICS.

Against this backdrop, this chapter evaluates bank performance and examines the impact of the 2007–2008 financial crisis across the BRIC banks while controlling for the effects of country-, industrial-, and bank-level differences to address the heterogeneity of the sample. This study also tests for the "quiet life" hypothesis and presents new empirical evidence to theoretical debates in the existing literature from an emerging market perspective. Given the high policy relevance of the concentration–performance relation, this study provides insights into banking industries in the BRICs with important implications for policy makers engaging in formulating banking policies not limited to the BRIC countries but also other developing countries. This chapter follows the micro approach to examining the risk–performance relation in the BRICs' banking markets. The findings enrich our understanding of how BRIC banks have withstood the storm wave of the 2007–2008 global financial crisis, which are of particular interests to bankers, practitioners, and regulators.

4.2 The Background of BRICS

4.2.1 An Overview of BRICS' Economies

The term "BRICs" was coined by O'Neill (2001) in a Goldman Sachs' report focusing on larger emerging market economies—Brazil, Russia, India and China. The report pointed out that this group of emerging countries represented a significant share of the world's production and population—accounting for 23.3% of world GDP (on a PPP basis) and comprising 42.5% of world total population as of the end 2000. BRIC started as a formal grouping during the 1st meeting of BRIC Foreign Ministers on the margins of General Debate of the UN General Assembly (UNGA) in New York in 2006 and the four countries initiated a regular informal diplomatic coordination, which led to the 1st BRIC Summit held in Yekaterinburg, Russia, on 16 June 2009. This group was further extended by the inclusion of South Africa and became BRICS in 2011—a new promising political-diplomatic entity.

Since the Yekaterinburg Summit, member states' leaders have been holding annual summits and BRICS has evolved incrementally around two main pillars—coordination in multilateral fora focusing on economic and political governance and cooperation between member states. The cooperation pillar has achieved significant progress with a broad agenda developed in areas such as finance, agriculture, economy and trade, combating transnational crime, science and technology, health, education, corporate and academic dialogue and security, among others. The financial front of cooperation has received a special focus. At the 4th BRICS summit in New Delhi, India (2012), the member states proposed to establish the BRICS Development Bank. The idea was agreed by BRICS leaders at the 5th BRICS summit in Durban, South Africa (2013), the agreement to establish the New Development Banks was signed during the 6th BRICS summit in Fortaleza, Brazil (2014). On 7 July 2015, the New Development Bank came into existence at the 7th BRICS summit in Ufa, Russia. It was headquartered in Shanghai, China and became fully operational in February 2016 with a reserve currency pool of $100 billion set up by the member states. The mission of the New Development Bank is to mobilize resources thereby supporting infrastructure and sustainable development in BRICS and other emerging economies for faster development through innovation and cutting-edge technology. The New Development Bank focuses on sustainable infrastructure and development with 60% of total lending extending to the renewable energy industry. In 2016, the bank provided loans of USD 1.5 billion assisting projects in renewable and green energy and transportation (www.ndb.int).

As of the end 2015, BRICS' share in world GDP was 22.4% and in world population 42%. Figure 4.1 shows the GDP growth rate of BRICS over the period 2000–2015, in comparison with that of the developed countries represented by the US and the EU. The average growth rate of BRICS is 5.35%—three times that of the US and the EU (1.71%) over the period 2000–2015. Like the developed economies, all BRICS economies were hit by the 2007–2008 financial crisis. In 2009, while India and China managed to maintain a high growth rate of 8.48% and 9.4%, respectively, Brazil experienced a negative growth of −0.13% and Russia slipped down to −7.82%. BRICS states rapidly recovered to a growth rate of 7.53% in Brazil, 4.5% in Russia, 10.26% in India, and 10.4% in China in 2010, faster than the US of 2.53% and the EU of 2.16%.[1] Since 2010, the BRICS economies deteriorated. In 2012, India picked up a steady growth rate, China and South Africa slowed down. Brazil and Russia slipped further down to a negative growth rate in 2015, posing a threat to the future development of BRICS.

As Latin America's largest economy, Brazil has made significant economic and social progress over the past decade, lifted 29 million people out of poverty and reduced inequality significantly with the Gini coefficient dropping by 6.6 percentage points between 2003 and 2014. Brazil experienced a deep recession with its GDP contracting by 3.8% in 2015 and 3.6% in 2016, as a result of the combination of the fall in commodity prices, failure to make necessary policy adjustments, and political turmoil, while it held a healthy level of reserves of US$ 358 billion

[1]Data are from World Bank. Annual percentage growth rate of GDP is at market prices based on constant local currency.

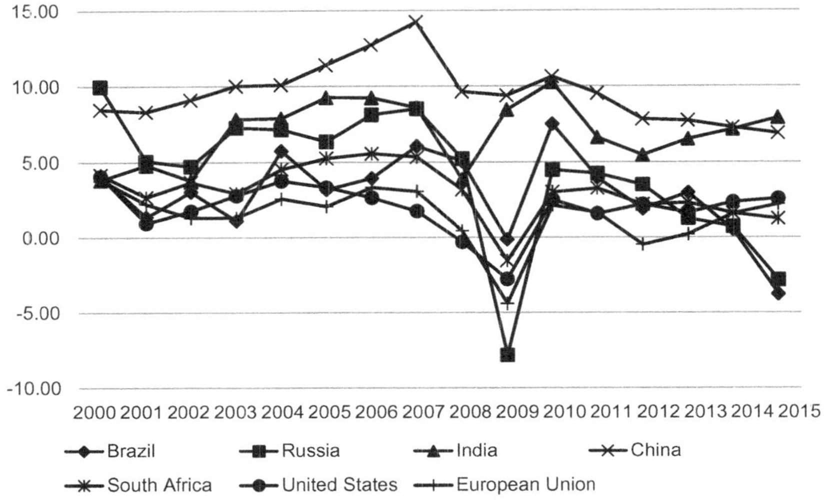

Fig. 4.1 GDP growth rate in BRICS (2000–2015). *Data source* The World Bank

at the end of 2015. The new President—Michel Temer announced a reform agenda with fiscal adjustment measures to address these issues after he took office on 31 August 2016. Despite low popularity, the Temer government has started to tackle some of the tough problems, such as budget deficit, and from the early months of 2017 there are signs that the recession is ending with the recognition of the need for some important changes to build a more sustainable future.

Russia has undergone drastic changes since the collapse of the Soviet Union in the late 1990s. Driven by rising oil prices, Russia with a commodity-based growth model achieved an average annual growth rate of 7% during 1998–2008. After this period of high economic growth, the economy has weakened since 2012 and went into a deep recession in 2015 caused by the lagged second phase structural reforms to remedy structural limitations, the unsustainable commodity-based growth model that was further hampered by the sharp fall in oil prices, and Western economic sanctions introduced in 2014. It has been recovering from the recession since 2016, driven by firmer oil prices, strong external position, and effective policy response. The authorities implemented an economic package, including a flexible exchange rate regime, enhanced banking sector in terms of capital and liquidity, limited fiscal stimulus, and regulatory forbearance, to restore public confidence and stabilize the financial system. However, the effects of sanctions are still significant, which deter investment and suppress growth. Future reforms should focus on reducing the economy's dependence on oil and other commodities.

India has the largest number of poor people in the world. The Indian government changed its economic policies since the beginning of the 2000s and soon enjoyed fast growth rate competing with China. India is classified as a lower-middle-income economy after the World Bank changing to a more precise description of economies in 2016. India lifted 133 million people out of poverty during the period 1994–2012, while 42% of the Indian population are still living below the poverty line according the World Bank and the figure is at least 28–30% even by the government's optimistic estimates. Income inequality has become increasingly serious with a remarkable rising trend in the consumption of the top 20% of the population but a rapid decline in that of the bottom 80% of the rural population. In contrast to Russia, India took advantage of the real positive effect of the sharp decline in oil and commodity prices. The Indian economy rapidly recovered from the 2008 global financial crisis. Its currency and stock markets largely remained resilient even during the crisis. It maintained a more than 7% growth rate overtaking China in 2015. Despite the cash crisis following the Prime Minister Narendra Modil's sudden ban on most of India's cash on 8 November 2016, India maintained a growth rate around 7%. On the other hand, banking crisis presents a key challenge for the sustainable growth of the Indian economy.

Since the commencement of the market-oriented reforms in 1978, China has experienced rapid economic and social development at an average annual growth rate of more than 9%, lifted more than 800 million people out of poverty. China made an economic miracle as the fastest and sustainable expanding economy in world history. It has been the largest contributor to the world economic recovery after the global financial crisis in 2008, with strong fiscal support and loose monetary policy. Since 2012, China's GDP growth has gradually entered into a new normal trajectory of lower but steady and sustainable growth. GDP growth rate fell to 7.4% in 2015 and down to the slowest rate in 26 years of 6.7%

in 2016 even after the government used more credit-fuelled stimulus to meet its economic growth target. The banking sector extended a record of $1.8 trillion of loans in 2016, posing a significant risk of explosive debt levels of the economy. More than three decades of rapid economic expansion comes with many challenges, such as an enlarged inequality gap, rapid urbanization, environmental sustainability, external imbalances, and aging population, which need to be dealt with properly by significant policy adjustments to promote sustainable growth in China.

Since South Africa's peaceful political transition in 1994 through the first election that opened to all its citizens, the African National Congress (ANC) has been driving the policy agenda and made considerable efforts on economic development. Poverty was halved from 34% in 1996 to 17% in 2008, as a result of improved social safety nets and real income growth, and decelerated inflationary pressure on households. After recovery from the recession in 2010, economic growth has been deteriorated mainly due to structural challenges and weak global growth in the post-crisis era. Poverty barely changed at an estimate of 15.9% in 2016 by the World Bank and unemployment reached a 13-year high of 27.7% in the first quarter of 2017. GDP growth was 1.3% in 2015, dropped to only 0.3% in 2016, and entered into recession after contracting by 0.7% in the first quarter 2017. This slowing down in economic growth was collectively driven by depressed commodity demand from China, low global commodity prices, weak manufacturing, low investment, erratic capital flows and low consumer and business confidence, posing a gloomy outlook to South Africa's economy.

4.2.2 The Evolution of the Banking Systems in BRICS

The banking systems in the BRICS countries have experienced rather different evolutionary processes. The first commercial bank in Brazil dated back to the early 19th century. The Central Bank of Brazil was established in 1964 as part of the financial reform to support the industrialization plan and fight against inflation. The reform specialized financial institutions and laid the foundation for the Brazilian Financial System referencing to the American financial model. The Brazilian banking system has two distinct features. First, Brazil experienced historical hyperinflation—three digits in the 1980s and well over 1000% in the 1990s. Brazilian banks survived and benefited from inflation by raising low-cost liabilities that were invested in short term securities at much higher interest rates. The high returns from this kind of transactions (known as the "float") covered up the deficiencies of the banking system and dis-incentivized the development of normal banking practices. Second, the Brazilian banking market has the highest cost of financial intermediation in the world in terms of both absolute interest rates and spreads (Miccolis-Anwar 2007).

State banks in Brazil played a critical role in financing state-level developments and deficits. In the 1980s, most state banks became rather weak, which was hampered by the worsening economic conditions and public sector deficits. In 1994, the Brazilian government implemented the Real Plan to stabilize the economy and control inflation. Without inflationary gains some banks went bankrupt. To avoid a systematic banking crisis, the federal government launched the "Program of Incentives for the Restructuring and Strengthening of the National Financial System – PROER" and the Credit Guarantee Fund to assure public confidence. Subsequently state banks underwent significant reforms of restructuring, privatization, or liquidation (Beck et al. 2005). Caused by significant M&A activities, the Brazilian banking system is highly consolidated with top six-bank concentration ratio of 80% in term of banking total assets, while state banks have maintained a solid position despite the emergence of large private conglomerates. The Brazilian banking sector has been adversely affected by the economic recession, leading to eroded profitability and asset quality and declined total credit. Nevertheless, the financial sector remains well-capitalized even according to more stringent international rules.

The Russian banking system emerged only in the early 1990s after the collapse of the Soviet Union in the late 1980s. The Bank of Russia (the Central Bank of the Russian Federation) assumed central banking functions and five state banks were commercialized to serve enterprises in their assigned sectors in the economy. These five state banks were created in 1987 by taking over commercial operations from the State Bank, namely USSR Promstroybank (industry), USSR Agroprombank (agriculture/industrial), USSR Zhilsotzbank (housing and social security), USSR Vnesheconombank (foreign trade) and USSR Sberbank (the savings bank). Without much surprise, the sudden death of the centrally-controlled economic system invited a disaster: the economy collapsed, GDP fell dramatically, and inflation rocketed to 2510% in 1992 (Heffernan 2005). The repercussions for the banking system were significant, leading to a series of systemic mini-crises in 1994, 1995, 1998, and 2004. The causes of these crises are a combination of numerous factors, including the absence of a regulatory and supervisory system until 1995, a massive and uncontrolled privatization schemes from 1992, the "pocket banks" serving business groupings or state institutions, under-capitalization, the lack of modern banking skills, and resultant poor asset quality (Tompson 2004).[2] After the crisis in 1998, the Bank of Russia took decisive steps to reform the banking system and made impressive progresses. After the implementation of the Banking Sector Development Strategy over 2005–2008, the Russian government ambitiously aimed at positioning the banking system on international financial markets during the period 2009–2015. However, due to the weak macroeconomic conditions, the banking performance deteriorated with lowering profitability and rising NPLs ratios. The authorities undertook a number of measures to prevent the financial system from collapsing, including forbearance measures to ease financial market stress on banks, regulatory changes, and recapitalization of major state banks. One of the important moves is the establishment of the Central Bank of the Russian Federation (CBR) as a unified or "Mega Regulator" in 2013. This not only symbolizes the far reaching changes to the legal and supervisory landscape in the Russian banking sector, but also facilitates greater cross-sectoral oversight in the financial system (IMF 2016).

Currently, the Russian banking system consists of more than 600 banks and the top three-bank concentration ratio is 60% in term of total assets and 71% of total loans as of 2015. The market has become more concentrated over time, compared with top three-bank concentration ratio of 53% (total assets) and 64% (loans) in 2012.

---

[2] The "pocket banks" were controlled by a single shareholder or a small group of related shareholders and they were used as a tool of business groupings or state institutions (Tompson 2004).

Since the independence in 1947, India has been a democratic nation without experiencing a centrally-controlled economic system as in the former Soviet Union and China. The financial system was quite unrestricted until the 1960 s when the state took control to facilitate the 5-year national economic plans. The government nationalized the 14 largest commercial banks in 1969 and further 6 in 1980 to support the implementation of the national economic plans by channelling funds to priority sectors and minimizing the cost of state borrowing. However, in 1991 India was faced with severe balance of payment crisis due to a rapidly growing fiscal deficit and rising oil prices.[3] In response, the Indian government initiated a systematic economic reform programme toward a market-oriented economy, along with financial deregulation and liberalization. From 1996, the government partially privatized state banks to avoid costly capital injections while maintaining 60–80% shareholding (Heffernan 2005), but the pace of banking reform was slow. The current banking sector is dominated by state ownership with poor asset quality, excessive supervision, and weak financial institutions. It also faces moral hazard and incentive problems stemming from the public belief that state banks will never be allowed to fail. A striking feature of the Indian banking system is the preferential lending requirements set by the Indian authority. Domestic banks and foreign banks are required to lend 40% and 32%, respectively, of their adjusted net bank credit (or credit equivalent of off-balance sheet exposures whichever is higher) to the priority sectors. As of the end 2016, the banking system consists of 26 state banks, 20 private banks, 43 foreign banks, 56 regional rural banks, 1589 urban cooperative banks and 93,550 rural cooperative banks, in addition to cooperative credit institutions. As the state-controlled banks have lent too much to support the economy, non-performing loans grew rapidly to two digit figures and banking crisis gradually set in since 2015 and no sign of an ending this slow-motion crisis in 2017, according to Bloomberg reports (Sharma 2017).

The first bank in South Africa—the Lombard Bank was established in the Cape in 1793. It was a state bank and was entrusted to issue

[3]Rising oil prices were caused by the first Gulf War in 1990–1991.

government notes. The first private bank in South Africa—the Cape of Good Hope Bank was opened in 1837. The South African Reserve Bank—the central bank of the Republic of South Africa, was established in 1921 with private shareholders other than governments (www.resbank.co.za). After nearly a century of evolvement, South Africa has a well-developed banking system better than many other emerging market countries and comparable with those in many developed countries. The total financial sector assets amounted nearly three times of GDP in 2014, of which two thirds were held by unusually large non-banking financial institutions. With the slowing down of economic growth since 2008, banks have increasingly exposed to credit risk as households and firms under pressure of high interest rates and deteriorated asset quality became more apparent in 2014. However, the banking risks have been mitigated by relatively high capital buffers and a high level of effective banking regulation and supervision (IMF 2014). The South African banking system is highly concentrated with the top five-bank concentration ratio of 90.5% by total assets, which gives major financial institutions significant market power in pricing and hence higher profitability.

4.3 Research Methodology

4.3.1 Models and Variables

The preferred estimation technique is the stochastic frontier analysis (SFA) which pre-specifies a functional form and decomposes error terms into a random error (v_i) and inefficiency (u_i) (Aigner et al. 1977). SFA is more appropriate for emerging markets where measurement errors and uncertainties of the economic environment are more likely to prevail. This study estimates a common frontier composed from all banks in the sample and employs an output distance function approach in a one-step estimation setting (Battese and Coelli 1995). For a cross-countries study, bank efficiencies can be measured against a common frontier or nation-specific frontiers. When using a common frontier, the analysis is informative for policy makers as measured efficiencies are comparable and studies have made good progress in controlling country differences through econometric methods. When using nation-specific frontiers, measured efficiencies are not comparable and therefore such comparisons are less informative regarding the policy and research questions in relation to the international financial institutions (Berger 2007).

The output distance function is first introduced by Shephard (1970) and has been increasingly applied to empirical efficiency studies. A major advantage is that a distance function represents multiple-outputs and multi-inputs production technology which facilitates efficiency study for industries using such technology without requiring price information as the cost/profit function does. When price information is unavailable or inaccurately measured and/or behaviour assumptions of cost-minimisation or profit-maximisation are inappropriate, traditional dual approach is inapplicable to account for multi-outputs production technology by estimating a cost function and/or a profit function. So a distance function approach is an alternative to the dual approaches (Cuesta and Orea 2002; Coelli and Perelman 1996).

Following Lovell et al. (1994), based on the common definition of production technology that transforms inputs into outputs, the output distance function is defined in terms of the output set $P(x)$ as in Eq. (4.1):

$$D_O(x,y) = \min\{\theta : (y/\theta) \in P(x)\} \tag{4.1}$$

$D_O(x,y)$ is non-decreasing, positively homogeneous and convex in the output vector y and non-increasing in the input vector x.

An empirical representation of the output distance function in a translog form is given in Eq. (4.2) for a firm producing m outputs using n inputs:

$$\begin{aligned} \ln D_o\left(x^t, y^t, t\right) = {} & \alpha_0 + \sum_{k=1}^{n} \alpha_k \ln x_k^t + \sum_{j=1}^{m} \beta_j \ln y_j^t + \frac{1}{2}\sum_{k=1}^{n}\sum_{h=1}^{n} \alpha_{kh} \ln x_k^t \ln x_h^t \\ & + \frac{1}{2}\sum_{j=1}^{m}\sum_{l=1}^{m} \beta_{jl} \ln y_j^t \ln y_l^t + \sum_{k=1}^{n}\sum_{j=1}^{m} \gamma_{kj} \ln x_k^t \ln y_j^t \\ & + \varphi_t t + \frac{1}{2}\varphi_{tt} t^2 + \sum_{k=1}^{n} \xi_{kt} \ln x_k^t t + \sum_{j=1}^{m} \tau_{jt} \ln y_j^t t, \end{aligned} \tag{4.2}$$

where x is input, y is output, and t is a time trend.

$D_o(x^t, y^t, t)$ is homogeneous of degree 1 in y, which give following constraints:

$$\sum_{j=1}^{m} \beta_j = 1, \sum_{l=1}^{m} \beta_{jl} = 0(j = 1, 2, \ldots M), \sum_{j=1}^{m} \gamma_{kj} = 0(k = 1, 2, \ldots N), \sum_{j=1}^{m} \tau_{jt} = 0(j = 1, 2, \ldots M), \beta_{jl} = \beta_{lj} \text{ and } \alpha_{kh} = \alpha_{hk}.$$

Rearranging the Eq. (4.2), we have the following for individual firm i

$$\begin{aligned} \ln D_{oi}^t - \ln y_{mi}^t = \alpha_0 &+ \sum_{k=1}^{n} \alpha_k \ln x_{ki}^t + \sum_{j=1}^{n} \beta_j \ln \left(y_{ji}^t\right)^* \\ &+ \frac{1}{2} \sum_{k=1}^{n} \sum_{h=1}^{n} \alpha_{kh} \ln x_{ki}^t \ln x_{hi}^t \\ &+ \frac{1}{2} \sum_{j=1}^{m-1} \sum_{l=1}^{m-1} \beta_{jl} \ln \left(y_{ji}^t\right)^* \ln \left(y_{li}^t\right)^* \\ &+ \sum_{k=1}^{n} \sum_{j=1}^{m-1} \gamma_{kj} \ln x_{kj}^t \ln \left(y_{ji}^t\right)^* \\ &+ \varphi_t t + \frac{1}{2} \varphi_{tt} t^2 + \sum_{k=1}^{n} \xi_{kt} \ln x_{ki}^t t \\ &+ \sum_{j=1}^{m-1} \tau_{jt} \ln \left(y_{ji}^t\right)^* t + v_i^t, \end{aligned} \tag{4.3}$$

where $\left(y_{ji}^t\right)^* = y_{ji}^t / y_{mi}^t (j = 1, 2, \ldots m - 1)$.

By definition $\ln D_{oi}^{t} \leq 0$. When defining $u_i^t = -\ln D_{oi}^{t}$ (i.e., u_i^t follows a non-negative truncated normal distribution); $v_i^t \sim N(0, \sigma_v^2)$ (i.e., v_i^t follows a standard normal distribution); and u_i^t and v_i^t are independent, Eq. (4.3) becomes the standard setting of a stochastic frontier model.[4]

Follows Jiang et al. (2009), two empirical models are specified, namely the income-based model and the earning asset-based model. When defining inputs and outputs, the intermediation approach (Sealey and Lindley 1977) is modified by treating total deposits as an output. The income-based model focuses on the efficiency of generating income and defines two inputs (total interest expense and non-interest expense) and two outputs (net interest income and non-interest income). The earning assets-based model explores the efficiency of growing earning assets and defines three inputs (total interest expense, labor, and physical capital) and four outputs (net loans, total securities, total deposit, and non-interest operating income). Following the literature, non-interest expenses is used as the proxy for labor (Hasan and Marton 2003) and non-interest income is included to capture the effect of the diversification in bank activities, such as off-balance sheet activities.

The technical inefficiency effect model is shown in Eq. (4.4).

$$u_{it} = \delta_0 + \delta_1 CR_{ji} + \sum_{a=2}^{6} \delta_a Risk_{it} + \sum_{b=7}^{18} \delta_b Control + \delta_{19} t + \varepsilon_{it} \quad (4.4)$$

where CR_{ji} is the concentration ratio for the country j in year t; $Risk_{it}$ is a vector of risk-taking variables for bank i in year t; *Control* is a vector of control variables; t is a time trend to capture the catching up effect against the shifting frontier.

Market concentration is defined as the sum of the market share (in terms of total assets) of the five largest banks. *Capital risk* is proxied by the ratio of equity to total assets (E/A) and a bank with a lower E/A ratio faces higher risk of failure. *Credit risk* is measured by the ratio of

[4]Simultaneous equation bias may exist when both inputs and outputs are included in the distance function as regressors. But after the normalization procedure, output ratios may be treated as exogenous (Coelli and Perelman 1996).

NPLs to total loans and a higher ratio indicates that the bank is more likely to suffer losses from loan defaults. *Market risk* is captured by the ratio of interbank borrowing to total borrowing and a higher ratio suggests that the bank relies more on interbank borrowing and therefore more vulnerable to the movements of market rates. One may argue that market risks also include risk arising from the movement of foreign exchange rates and the ratio of interbank borrowing may not be an adequate measure. We consider that our sample only includes domestic commercial banks and these banks' exposure to foreign exchange risk is small given their involvement in the international financial markets. *Liquidity risk* is measured by the ratio of liquid assets to total assets and the higher the ratio, the lower the risk that a bank may fail to meet its liabilities when they fall due. *Overall risk* is proxied by the ratio of loan loss reserve to NPLs that indicates the bank's ability to absorb losses from NPLs before eroding the bank's capital. A bank with a higher ratio faces lower risk of going bankrupt.

The first control variable is the 2007–2008 financial crisis and the dummy equals zero before 2008 and one thereafter. The country level control variables include *GDP* growth to reflect the macroeconomic environment, and *Country dummies* to take into account of the differences in institutional framework and legal systems across BRICs. At the industrial level, the share of state-owned banks and the share of foreign banks (in terms of total assets) are employed to gauge the performance effect of ownership. The importance of the stock market reveals the impact of capital markets on bank performance. Following the "Financial Structure Dataset" from the World Bank, the importance of the stock market is defined as the average of the structure activity and the structure size. The higher the value, the more market-based is a country's financial system. The structure activity is defined as the ratio of two ratios: (1) the ratio of stock market total value traded to GDP, and (2) the ratio of private credit by deposit money of banks to GDP; the structure size is also defined as the ratio of two ratios: (1) the ratio of stock market capitalization to GDP, (2) the ratio of private credit by deposit money of banks to GDP. The higher the value, the more market-based is a country's financial system. The effect of net interest spread is also controlled given the significant differences across the BRIC banks. At the bank level, we consider the impact of Bank size (dummy equals 1 if a bank's total assets are greater than the average total assets of the sample and 0 otherwise), Listing status (dummy equals 1 for publicly listed banks and 0 otherwise), Revenue diversification (the share of non-interest income in total income), and Assets diversification (the share of security in total earning assets).

4.3.2 Data

This chapter restricts the sample to the major domestic commercial banks in the BRIC economies over 2003–2010 with 1001 bank-year observations. South Africa was included in BRICS in 2011 and hence excluded from our sample. The sample period ends in 2010 for comparison purposes as findings are more comparable with those from Chap. 3 that investigates bank performance in China. After 2010, the banking sectors as well as the economies of BRICS have experienced significant changes with difference research foci, which are beyond the scope of this book and shows the direction for future research. Banks are selected if they are on the list of the world 1000 biggest banks by The Banker and data are available from the Bankscope. Data are collected from multiple sources, such as BankScope, the Central Banks' website, World Bank, and IMF.

Table 4.1 presents descriptive statistics of the sample, providing a snapshot of the banking sectors in BRIC. The BRIC's banking markets are relatively concentrated with an average five-bank concentration ratio of 61%, ranging from 72% in China, followed by 64% in Brazil, to just below 50% in both India and Russia. The Chinese banking market is the largest, 5 times greater than the smallest one in Russia. State banks dominate in the banking sectors in India and China, while foreign banks play a relatively more important role in Brazil and Russia. The capital markets are more important in India and Russia relative to Brazil and China. Data also reveal that Russian and Brazilian banks are in favour of a diversification strategy, while Chinese banks seem to embrace a focus strategy.

Table 4.1 Descriptive statistics

	Full sample obs: 1001		Brazil obs: 92		India obs: 219		Russia obs: 184		China obs: 506	
	Mean	S.D.	Mean	S.D.	Mean	S.D.	Mean	S.D.	Mean	S.D.
Inputs and outputs variables										
Operating income*	1643	4164	3881	5147	1060	1889	974	2145	1731	5012
Net interest income*	1260	3342	2779	3540	628	997	600	1565	1498	4211
Total non-interest operating income*	382	1028	1102	1705	432	1001	374	762	233	898
Net loans*	22890	66374	16946	25095	14020	22410	8689	19697	32974	89650
Total securities *	11141	36456	17711	23406	7427	11658	1798	4433	14952	49061
Total customer deposits*	32858	109773	16874	24922	18924	28651	7985	20768	50840	150195
Total interest expense*	1021	2281	2672	3428	1155	1857	572	1170	826	2364
Total non-interest expenses*	1103	2657	2795	3741	746	1408	748	1671	1079	2994
Fixed assets*	492	1543	343	534	206	242	422	1029	668	2045
Inefficiency effects variables										
Market concentration	61	12	64	3	47	3	48	4	72	2
Risk-taking										
Capital risk	8	7	10	4	6	2	16	12	5	3
Credit risk	5	8	9	6	3	3	5	9	6	9
Market risk	22	22	49	20	10	8	50	25	13	9

(continued)

Table 4.1 (continued)

	Full sample obs: 1001		Brazil obs: 92		India obs: 219		Russia obs: 184		China obs: 506	
	Mean	S.D.	Mean	S.D.	Mean	S.D.	Mean	S.D.	Mean	S.D.
Liquidity risk	34	21	29	21	9	3	26	11	48	15
Overall risk	178	189	75	23	66	23	287	258	140	160
Control variables										
GDP	8.6	3.9	4.0	2.5	8.3	1.5	4.7	5.3	11	1.6
Share of state-owned banks	60	14	32	3	73	2	40	3	67	1
Share of foreign banks	7.1	6.6	20.9	1.5	7.5	0.6	13.9	4.7	1.9	0.3
Importance of stock market	1.2	0.89	1.3	0.37	2.0	0.75	2.1	0.49	0.5	0.26
Net interest spread	7.9	10.41	37.7	3.37	4.9	0.59	6.5	0.97	3.3	0.18
Bank size *	50455	153975	45953	63842	24751	38970	13471	28521	75848	209350
Revenue diversification	19.3	20.5	20.6	18.3	32.6	11.1	39.5	28.1	6.0	5.5
Assets diversification	24.7	14.0	46.9	18.0	34.6	6.8	14.3	9.0	20.1	9.4

Note (1) * Values are in million US dollars (2005 price level); (2) NPL—non-performing loans; LLR—loan loss reserve (3) Operating Income = Net Interest Income + Total Non-Interest Operating Income, Pre-Impairment Operating Profit = Operating Income – Total Non-Interest Expenses (overheads), Operating Profit = Pre-Impairment Operating Profit – Loan Impairment Charge – (Securities and Other Credit Impairment Charges)

Turning to the risk-taking variables, the BRIC banking sectors are generally under-capitalized with an average E/A ratio of 8%, ranging from the highest of Russian banks at 16% to the lowest of Chinese banks at 5%. The average NPL ratio is 5%, higher than an international level of 1–3% for a healthy bank. Indian banks and Brazilian banks have the lowest and the highest NPL ratio at 3% and 9%, respectively. The BRIC banks on average source 22% of their total borrowings from the interbank markets with large variations from 50% for Brazilian and Russian banks to only 10–13% for Indian and Chinese banks. The BRIC banks as a whole hold one-third of total assets as liquid assets with substantial variance from only 9% in India to 48% in China. Brazilian banks and Indian banks tend to take more overall risk with a relatively low LLR/NPL ratio of 75% and 66%, respectively, in contrast to Russian banks with a ratio of 287% and Chinese Banks with a ratio of 139%. In summary, Indian banks take on the highest liquidity risk and overall risk but assume the lowest market risk and credit risk; Brazilian banks confront the highest credit risk and market risk; Russian banks are relatively safe in terms of capital risk and overall risk; and Chinese banks are faced with the greatest capital risk but the lowest liquidity risk.

4.4 Empirical Analysis

4.4.1 Results from Frontier Estimations

Table 4.2 reports the one-step maximum-likelihood estimation results from the above model specifications. Gamma ($\gamma \equiv \sigma_u^2/\sigma_v^2 + \sigma_u^2$) is 0.93 in the income-based model and 0.69 in the earning assets-based model, indicating a high proportion of the error terms attributable to inefficiencies. Log Likelihood statistics and LR test also confirm the good fit of the models. Moreover, all elasticities are significant and

Table 4.2 Estimation results

	Income-based		Earning assets-based	
	Coefficient	*t*-value	Coefficient	*t*-value
Frontier Regression				
Scale elasticity	0.97		0.98	
Sigma-squared ($\sigma^2 \equiv \sigma_V^2 + \sigma_U^2$)	0.60	11.86	0.10	12.01
Gamma ($\gamma \equiv \sigma_U^2/\sigma_V^2 + \sigma_U^2$)	0.93	99.58	0.69	17.68
Log likelihood	−110.56		149.22	
LR test	615.19		341.85	
Inefficiency Effects Analysis				
2007–2008 global financial crisis	0.62	4.39	0.98	9.32
Market concentration	15.63	10.36	2.01	3.45
Risk-taking variables				
Capital risk	−1.31	−1.31	0.89	3.62
Credit risk	3.35	6.55	0.81	4.67
Market risk	3.37	9.96	0.74	6.16
Liquidity risk	2.62	5.65	1.35	11.63
Overall risk	−0.004	−3.27	−0.002	−9.55
Control variables				
Country level				
GDP growth	0.97	0.78	4.09	6.22
Brazil	−2.13	−3.41	6.26	8.15
India	2.94	4.85	0.43	1.89
Russian	2.87	4.15	5.67	9.13
Industrial level				
Share of state-owned banks	7.23	5.03	17.77	12.18
Share of foreign banks	12.72	9.09	5.22	4.76
Importance of stock market	0.93	3.71	−0.72	−8.94
Net interest spread	3.53	2.41	−3.40	−2.81
Bank level				
Bank size	0.25	1.85	−0.25	−3.83
Listing status	−0.81	−6.52	−0.19	−5.90
Revenue diversification	−0.60	−1.94	0.84	7.12
Assets diversification	3.24	7.57	1.57	8.74
Time	−0.16	−2.86	0.05	4.16
Constant	−21.19	−9.93	−15.34	−12.19

Note (1) As the dependent variable in the inefficiency effect model is the estimated inefficiencies, a negative sign of the estimated coefficient indicates that the particular variable has a positive effect on efficiency and *vice versa*; (2) The country dummy of China is excluded from the estimation for comparison purposes

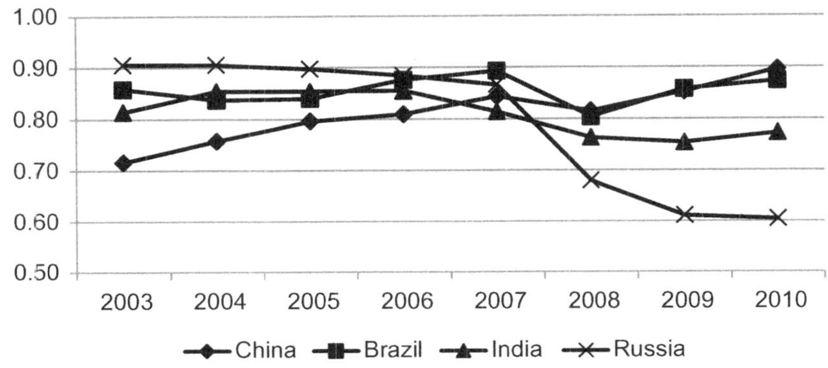

Fig. 4.2 The technical efficiency level from the income-based model

possess the expected signs at the geometric mean, fulfilling the property of monotonicity of the output-oriented distance function.[5] The scale elasticity, defined as the negative of the sum of input elasticities (Färe and Primont 1996), is 0.97 in the income-based model and 0.98 in the earning assets-based model, consistently suggesting decreasing economies of scale for the BRIC banks.

The estimated average efficiency of the BRIC banks over 2003–2010 is 81% from the income-based model and 84% from the earning assets-based model. As shown in Figs. 4.2 and 4.3, unsurprisingly the banking sectors in BRIC were all negatively affected by the 2007–2008 global financial crisis with a precipitous drop in performance. In the income-based model (shown in Fig. 4.2), from 2007 to 2008, China was the least affected country with a reduction in efficiency by 3 percentage points from 84 to 81%, while Russia recorded the biggest drop by 18 percentage points from 86 to 68%. Prior to the 2007–2008 crisis, the performance of the BRIC banks was stable at a relatively high level of 80–90%, except for Chinese banks that steadily caught up from 71% in 2003 to 84% in 2007. After 2008, the efficiency level of the BRIC banks dispersed: Chinese and Brazilian banks' performance recovered

[5]Table 4.2 only reports scale elasticities and full results are available from the authors upon request.

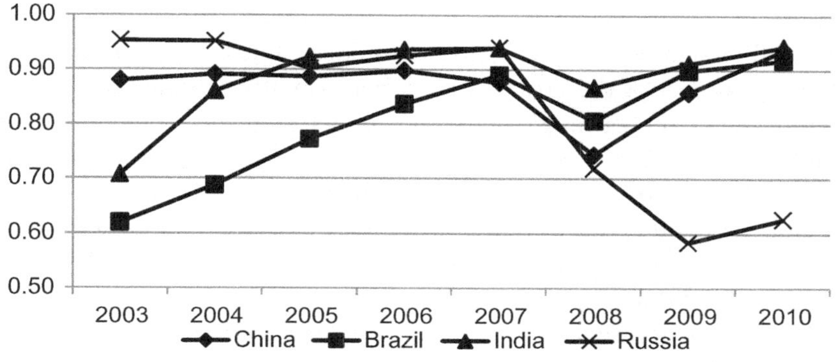

Fig. 4.3 The technical efficiency level from the earning assets-based model

rapidly to 90%; Indian banks stabilized their performance at a level around 75%; and Russian banks suffered further losses by 8 percentage points down to 60% in 2010.

The earning assets-based model (Fig. 4.3) shows a slightly different picture. The 2007–2008 crisis wiped out bank efficiency by 8 percentage points in Brazil and India, 13 percentage points in China, and 22 percentage points in Russia. Prior to the 2007–2008 crisis, Brazilian and Indian banks steadily improved their efficiency to 90%, a figure that had been enjoyed by Chinese and Russian banks. After the crisis, all BRIC banks recovered quickly and reached their highest efficiency levels in 2010, except for Russian banks with further efficiency losses by 14 percentage points in 2009. Russian banks were the most efficient banks prior to the 2007–2008 crisis but became the most inefficient ones after the crisis.

4.4.2 Results from the Inefficiency Effect Model

The results from the technical inefficiency effect model are reported in Table 4.2. We performed a test for the possible multi-collinearity. The mean variance inflation factor (VIF) is 3.9 (well below 5) for all variables in the inefficiency effect model excluding country dummies, suggesting that a multi-collinearity problem is not a major issue. The estimated coefficients on *2007–2008 Global Financial Crisis* are positive at the 1% significance level in both models, statistically confirming a negative impact of the crisis on bank performance. The impact is more significant in the earning asset-based model than in the income-based model. The possible reason is that during the crisis period banks became more cautious in lending and their lending ability was also restricted by the availability of funding, while income could be sustained by increased spreads between the lending and borrowing rates with the latter being held down by central banks.[6]

We find a negative impact of *market concentration* (market power) on efficiency, which is stronger on income generation than on earning assets growth. The results provide strong evidence for the "quiet life hypothesis." The BRIC banks with market power tend to relax their efforts and reap the "monopoly profit" of a "quiet life." These banks may also become inefficient due to the pursuance of objectives other than profit maximization, the costs of gaining and maintaining market power, and the costs of keeping incompetent managers (Berger and Hannan 1998).

As expected, various risks have significant and differential impacts on bank performance. *Capital risk* affects bank performance differently in two models. In the income-based model, the estimated coefficient is negative and marginally significant at the 10% significance level, indicating that banks with low capital risk are more efficient in drawing income, consistent with the extant literature (Mester 1996; Brissimis et al. 2008; Altunbas et al. 2000). In the earning assets-based model, the effect of capital risk is positive at the 1% significance level, consistent with the recent work of Altunbas et al. (2007). The implication is that over-capitalization may induce inefficiency by restricting earning assets growth. *Credit risk* has a negative and statistically significant impact on bank performance, in line with the findings of Berger and De Young (1997), Altunbas et al. (2000), and Brissimis et al. (2008). Banks taking excessive credit risk are associated with poor performance, which

[6]For instance, the spreads increased by 2.45 percentage points in Brazil and 1.58 percentage points in Russia.

lend support to the "bad luck" hypothesis. This impact is more prominent in the income-based model than in the earning assets-based model. *Market risk* also exhibits a negative influence on bank performance. Indeed, greater exposure to interbank markets induces not only market risk but also liquidity risk. Interbank markets are vital for banks' liquidity management when the markets function smoothly in normal times, while overreliance on interbank borrowing may cause severe liquidity problems in crisis periods. Our results show that *liquidity risk* positively affects bank performance in both models. Banks taking less liquidity risk are inefficient, consistent with the trade-off between liquidity and profitability and existing studies (Altunbas et al. 2000, 2007; Brissimis et al. 2008). The effect of *overall risk* on bank performance is negative and statistically significant, but the magnitude is rather small. Our finding is in contrast to Altunbas et al. (2007) that find efficient banks taking on more risk using the ratio of loan loss reserve to total assets as a measure of overall risk.[7]

Turning to the control variables, at the country level, the estimation results suggest that *GDP growth* has no impact on bank performance in the income-based model but a statistically significant and negative impact in the earning assets-based model. The BRIC banks seem not to have benefited from efficiency gain from the faster than world average GDP growth rates in their respective economies, partially reflecting their role in supporting economic growth rather than improving performance. The coefficients on *country dummies* suggest that Brazil and China have the more favourable institutional environment for banks to draw income and to expand earning assets, respectively.

At the industrial level, *the share of state ownership* is found to be negatively associated with bank performance. This finding is consistent with the literature in most developing and transition economies, but in contrast to most single-country studies in Brazil, Russia, and India that find state banks are more efficient. *The share of foreign banks* affects domestic banks' performance negatively, consistent with Claessens et al. (2001).

---

[7]More than 75% of BRIC banks' total earning assets are loans and this study employs the NPL coverage ratio as the proxy for overall risk.

The importance of the stock market has a significant impact on bank performance and banks in a more capital market-based financial system are more efficient in expanding earning assets while becoming inefficient in raising income. This is because high-quality borrowers may raise funds from the capital markets, while they would go to banks for funding in a more bank-based financial system. A larger *net interest spread* has no impact on raising income but helping expanding earning assets. In fact, a larger spread pushes up interest rates, which exaggerates the adverse selection effect and undermines bank performance in generating incomes. On the other hand, excessive risks taken by banks due to adverse selection induce moral hazard problems that banks may lend recklessly to boost earning assets.

At the bank-specific level, we also observe some interesting findings. Bank-specific characteristics have significant and distinct impacts on bank performance: *Large banks* outperform small banks in growing earning assets but not in raising incomes; *listed banks* perform better than unlisted ones; and the *diversification* strategy has a negative impact on bank performance with an exception of efficiency gains from the diversification of revenue sources in the income-based model.

4.4.3 Robustness Tests

To test the robustness of our model specifications, we exclude the bank-level control variables in turn while keeping variables with proven influences on bank performance according to the literature. Results are reported in Table 4.3 for the income-based model and Table 4.4 for the earning assets-based model. The columns (1) of these tables are the chosen specifications. The test results indicate that our chosen models are robust to the inclusion of a variety of bank-specific characteristics. All estimated coefficients on market concentration and risk variables possess the same signs without substantial changes in the significance level. One exception is the capital risk that is slightly sensitive to the exclusion of the bank-level control variables, but the effects are not significant enough to change our conclusion regarding capital risk. As to the country level and the industrial level control variables, the results also suggest that our final specifications are robust.

Table 4.3 Robustness test: The income-based model

	(1)		(2)		(3)		(4)		(5)		(6)		(7)	
	δ_S	*t*-value	δ_S	*t*-value	δ_S	*t*-value	δ_S	*t*-value	δ_S	*t*-value	δ_S	*t*-value	δ_S	*t*-value
2007–2008 financial crisis dummy	0.62	4.39	0.84	4.35	0.77	4.57	0.77	5.23	0.71	4.00	0.77	4.68	0.88	4.50
Market concen-tration	15.63	10.36	18.43	9.75	16.57	11.59	16.20	13.30	14.58	11.62	15.18	12.21	14.29	8.81
Risk-taking variables														
Capital risk (equity/assets)	−1.31	−1.31	−1.05	−1.23	−0.98	−1.36	−1.55	−2.84	−0.31	−0.34	0.05	0.06	−0.06	−0.07
Credit risk (NPL ratio)	3.35	6.55	3.42	6.51	3.38	6.31	3.34	6.19	3.56	6.41	3.60	6.52	3.60	6.04
Market risk	3.37	9.96	3.72	9.32	3.65	10.02	3.16	10.23	3.54	8.68	3.30	9.54	3.44	8.65
Liquidity risk	2.62	5.65	2.65	6.23	2.59	5.74	2.54	5.50	2.71	4.61	2.12	4.72	2.13	4.04
Overall risk	−0.004	−3.27	−0.005	−7.46	−0.005	−7.96	−0.004	−8.01	−0.006	−9.12	−0.006	−9.43	−0.006	−8.14
Control variables														
GDP growth rate	0.97	0.78	1.73	1.17	1.27	0.89	1.64	1.43	1.06	0.87	1.19	1.01	1.91	1.24
Brazil	−2.13	−3.41	2.43	1.16	0.72	0.27	−2.44	−3.15	−0.54	−0.60	−0.25	−0.24	1.45	0.82
India	2.94	4.85	3.83	5.77	3.24	4.37	2.69	4.37	3.59	6.53	3.53	5.62	3.08	4.49
Russian	2.87	4.15	6.36	3.75	5.01	2.48	2.57	3.76	3.59	2.80	3.32	2.60	4.45	3.03

(continued)

Table 4.3 (continued)

	(1)		(2)		(3)		(4)		(5)		(6)		(7)	
	δ_S	*t*-value	δ_S	*t*-value	δ_S	*t*-value	δ_S	*t*-value	δ_S	*t*-value	δ_S	*t*-value	δ_S	*t*-value
Share of state-owned banks	7.23	5.03	13.07	3.72	11.02	2.80	7.27	4.69	10.32	3.12	9.16	2.90	12.73	2.95
Share of foreign banks	12.72	9.09	4.00	0.84	5.54	0.99	16.25	13.87	13.45	9.39	14.33	12.39	12.58	4.70
Importance of stock market	0.93	3.71	0.99	3.88	1.00	4.40	0.95	3.75	0.59	2.85	0.56	2.27	0.63	2.39
Listing status	−0.81	−6.52	−0.83	−6.17	−0.78	−7.99	−0.81	−6.96	−0.99	−6.91	−1.03	−6.52	−1.04	−6.20
Net interest spread	3.53	2.41			2.62	1.08	2.84	2.24	5.57	2.06				
Bank size	0.25	1.85	0.30	2.47			0.18	1.34	0.42	3.51	0.47	3.22		
Revenue diversification	−0.60	−1.94	−0.73	−3.28	−0.72	−2.33			−0.44	−1.34				
Assets dversification	3.24	7.57	3.21	7.77	3.22	6.94	3.22	8.18						
Time	−0.16	−2.86	−0.19	−3.47	−0.18	−4.30	−0.21	−3.86	−0.19	−3.47	−0.21	−3.37	−0.26	−3.75

Table 4.4 Robustness test: The earning assets-based model

	(1)		(2)		(3)		(4)		(5)		(6)		(7)	
	δ_S	*t*-value	δ_S	*t*-value	δ_S	*t*-value	δ_S	*t*-value	δ_S	*t*-value	δ_S	*t*-value	δ_S	*t*-value
2007–2008 financial crisis	0.98	9.32	0.57	1.17	0.27	5.90	0.08	2.20	0.37	7.88	0.11	3.21	0.12	3.91
Market concentration	2.01	3.45	1.53	1.46	0.18	0.36	0.68	1.61	1.10	2.08	0.69	1.75	0.72	3.05
Risk-taking variables														
Capital risk	0.89	3.62	0.64	4.22	0.20	1.06	0.09	0.39	0.39	1.43	0.05	0.27	−0.01	−0.08
Credit risk	0.81	4.67	0.75	1.35	0.44	4.67	0.31	2.00	0.43	2.68	0.29	2.03	0.22	1.65
Market risk	0.74	6.16	0.72	7.59	0.35	5.21	0.51	5.69	0.48	4.23	0.49	6.10	0.40	6.30
Liquidity risk	1.35	11.63	1.29	1.63	0.61	23.46	0.27	3.19	0.74	5.94	0.25	3.00	0.20	3.20
Overall risk	−0.002	−9.55	−0.001	−2.22	−0.001	−2.16	−0.002	−5.36	−0.001	−3.13	−0.003	−14.8	−0.002	−10.6
Control variables:														
GDP growth rate	4.09	6.22	2.06	0.89	1.59	3.42	0.50	0.94	1.42	2.63	0.82	1.59	0.82	1.94
Brazil	6.26	8.15	3.70	3.93	1.92	6.69	2.00	5.14	2.69	6.03	2.67	8.29	2.32	8.08
India	0.43	1.89	0.33	0.52	0.03	0.15	−0.15	−1.00	0.33	1.62	−0.03	−0.20	−0.02	−0.21
Russian	5.67	9.13	3.62	6.16	1.89	18.07	1.93	6.80	2.34	6.45	2.14	7.85	1.95	9.11
Share of state-owned banks	17.78	12.18	12.46	12.67	6.78	17.94	7.67	10.20	8.34	8.94	8.18	11.95	7.41	11.96
Share of foreign banks	5.22	4.76	4.98	7.77	3.20	2.61	0.96	1.55	4.15	7.04	0.99	1.69	1.27	2.09
Importance of stock market	−0.72	−8.94	−0.43	−1.62	−0.30	−12.04	−0.09	−2.09	−0.36	−7.05	−0.11	−2.63	−0.10	−3.10

(continued)

Table 4.4 (continued)

	(1)		(2)		(3)		(4)		(5)		(6)		(7)	
	δ_S	*t*-value	δ_S	*t*-value	δ_S	*t*-value	δ_S	*t*-value	δ_S	*t*-value	δ_S	*t*-value	δ_S	*t*-value
Listing status	−0.19	−5.90	−0.13	−6.75	−0.12	−9.29	−0.06	−2.25	−0.12	−3.52	−0.06	−2.41	−0.06	−2.48
Net interest spread	−3.40	−2.81			−0.36	−0.43	2.14	2.44	−0.96	−1.07				
Bank size	−0.25	−3.83	−0.18	−2.36			−0.13	−3.30	−0.16	−3.58	−0.14	−3.37		
Revenue diversification	0.84	7.12	0.67	4.47	0.33	3.05			0.56	5.41				
Assets diversification	1.57	8.74	0.98	6.44	0.74	6.64	0.57	3.21						
Time	0.05	4.16	0.037	1.75	0.02	2.16	0.32	8.87	0.03	2.85	0.27	7.13	0.13	9.15

Moreover, as SFA is criticized for the predetermination of a functional form and the distributional assumptions of the random errors and inefficiencies, we also employ data envelopment analysis (DEA) to check the robustness of our results. The average efficiency level from DEA models is 66% in the income-based model and 79% in the earning assets-based models, which is lower than 81% and 84% from the corresponding SFA models. These results are consistent with the literature that the nonparametric techniques generally give lower efficiency estimates (Berger and Humphrey 1997). As to the inefficiency effect analysis, results from the DEA models are qualitatively consistent with those from the SFA models relating to our main concern of market concentration and risk variables. The significance level of the estimated coefficients from the DEA models has generally decreased and the income-based model appears to be more robust than the earning assets-based model.

4.5 Conclusion

This chapter takes a comparative approach and puts the Chinese banking system into the context of emerging economics, in particular, the BRICS. The banking sectors in BRICS have evolved distinctively while supporting remarkable economic growth in these countries. The banking sectors in BRICS all have experienced significant changes during financial reforms, such as deregulation, re-regulation, and privatization, with the goal to improve bank performance and better serve economic development. This chapter compares bank efficiency among the BRIC economies and investigates the impact of market concentration and risk-taking on bank efficiency. Using a sample of commercial banks in BRIC over the period 2003–2010, the main findings are as follows, which are robust to alternative model specifications and estimation techniques. First, the average technical efficiency of BRIC banks is 81% in the income-based model and 84% in the earning assets-based models. On average, the Chinese and Brazilian banks outperform the Indian and Russian ones, indicating that China and Brazil have more favourable institutional infrastructure. Second, the 2007–2008 financial crisis has a significant adverse impact on bank performance and BIRC banks recovered immediately in 2009, except for Russian banks that suffered further efficiency losses. China was the least affected country, while Russia was hit hardest with the largest drop in bank efficiency. Interestingly, the BRIC banks do not benefit from their fast-growing economies as our results show that GDP growth has little impact on bank performance. Third, we find a negative association between market concentration and performance, implying that the "quiet life" hypothesis holds in the BRIC banking markets. Fourth, we observe a negative association between performance and credit risk, market risk, and overall risk but a trade-off between performance and liquidity risk. The implication is that banks may improve performance by taking less credit risk, market risk, and overall risk, which enhance the stability of the banking sector. Finally, results from a wide range of control variables at the country, industrial, and bank level are also independently valuable. Brazil and China have more favourable institutional infrastructure for banks to operate more efficiently. State ownership and foreign banks have negative impacts on bank performance. Listed banks subject to market disciplines and public scrutiny perform better. Our results provide important policy implications for bankers and regulators in BRICS as well as other developing and transition countries.

In the post-crisis era, banking sectors in BRICS and other emerging economies face more challenges and uncertainties as well as opportunities. Future research is needed to gain better understanding of the banking markets in these economies. Future research may address the following issues. First, banking reforms in these countries are still ongoing with rapid development in shadow banking and financial deepening, which are affected by the macroeconomic conditions. Future research should follow up on how these developments interact with each other and influence the economy. Second, future work may take a macro approach to investigate the connections between performance, financial stability, and competition from an emerging market perspective thereby providing information for policy makers. Last but not least, the impacts of the newly established New Development Bank initiated by BRICS require more research attention.

References

Aigner, D., C.A.K. Lovell, and P. Schmidt. 1977. Formulation and Estimation of Stochastic Frontier Production Models. *Journal of Econometrics* 6 (21): 37.

Allen, F., and D. Gale. 2004. Competition and Financial Stability. *Journal of Money, Credit, and Banking* 36 (453): 480.

Allen, F., E. Carletti, and R. Marquez. 2011. Credit Market Competition and Capital Regulation. *Review of Financial Studies* 24 (983): 1018.

Altunbas, Y., M.H. Liu, P. Molyneux, and R. Seth. 2000. Efficiency and Risk in Japanese Banking. *Journal of Banking & Finance* 24 (1605): 1628.

Altunbas, Y., S. Carbo, E.P.M. Gardener, and P. Molyneux. 2007. Examining the Relationship Between Capital, Risk and Efficiency in European Banking. *European Financial Management* 13 (49): 70.

Ariff, M., and L. Can. 2008. Cost and Profit Efficiency of Chinese Banks: A Non-Parametric Analysis. *China Economic Review* 19 (260): 273.

Arena, M. 2005. Bank Failures and Bank Fundamentals: A Comparative Analysis of Latin America and East Asia During the Nineties Using Bank-Level Data. Bank of Canada Working Paper 2005-19.

Battese, G.E., and T.J. Coelli. 1995. A Model for Technical Inefficiency Effects in a Stochastic Frontier Production Function for Panel Data. *Empirical Economics* 120 (325): 332.

Bain, J.S. 1956. *Barriers to New Competition*. Cambridge: Harvard University Press.

Beck, T., J.M. Crivelli, and W. Summerhill. 2005. State Bank Transformation in Brazil—Choices and Consequences. *Journal of Banking & Finance* 29 (2223): 2257.

Berger, A.N. 2007. International Comparisons of Banking efficiency. *Financial Markets, Institutions & Instruments* 16 (3): 119–144.

Berger, A.N., G.R.G. Clarke, R. Cull, L. Klapper, and G.F. Udell. 2005. Corporate Governance and Bank Performance: A Joint Analysis of the Static, Selection, and Dynamic Effects of Domestic, Foreign, and State Ownership. *Journal of Banking & Finance* 29 (2179): 2221.

Berger, A.N., and R. De Young. 1997. Problem Loans and Cost Efficiency in Commercial Banking. *Journal of Banking & Finance* 21 (849): 870.

Berger, A.N., I. Hasan, and M. Zhou. 2009. Bank Ownership and Efficiency in China: What will Happen in the World's Largest Nation? *Journal of Banking & Finance* 33: 113–130.

Berger, A.N., and T. Hannan. 1998. The Efficiency Cost of Market Power in the Banking Industry: A Test of the "Quite Life" and Related Hypothesis. *Review of Economics and Statistics* 80 (454): 465.

Berger, A.N., and D.B. Humphrey. 1997. Efficiency of Financial Institutions: International Survey and Directions for Future Research. *European Journal of Operational Research* 98 (2): 175–212.

Bhattacharyya, A., C.A.K. Lovell, and P. Sahay. 1997. The Impact of Liberalisation on the Productive Efficiency of Indian Commercial Banks. *European Journal of Operations Research* 98 (332): 345.

Bongini, P., S. Claessens, and G. Ferri. 2000. The Political Economy of Distress in East Asian Financial Institutions. World Bank Policy Research Working Paper 2265.

Bonin, J.P., I. Hasan, and P. Wachtel. 2005. Bank Performance, Efficiency and Ownership in Transition Countries. *Journal of Banking & Finance* 29 (31): 53.

Boyd, J.H., and G. De Nicolo. 2005. The Theory of Bank Risk Taking and Competition Revisited. *Journal of Finance* 60 (1329): 1343.

Brissimis, S.N., M.D. Delis, and N.I. Papanikolaou. 2008. Exploring the Nexus Between Banking Sector Reform and Performance. *Journal of Banking & Finance* 32 (2674): 2683.

Claessens S., A. Demirguc-Kunt, and H. Huizinga. 2001. How does Foreign Entry Affect Domestic Banking Markets? *Journal of Banking and Finance* 25: 891–911.

Coelli, T., and S. Perelman. 1996. Efficiency Measurement, Multi-Output Technologies and Distance Functions: With Application to European Railways. CREPP Working Paper 96 (05), University of Liege.

Cuesta, R.A., and L. Orea. 2002. Mergers and Technical Efficiency in Spanish Savings Banks: A Stochastic Distance Function Approach. *Journal of Banking & Finance* 26: 2231–2247.

Das, A., and S. Ghosh. 2009. Financial Deregulation and Profit Efficiency: A Nonparametric Analysis of Indian Banks. *Journal of Economics and Business* 61 (509): 528.

Delis, M.D., and E.G. Tsionas. 2009. The Joint Estimation of Bank-Level Market Power and Efficiency. *Journal of Banking & Finance* 33 (1842): 1850.

Demsetz, H. 1973. Industry Structure, Market Rivalry and Public Policy. *Journal of Law and Economics* 16 (1): 9.

Färe, R., and D. Primont. 1996. The Opportunity Cost of Duality. *Journal of Productivity Analysis* 7 (213): 224.

Fonseca, A.R., and F. Gonzalez. 2010. How Bank Capital Buffers Vary Across Countries: The Influence of Cost of Deposits, Market Power and Bank Regulation. *Journal of Banking & Finance* 34 (892): 902.

Fiordelisi, F., D. Marques-Ibanez, and P. Molyneux. 2011. Efficiency and Risk in European Banking. *Journal of Banking & Finance* 35 (1315): 1326.

Fries, S., and A. Taci. 2005. Cost Efficiency of Banks in Transition: Evidence from 289 Banks in 15 Post-Communist Countries. *Journal of Banking and Finance* 29 (1): 55–81.

Fungáčová, Z., L. Solanko, and L. Weill. 2010. Market Power in the Russian Banking Industry. *International Economics* 124: 127–145.

Hasan, I., and K. Marton. 2003. Development and Efficiency of the Banking Sector in a Transition Economy: Hungarian Experience. *Journal of Banking and Finance* 27 (12): 2249–2271.

Heffernan, S. 2005. *Modern Banking*. London: Wiley.

Hicks, J.R. 1935. Annual Survey of Economic Theory: The Theory of Monopoly. *Econometrica* 3 (1): 20.

IMF. 2014. Country Report: South Africa. IMF Financial Sector Assessment Program.

IMF. 2016. Country Report: Russian Federation. IMF Financial Sector Assessment Program.

Jia, C. 2009. The Effect of Ownership on the Prudential Behavior of Banks—The Case of China. *Journal of Banking & Finance* 33: 77–87.

Jiang, C., S. Yao, and G. Feng. 2013. Bank Ownership, Privatization, and Performance: Evidence from a Transition Country. *Journal of Banking & Finance* 37: 3364–3372.

Jiang, C., S. Yao, and Z. Zhang. 2009. The Effects of Governance Changes on Bank Efficiency in China: A Stochastic Distance Function Approach. *China Economic Review* 20 (717): 731.

Karas, A., K. Schoors, and L. Weill. 2010. Are Private Banks More Efficient than Public Banks? Evidence from Russia. *The Economics of Transition* 18 (209): 244.

Keeley, M.C. 1990. Deposit Insurance, Risk and Market Power in Banking. *American Economic Review* 80 (1183): 1200.

Koetter, M., J.W. Kolari, and L. Spierdijk. 2012. Enjoying the Quiet Life Under Deregulation? Evidence Form Adjusted Lerner Indices for U.S. Banks. *Review of Economics and Statistics* 94 (2): 462–480.

Kumbhakar, S.C., and S. Sarkar. 2003. Deregulation, Ownership, and Productivity Growth in Banking Industry: Evidence from India. *Journal of Money Credit and Banking* 35 (3): 403–424.

Kwan, S., and R. Eisenbeis. 1997. Bank Risk, Capitalization and Operating Efficiency. *Journal of Financial Services Research* 12 (117): 131.

Lovell, C.A.K., S. Richardson, P. Travers, and L.L. Wood. 1994. Resources and Functioning: A New View of Inequality in Australia. In *Models and Measurement of Welfare and Inequality*, ed. W. Eichhorn. Berlin: Springer-Verlag.

Mannasoo, K., and D. Mayes. 2009. Explaining Bank Distress in Eastern European Transition Economies. *Journal of Banking & Finance* 33 (244): 253.

Maudos, J., and J. Fernández de Guevara. 2007. The Cost of Market Power in Banking: Social Welfare Loss vs. Cost Inefficiency. *Journal of Banking & Finance* 31 (2103): 2135.

Mester, L.J. 1996. A Study of Bank Efficiency Taking into Account Risk-Preferences. *Journal of Banking & Finance* 20 (1025): 1045.

Miccolis-Anwar, C. 2007. Causes and Effects and Changes in the Brazilian Banking System. Fordham Economics Discussion Paper Series 2007-02.

O'Neill, J. 2001. Building Better Global Economic BRICs, *Global Economics paper* No. 66. Godman Sachs.

Ray, S., and A. Das. 2010. Distribution of Cost and Profit Efficiency: Evidence from Indian Banking. *European Journal of Operational Research* 201 (1): 297–307.

Sanyal, P., and R. Shankar. 2011. Ownership, Competition, and Bank Productivity: An Analysis of Indian Banking in the Post-Reform Period. *International Review of Economics and Finance* 20 (225): 247.

Sathye, M. 2003. Efficiency of Banks in Developing Economy: The Case of India. *European Journal of Operational Research* 148 (662): 671.

Schaeck, K., M. Cihak, and S. Wolfe. 2009. Are Competitive Banking Systems More Stable? *Journal of Money, Credit, and Banking* 41: 711–734.

Sealey, C.W., and J.T. Lindley. 1977. Inputs, Outputs and a Theory of Production and Cost at Depository Financial Institutions. *Journal of Finance* 32 (1251): 1266.

Sensarma, R. 2005. Cost and Profit Efficiency of Indian Banks During 1986–2003. *Economic and Political Weekly* 40 (1198): 1209.

Sharma, M. 2017. India's Slow-Motion Bank Crisis. Bloomberg View. https://www.bloomberg.com/view/articles/2017-02-27/no-end-in-sight-to-india-s-slow-motion-bank-crisis.

Shephard, R.W. 1970. *Theory of Cost and Production Functions*. Princeton: Princeton University Press.

Staub, R., G. Souza, and B. Tabak. 2010. Evolution of Bank Efficiency in Brazil: A DEA Approach. *European Journal of Operational Research* 202 (204): 213.

Styrin, K. 2005. What Explains Differences in Efficiency Across Russian Banks? Economics Education and Research Consortium, Russia and CIS, Final report, Moscow.

Tabak, B.M., G.M.R. Gomes, and M. da S. J. Medeiros. 2015. The Impact of Market Power at Bank Level in Risk-Taking: The Brazilian Case. *International Review of Financial Analysis* 40: 154–165.

Tecles, P.L., and B.M. Tabak. 2010. Determinants of Bank Efficiency: The Case of Brazil. *European Journal of Operational Research* 207 (1587): 1598.

Tompson, W. 2004. Banking Reform in Russia: Problems and Prospects. OECD Economics Department Working Papers, No. 410, OECD publishing.

Williams, J., and N. Nguyen. 2005. Financial Liberalization, Crisis, and Restructuring: A Comparative Study of Bank Performance and Bank Governance in South East Asia. *Journal of Banking & Finance* 29 (2119): 2154.

Yao, S., C. Jiang, G. Feng, and D. Willenbockel. 2007. On the Efficiency of Chinese Banks and WTO Challenges. *Applied Economics* 39 (629): 643.

Zhang, J., C. Jiang, B. Qu, and P. Wang. 2013. Market Concentration, Risk-Taking, and Bank Performance: Evidence from Emerging Economies. *International Review of Financial Analysis* 30: 149–157.

Zhang, J., B. Qu, and W. Wang. 2012. Bank Risk Taking, Efficiency, and Law Enforcement: Evidence from Chinese City Commercial Banks. *China Economic Review* 23 (2): 284–295.

Zhao, T., B. Casu, and A. Ferrari. 2010. The Impact of Regulatory Reforms on Cost Structure, Ownership and Competition in Indian Banking. *Journal of Banking & Finance* 34 (246): 254.

5

Banking Competition in China

Preamble

Competition is important in any industry, with impacts on a wide range of issues such as productivity, innovation, and consumer welfare. In banking, competition is even more important because of its externalities beyond the banking industry. Anti-competitive behaviour of banks may have far-reaching influences on social welfare and well-being of the economy with implications for not only banking and financial services sector regulation and supervision but also financial stability and macroeconomic policy. The market-oriented banking reform in China started from deregulation in order to increase competition in the sector. After nearly four decades of reform, the banking sector has undergone significant changes and it is of great interest to understand whether the sector has become more competitive. This chapter addresses this issue by assessing the degree of banking competition and its evolution over the period 1995–2015 using multiple competition measures.

This chapter is organized as follows. Section 5.1 introduces a variety of competition measures and discusses their respective merits and shortcomings. Section 5.2 reviews literature on banking competition.

C. Jiang and S. Yao, *Chinese Banking Reform*, The Nottingham China Policy Institute Series, DOI 10.1007/978-3-319-63925-3_5

Section 5.3 outlines research methodologies to obtain a variety of competition measures. Section 5.4 analyzes the empirical results, and Sect. 5.5 concludes.

5.1 Measures of Competition

5.1.1 Structural Approach

In the literature, a number of competition measures have been widely used to capture the competitive features of the banking industry, broadly falling into two approaches—the structural approach and non-structural approach. The structural approach measures competition based on the structural characteristics of the banking market that are exogenous and observable. The central argument is that a more concentrated market is less competitive. Structural measures include market shares, concentration ratio for the top n largest firms (CRn), and Hrschman–Herfindahl index (HHI).

The structural approach focuses on the relationship between competition and performance usually by testing two competing hypotheses: the Structure—Conduct—Performance (SCP) hypothesis and the efficient structure hypothesis. SCP emerged in the 1930s and developed in the 1950s (Bain 1956, 1959; Mason 1957), and subsequently dominated industrial economics in the 1960s and the 1970s. The SCP paradigm offers important insights on empirical regularities of market based on statistical inferences. SCP provides a theoretical causal explanation for the relationship between market concentration and firm performance. A highly concentrated market dominated by a small number of large firms (structure) induces collusive behaviour among these large firms (conduct), that is, setting higher prices for excess return, which leads to superior performance. On the contrary, the efficient structure hypothesis (Demsetz 1973) argues that large banks outperform small banks because larger banks' higher operating efficiency level enables them to gain market shares, resulting in a more concentrated market. The causality runs from bank efficiency (performance) to market concentration.

Recent studies indicate that using market concentration as the indicator of banking competition has limitations and the link between concentration and competition indeed is very weak in banking (Maudos and Fernández de Guevara 2004; Claessens and Laeven 2004). For example, HHI decreases with a fall in entry barriers as banks are assumed to be symmetric in a Cournot model, while with variations in bank efficiency, intensified competition reallocates output to more efficient banks, which raises HHI (Carbó et al. 2009).

5.1.2 Non-structural Approach

It is argued that the competitive environment is not necessarily determined by the market structure, but market power. The traditional performance-based measure of market power is the Lerner index (Lerner 1934) that captures the ability of a bank to set prices above marginal costs. It measures the varying degrees of competition by the deviation between observed prices and marginal costs. Under the monopolist's profit maximization condition, Lerner index is defined as the ratio of the mark-up (price minus marginal cost) to price ((P – MC) /P). The Lerner index is close to zero in a perfectly competitive market and approaches one in a monopolistic market. Theoretically, the monopolist achieves profit maximization when the Lerner index is equal to the inverse price elasticity of market demand. As such, the Lerner index takes into account market concentration, demand condition, and performance (as profit relative to marginal costs). The Lerner index is widely used in the banking literature (e.g., Berger et al. 2009; Beck et al. 2013). A key advantage of the Lerner index is that market power can be measured at bank level, which allows more comprehensive analysis, such as factors explaining the variations in market power across banks and over time. Estimating Lerner index requires information on prices and marginal costs. Prices can be obtained as observed mean output prices, while marginal costs are usually unobservable except for the case of constant returns to scale where marginal costs equal average cost. Marginal costs are estimated from a cost function, assuming that banks are fully efficient. As both output prices and marginal costs are estimated, the Lerner index is more likely subject to measurement errors. For example, when banks fail to minimize costs or maximize profit, their inefficiency is incorporated into the empirical measures of the price-cost mark-up (Kumbhakar et al. 2012). Recent studies attempt to address the issue. Efficiency-adjusted Lerner indices, developed by Koetter et al. (2012) take into account both mark-ups and inefficiency by simultaneously estimating banks' cost and profit efficiency scores, while the stochastic frontier estimator of market power, developed by Kumbhakar et al. (2012), can reliably estimate market power without input prices and constant returns to scale.

During the past half century, a variety of non-structural market power measures have been developed, from those measuring competition between oligopolists (Iwata 1974)[1] to those testing for competitive behaviour in contestable markets (e.g., Bresnahan 1982; Lau 1982; Panzar and Rosse 1987). A contestable market has no entry or exit barriers and sunk costs, and firms have access to the same level of technology, thereby market concentration becomes irrelevant (Baumol et al. 1982). The New Empirical Industrial Organization, known as the NEIO approach, is based on the contestable market theory to derive market power measures from a regression (e.g., based on a supply relation) that incorporates more industrial and firm-specific details to controls for factors that affect marginal costs. It requires data on all cost determinants including output and input prices. The NEIO approach does not directly estimate marginal costs but measures the departure of firms' performance with respect to expected outcomes under perfect competition. In contrast to the structural approach that focuses on incumbents, the contestable market theory considers the influence of existing incumbents and potential competitors. The central argument is that the competitive behaviour of banks depends on (actual or potential) entry and exit conditions. Low entry and exit barriers encourage firms to behave competitively to deter new entry even if the existing

[1]The Iwata (1974) model estimates conjectural variation values for firms that offer homogenous products. It is not widely employed in the banking literature.

market is concentrated. The contestability as a measure of the degree of competitive behaviour in the market is not necessarily related to concentration or the number of banks but related to deviations from competitive pricing. New entrants may have smaller market share, while they can potentially force incumbents to change behaviour, for example, adopting competitive pricing to make the market less attractive to new entrants. Based on the contestable market theory, two widely used market power measures—the Bresnahan–Lau statistics (Bresnahan 1982; Lau 1982) and PRH statistics (Panzar and Rosse 1987) are derived from the equilibrium assumptions of profit maximization.

The literature on oligopoly behaviour indicates that the competition among major firms in concentrated markets can be rather fierce and firms may attempt to adapt strategically in response to their competitors' reactions (conjectural variations). Hence, the degree of market competition is determined by the strategic reactions of firms. A high conjectural variation implies a high level of awareness of the interdependence with other firms in terms of output and prices. Under perfect competition conditions, conjectural variation among banks is zero as output price equals marginal costs, while it equals one under monopolistic market condition. Bresnahan (1982), Lau (1982) estimate the average conjectural variation of banks using the first order condition of profit maximization and obtain mark-up test statistics that capture varying degrees of market power (competition) in terms of firms' deviations from marginal cost pricing. The Bresnahan–Lau method, popularized by the empirical approach suggested in Bresnahan (1989), applies to aggregate industry time-series data to measure the average degree of competition for a long period. Delis and Tsionas (2009) propose a method of estimating this competition measures at bank level using the local maximum likelihood (LML) technique. The mark-up test statistics take values between 1 and 0 where 1 indicates perfect competition and 0 suggests perfect collusion. The Bresnahan–Lau method was first applied to the banking industry by Shaffer (1989, 1993), followed by subsequent applications such as those by Neven and Röller (1999), Uchida and Tsutsui (2005).

Rosse and Panzar (1977), Panzar and Rosse (1987) developed a test to differentiate oligopolistic, competitive, and monopolistic markets by investigating to what extent a firm's revenues changes due to a change in factor input price. Theories suggest that an increase in input prices will increase costs, marginal costs, and total revenues in a perfect competitive market, and it will increase marginal costs but reduce equilibrium output and total revenue in a monopolistic market. Based on reduced-form revenue equations at the firm level, the test *H*-statistics measures the elasticity of revenue with respect to input prices to reflect competition conditions, assuming low entry and exit barriers and a homogeneous cost structure across banks (both potential competitors and existing established banks). The main argument is that in a contestable market existing firms adopt marginal cost pricing that effectively deter potential competitors from entering into the market. It uses bank-level data that take into account bank-specific differences in the production function and requires no information about equilibrium output prices and quantities for the bank and/or industry. Banks are treated as profit-maximizing, single-product firms producing intermediation services. *H*-statistics takes a value of 1 implying perfect competition, a value of 0 or less indicating perfect collusion, and a value between 1 and 0 suggesting monopolistic competition. The numerical value of H within the range $0 < H < 1$ can be interpreted as a measure of the intensity of competition. When estimating *H*-statistics, markets are assumed to be in long-run equilibrium at each point in time and misspecification bias arises when markets are out of equilibrium. A dynamic panel estimator with a lagged dependent variable in the revenue equation addresses the issues of non-instantaneous adjustment toward equilibrium in response to market shocks and provides unbiased estimates of *H*-statistics (Goddard and Wilson 2009). The theoretical foundation of profit-maximizing equilibrium conditions and the simplicity of econometric setup and implementation make *H*-statistics an appealing indicator of competition in the banking literature (Claessens and Laeven 2004; Bikker et al. 2012). Applications are extensive, such as those by Bikker and Haaf (2002), Bikker (2004), Claessens and Laeven (2004), Carbó et al. (2009), Schaeck and Cihák (2012), among others.

A more recent development in measuring the degree of competition is the Boone indicator, proposed by Boone et al. (2005) and advanced by Boone (2008). The Boone indicator focuses on the nexus between profits and efficiency in a competitive banking market, calculated as the elasticity of profits with respect to marginal costs. The indicator is based on the efficient structure hypothesis (Demsetz 1973) and the underlying argument is that more efficient banks (i.e., banks with lower marginal/average costs) gain higher profits at the expense of their inefficient counterparts. As the market becomes more competitive, for given banks' efficiency levels, the profits of the more efficient banks grow faster than that of inefficient banks. This is consistent with the industrial organization literature that competition reallocates profits toward efficient firms (Olley and Pakes 1996; Stiroh 2000). The reallocation effect is monotonically increasing with the degree of competition due to more aggressive interaction among banks, representing a general feature of intensifying competition (Boone 2008). An increasing Boone indicator implies decreasing competition in the market and a more negative Boone indicator indicates a higher degree of competition.

The Boone indicator has a number of advantages. It can be estimated based on the widely available bank-level data and requires no exhaustive sample of all banks in the market (Boone 2008). It can measure the degree of competition for different segments of the banking market such as the loan market and different types of banks, in contrast to other measures that consider the entire banking market (Van Leuvensteijn et al. 2011; Schaeck and Cihák 2014). The Boone indicator requires neither restrictive assumption as *H*-statistic that requires market to be in long-run equilibrium nor faces criticism against the inability to capture product substitutability as the Lerner index (Vives 2008). The Boone indicator has rapidly gained popularity as a measure of competition among researchers (e.g., Schaeck and Cihák 2014; Van Leuvensteijn et al. 2011; Delis 2012; De-Ramon and Straughan 2016). The World Bank has included the Boone indicator as a measure of the degree of banking competition estimated by the Federal Reserve Bank of St. Louis, Missouri.

The persistence of profit hypothesis, developed by Mueller (1977, 1986), argues that sufficiently free entry and exit should quickly eliminate abnormal profit and induces convergence toward a same average profit level in the long run. If abnormal profits persist over years, possible reasons are the existence of entry barriers or the exploitation of monopoly power by banks—both indicate a lack of competition in the market. The empirical test of this in banking can be found in Berger et al. (2000), Goddard et al. (2004a, b), and Zhao et al. (2010).

Reliable measurement of banking competition is important given the vital role of the banking sector in any economy. There is no consensus as to which competition measure is superior over others. In general, concentration-based measures are not a reliable measure of competition. Most model-based measures ignore differences in bank product quality, design, and the attractiveness of innovations. In the literature, based on our survey of 40 studies on banking competition, the Lerner index and the *H*-statistics are the two most popular measures. The Lerner index has long been the only market power indicator available at bank level until recently the Boone indicator and the Bresnahan–Lau method can be estimated at bank level advanced by Delis (2012), Delis and Tsionas (2009), respectively. The relative profits measure of the Boone indicator is significantly and positively correlated with the price-cost margin and a useful empirical complement to these measures. The price-cost margin based measures or the Lerner index appear to be less robust as competition measures. Theoretical studies demonstrate that more intense competition can theoretically lead to higher price-cost margin values (e.g., Rosenthal 1980). When there are large variations in the cost structure among banks and marginal costs are subject to estimation biases (i.e., poor data quality), traditional measures such as the *H*-statistics and the Lerner index can be poor indicators of the degree of competition. The Boone indicator offers a more reliable measure of competition and it is less sensitive to cyclical changes (Boone 2008). The *H*-statistics is robust in small samples, while the Bresnahan-Lau model tends to exhibit an anticompetitive bias in small samples (Shaffer 2004). It is argued that the H-statistic may not robustly reflect a full range of oligopoly solution concepts than other measures such as the Lerner index (Brissimis et al. 2008). Bikker et al. (2009) argues that the *H*-statistics test may be intrinsically unsuitable for a sample with large variations in bank sizes in a single market and suggests that researchers should consider alternative measures, such as the Bresnahan-Lau approach. The disadvantage of this approach is data intensive though. Carbó et al. (2009) compared the structural and non-structural indicators of competition and found different results on the competitive behaviour within and across countries and over time. As such, researchers' choice largely depends on the research setting and data availability and some studies employ multiple measures to ensure the robustness of their results (Berger et al. 2009).

5.2 Literature on Banking Competition

Driven by forces such as globalization, technological change, and deregulation, the banking industry across the world has experienced dramatic changes. Following banking deregulation in the 1980s, researchers have paid extensive attention to competition in the banking markets. Assessing the degree of competition, the literature based on traditional measures suggests that monopolistic competition prevails at varying degrees in the major industrialized economies, including the European Union and the United States from the 1990s up to the global financial crisis in 2008. Among the EU member states, the banking systems are more competitive in Belgium, Luxembourg, and Portugal, while market powers are stronger in Denmark and Spain (Bikker and Haaf 2002; Claessens and Laeven 2004; Beck et al. 2013). The Italian banking sector was relatively stable with the Lerner index between 0.15 and 0.2 from 1983 to 1993 and then became even more competitive with the Lerner Index declining to 0.05–0.1 (Angelini and Cetorelli 2003). In the German banking sector, the competition level increased steadily and accelerated in the period 2001–2004 (Koetter and Poghosyan 2009). The market power of the loan market increased in all the EU member states with the exception of Sweden and the United Kingdom, while the market power in deposits weakened with the exception of Finland, Sweden, and the United Kingdom (Maudos and Fernández de Guevara 2007). The market power in the EU banking sector increased from in the late 1990s and early 2000s, suggested by the studies of Matthews et al. (2007)—for the United Kingdom—and Weill (2004)—for 12 major EU countries. Van Leuvensteijn et al. (2011) shows more fluctuations in market power relative to Delis (2012), while both suggest increasing market power in the EU banking sector except for Italy, the Netherlands, and the United Kingdom.

The frequently employed Rosse–Panzar *H*-statistics assume that markets are in long-run equilibrium at each point in time when the data are observed. Goddard and Wilson (2009) find evidence that the *H*-statistic is severely biased towards zero due to misspecification when the market is in an adjustment process towards equilibrium. They propose a dynamic model and find a monopoly model prevailing in the United Kingdom, the United States, and Japan during the period 2001–2007. More recently, researchers employ the Boone indicator and find that the French banking industry has more market power (Schaeck and Cihák 2010; Van Leuvensteijn et al. 2011), while the banking sectors in the Netherlands, the United Kingdom, Germany, and Spain are more competitive (Schaeck and Cihák 2010; Van Leuvensteijn et al. 2011).

Exploring the sources of bank competition, the literature places emphasis on factors such as deregulation, foreign bank entry, financial liberalization, institutions, capital regulation, and bank ownership. Since the late 1970s through to the 1980s, bank deregulation/liberalization started in the developed countries and followed by the developing economies. One of the main goals is to introduce more competition in banking. The NEIO literature finds no evidence of rising competition following the rapid deregulation and liberalization processes in Europe (Maudos and Fernández de Guevara 2004; Fernández de Guevara et al. 2005; Matthews et al. 2007). Bos et al. (2013) find that the interstate banking deregulation in the United States negatively affects competition and the consolidation movement is associated with rising price-cost margins that are higher than the optimal price-cost margins. Using a sample of 50 developed and developing countries, Claessens and Laeven (2004) find that bank competition is higher with greater foreign bank presence and fewer restrictions on entry and activities. Delis (2012) find that financial liberalization reduces bank market power in the developed countries with advanced institutions and this effect is weaker in countries with weaker institutions and a lower level of institutional development. Based on the Lerner index and the Boone indicator estimated from a sample of 146 countries over the period 1999–2011, Mirzaei and Moore (2014) find evidence that a concentrated banking system undermines competition in developing economies, but not in advanced and emerging economies. They also find that contestability and institutional development increase competition in the less-developed banking systems, while inter-industry competition and financial freedom are more important factors driving competition in the advanced banking systems.

The impact of banking competition has also been studied extensively. It is believed that competition has a positive effect on bank efficiency as a higher degree of competition encourages or forces banks to improve efficiency in order to remain in the market. The "quiet life hypothesis" argues that banks with market power tend to behave inefficiently as market power allows managers to enjoy monopoly rents (Hicks 1935). Banks may exercise market power leading to higher social costs because of lessened effort by managers to operate efficiently (Berger and Hannan 1998). Empirically, the relationship between competition and efficiency is not conclusive, perhaps because of the more complex nature of banking industry compared with other industries (Claessens and Laeven 2004). For EU banking, some studies (e.g., Casu and Girardone 2006; Brissimis et al. 2008) find a positive impact of competition on bank efficiency, and others (e.g., Weill 2004) suggest a negative relationship. Delis and Tsionas (2009) find that bank market power is adversely related with efficiency in the Economic and Monetary Union (EMU) banking system, evident for the "quite life hypothesis." Maudos and Fernández de Guevara (2007) investigate the relationship between market power and efficiency in the loan and deposit markets of the EU-15 countries over the period 1993–2002 and find a positive relationship between market power and cost X-efficiency, rejecting the quiet life hypothesis. They show that reduced market power leads to social welfare gains that are greater than the loss of bank cost efficiency.

The relation between bank competition and financial stability remains a controversial issue with two competing views. The competition-fragility view argues that higher competition encourages excessive risk taking, leading to instability while monopoly rents will increase charter value and less risk-taking (Allen and Gale 2004; Marcus 1984; Keeley 1990; Beck et al. 2006; Matsuoka 2013). On the contrary, the competition-stability view suggests that monopoly allows banks to charge higher interest rates, which in turn encourages borrowers to take excessive risks. Higher competition reduces financial costs, and borrowers are more likely to pay back loans, which lowers default risk (Boyd and De Nicolo 2005). This view is also supported by the general view of (larger banks) "too big to fail." Most studies find supportive evidence for the competition-fragility view, while Liu et al. (2013) find an inverted U-shaped relationship between regional bank competition and stability in the EU countries. More recent literature shows that the relationship between competition and financial stability varies with environmental factors, such as the level of financial development (financial markets and stock market), characteristics of the banking market, availability of safety net facility, regulatory and institutional framework in which banks operate, and information system. Using a large sample of banks from 79 countries, Beck et al. (2013) show evidence that competition has a stronger impact on banks' risk-taking behaviour in countries with more stringent restrictions, lower systemic risk and a higher level of financial development, more generous deposit insurance, and more effective systems of credit information sharing. Cipollini and Fiordelisi (2012) find that bank market power has a significant impact on bank financial distress, supporting the competition-fragility view based on an unbalanced panel of 308 European commercial banks between 1996 and 2009.

Research also documents significant influences of banking competition on a wide range of issues, such as financial innovation, capital regulation, and the transmission of monetary policy. Over the past two decades or so, innovation has been one of the forces shaping the banking industry worldwide. As in other industries, innovations are expected to increase efficiency of providing financial services, improve the quality and broaden the variety of financial products. However, the influences of competition on innovation are different from those in other industries due to revolutionary changes in financial institutions and instruments (Frame and White 2004). Bos et al. (2013) examines the relationship between competition and innovation and find an inverted-U relationship in the US banking industry over the period 1984–2004. A theoretical model, developed by Hakenes and Schnabel's (2011), indicates that capital regulation may not be able to prevent excessive risk-taking in banking under all circumstances. More stringent capital requirements may reduce the degree of competition in the loan market, which induces higher loan rates and hence higher risk-taking of firms. The model suggests that when competition has a destabilizing effect (the competition-fragility view), capital regulation may stabilize the banking sector. Theoretically, banking competition affects bank lending and hence has significant implications to the transmission of monetary policy (Aftalion and White 1978; VanHoose 1983, 1985). An increase in competition, due to increased market share or reduced informational asymmetries, may weaken the bank lending channel of monetary policy transmission, while an increase in competition may strengthen monetary policy transmission if any changes in the interest rates on deposits are more directly translated into changes in interest rates on loans (Olivero et al. 2011). The net effect of competition on monetary policy transmission becomes an empirical question. Adams and Amel (2005) find that the effect of monetary policy on the bank lending channel is weaker in more concentrated banking markets in the United States over the period 1996–2002. Using bank-level data in 10 Asian and 10 Latin American countries over the period 1996–2006, Olivero et al. (2011) find consistent evidence that banking competition weakens the transmission of monetary policy through the bank lending channel and the effect is stronger for banks in Latin American countries and relatively small, illiquid and under-capitalized banks.

The majority of existing literature on banking competition is cross-country studies and limited single-country studies, which mainly focus on the developed countries with a few exceptions for the emerging economies. Maudos and Solis (2011) examine the evolution of competition in the Mexican banking system over the period 1993–2005 when banking deregulation, liberalization, and consolidation took place. They cannot reject monopolistic competition and show a decrease in competition in the deposit market but an increase in the loan market. Fungáčová et al. (2010) analyze bank competition in Russia and find slightly improved bank competition over the period 2001–2006. They investigate whether market power depends on ownership and whether the privatization of state-controlled banks or relaxing of foreign bank entry improves competition in banking. Their evidence suggests enhanced market power for foreign-owned banks and reduced market power for state-controlled banks over the period under study, and the most competitive banks being foreign banks at the beginning and state-owned banks at the end of the period. Zhao et al. (2010) evaluates the impact of financial sector reforms on the dynamics of competition in India. They find evidence that deregulation fosters competition in the lending market and competition increased even in the re-regulation over 1992–2004.

With the rising importance of the Chinese banking industry in the world financial system, banking competition in China started to gain growing attention among researchers. Fu and Heffernan (2009) test the structure-performance relation employing a structural approach to measure competition. They find tentative evidence supporting the relative market power hypothesis that banks with large market shares exercise market power, suggesting monopolistic competition in China over the period 1985–2002. Fungáčová et al. (2013) examine the relationship between bank competition and efficiency for a sample of Chinese banks over the period 2002–2011. They find no increase in bank competition (measured by the Lerner index) over the period despite of improvement in bank cost efficiency. This relation is insignificant in Chinese banking, unlike findings from banks in Western countries that competition negatively Granger-causes cost efficiency. While studies adopting conventional approaches to measure competition suggest that bank competition in China declined or remained unchanged, Xu et al. (2013) employ the Boone indicator and report increased competition in the loan market over the period 1996–2008. They argue that conventional indicators such as the Lerner index and the Panzar–Rosse H-statistic do not offer reliable measures of competition in the loan market because of regulation on interest rate in China. Tang (2016) studies the joint effects of bank competition and risk-taking on profitability in the Chinese banking industry over the period 2003–2011 using both the Lerner index and Herfindahl–Hirschman index. The results do not support any impact of competition and risk on bank profitability.

5.3 Research Methodology and Data

5.3.1 Structural Measure of CRn and HHI

Top n-bank concentration ratio (CRn) is calculated as the sum of market share of top n largest banks in the market and a higher CRn indicates the banking market is less competitive. Herfindahl–Hirschman Index (HHI) is calculated as the sum of the squares of the average market share of each individual bank in the sample as in Eq. (5.1). The normalized HHI ranges from 0–1 and a higher value implies greater monopoly power.

$$HHI = \sum_{i=1}^{n} MS_i^2 \tag{5.1}$$

where *MS* is the market share of bank *i* and *n* is the number of banks in the market.

5.3.2 The Lerner Index of Market Power

The conventional Lerner index is defined in Eq. (5.2):

$$Lerner = \frac{p_{it} - MC_{ir}}{p_{it}} \tag{5.2}$$

Due to the lack of data to estimate separate prices for bank output, following the literature (e.g., Turk-Ariss 2010), this study defines a single output of total asset to proxy the total banking activities (we also use total loan as the single output for robustness check). Assuming that the flow of services produced by a bank is preoperational to its total assets, p_{it} is calculated as the ratio of total revenues to total assets where total revenue is the sum of gross interest income and total non-interest income. Marginal cost (MC) is obtained by estimating a translog cost function as specified in Eq. (5.3) with three inputs (funds, labour, and physical capital) and a single output (total assets or total loan). Due to data availability, price of labour and physical capital is calculated as total non-interest expenses divided by total assets. The price of fund is calculated as total interest expenses divided by total fund. Total cost is the sum of total interest expense and total non-interest expenses. The homogeneity of degree one on input prices is imposed by dividing all factor prices and total costs by the price of labour and physical capital (w_2).

$$\begin{aligned}\ln TC_{it} &= \alpha + \beta_1 \ln Y + \frac{1}{2}\beta_2 \ln Y^2 + \sum_{k=1}^{2} \gamma_k \ln W_k + \sum_{k=1}^{2} \delta_k \ln Z_k + \tau_1 T \\ &+ \frac{1}{2}\sum_{k=1}^{2}\sum_{j=1}^{2} \varphi_{kj} \ln W_k \ln W_j + \frac{1}{2}\sum_{k=1}^{2}\sum_{j=1}^{2} \phi_{kj} \ln Z_k \ln Z_j \\ &+ \tau_2 T^2 + \frac{1}{2}\sum_{k=1}^{2} \eta_k \ln Y \ln W_k + \frac{1}{2}\sum_{k=1}^{2} \kappa_k \ln Y \ln Z_k + \tau_3 T \ln Y \\ &+ \frac{1}{2}\sum_{k=1}^{2}\sum_{j=1}^{2} \ln W_k \ln Z_j + \sum_{k=1}^{2} \gamma_k T \ln W_k \\ &+ \sum_{k=1}\sum_{r=1} \sigma_{kr} \ln(W_k/w_2) \ln(Z_r/TA) + \tau_2 T^2 + \varepsilon \end{aligned} \quad (5.3)$$

where TC is the total cost of a bank in a given year; Y is output (total asset/total loan); W_k are input prices (price of funds, price of labour, and physical capital); Z_r are netputs; T is a time trend (with full intersection terms, including time).

Marginal costs are derived from Eq. (5.3) by taking the derivative with respect to total assets as in Eq. (5.4).

$$MC = \frac{TC_{it}}{Y_{it}} \left[\beta_1 + \beta_2 \ln Y_{ir} + \sum_{k=1}^{2} \phi_k \ln W_{it} + \delta Time \right] \quad (5.4)$$

5.3.3 Panzar and Rosse (1987) *H*-Statistics

The *H*-statistics is used to indicate whether the market is under perfect competition, monopolistic competition, or monopoly. The test is based on the properties of a reduced form log-linear revenue equation shown in Eq. (5.5):

$$\ln R_{it} = \alpha_0 + \sum_{j=1}^{J} \alpha_j \ln w_{jit} + \sum_{k=1}^{K} \beta_k \ln X_{kit} + yr + \varepsilon_{it} \tag{5.5}$$

where R represents the revenue of bank i at time t; w_j are input prices; the terms in X are bank-specific variables that affect the bank's revenue and cost functions; yr is a set of year dummies; and ε is stochastic disturbance term.

The H-statistics is the sum of the elasticities of the total revenue with respect to a bank's factor input prices: $H = \sum_{j=1}^{J} \alpha_j$. When H equals 1 ($H = 1$), the market is under perfect competition. When H is between 0 and 1 ($0 < H < 1$), the market is under monopolistic competition. Bikker and Haaf (2002) further interpret the numerical value of H as a continuous measure of the competition intensity particularly between 0 and 1, the higher values of H, the stronger competition.[2] When H is negative ($H \leq 0$), the market is under classical monopoly or collusive oligopoly. As shown in Shaffer (1982, 1983), a negative H may also suggest conjectural variations of oligopoly and short-run competition. The H-statistics test is based on a long-run equilibrium condition, which is commonly tested using Eq. (5.6) by replacing the dependent variable of total revenue in Eq. (5.5) with pre-tax profit to total assets ratio (π):

$$\ln \pi_{it} = \alpha_0 + \sum_{j=1}^{J} \alpha_j \ln w_{jit} + \sum_{k=1}^{K} \beta_k \ln X_{kit} + yr + \varepsilon_{it} \tag{5.6}$$

$E = \sum_{j=1}^{J} \alpha_j' = 0$ suggests that the markets are in long run equilibrium.

The empirical model specification includes two factor inputs. The price of fund is calculated as total interest expenses divided by total fund. The price of labour and physical capital is calculated as total non-interest expenses divided by total assets. Following the standard

[2] This "continuous" interpretation of the H-statistics is not spelt out in Panzar and Rosse (1987). The comparisons between countries or banks are correct subject to a stronger assumption of a constant price elasticity of demand.

approach from the literature, we control for a set of bank-specific characteristics that may affect the process of bank-generating revenue. Five control variables account for bank behavior, business structure, risk profile, and a full set of year dummies. The ratio of equity to total assets (E/A) controls for equity risk, the ratio of customer deposits to the sum of total deposits and short-term funding, the ratio of loan to total assets, and the ratio of non-earning assets to total assets capture the effects of differences in funding and asset structure across banks, and the ratio of other income to interest income accounts for bank-specific income structure.

The dependent variable is total revenue in Eq. (5.5) and return on asset (ROA) in Eq. (5.6). We use two different measures of revenue to check the robustness of results: (1) total revenue is defined as the sum of gross interest income and total non-interest income; and (2) gross interest income. Neither a reduced-form price equation nor the scaled revenue equation (using total assets to control size effect on revenue) can be used to infer the degree of competition due to potential upward bias (Bikker et al. 2009, 2012). This study estimates an un-scaled revenue equation that can yield a valid measure of the *H*-statistics for competitive conduct. Equations (5.5) and (5.6) are estimated with a fixed effect specification using a panel data set of banks.[3]

5.3.4 The Boone Indicator

Following the theoretical contribution (Boone et al. 2005; Boone 2008) and empirical literature (Van Leuvensteijn et al. 2011; Delis 2012; Schaeck and Cihák 2014), the measure of market power of banks—the Boone indicator can be estimated by regressing the log of profits on average costs. As banks with lower marginal costs (higher efficiency) are expected to be more profitable, the Boone indicator—β should be negative. A lower market power (higher competition) is implied by a larger absolute value of β. A set of bank-specific effects are included

[3]Following the literature, the choice of the fixed effect estimators over random effect estimators is confirmed by the Hausman test.

to account for the heterogeneity within the sample as in Schaeck and Cihák (2014). The empirical setup of the model is in Eq. (5.7).

$$\pi_{it} = \alpha_i + \beta_t d_t \ln(c_{it}) + \delta_t d_t + \gamma X_{it} + \varepsilon_{it} \tag{5.7}$$

where π_{it} are the profits of bank i at time t measured as return to assets, d_t is a time dummy; it c_{it} is average variable costs; X_{it} is a set of control variables, and ε_{it} is the error term.

Since marginal costs cannot be observed directly, following the literature (Boone et al. 2005; Schaeck and Cihák 2014), we use average costs, measured as a ratio to total income. The cost components are the sum of interest and non-interest expenses (personnel cost, administrative, and other operating expenses). Total income consists of interest income and non-interest operating income.

5.3.5 Data

The sample used in this chapter consists of 157 commercial banks in China over the period 1995–2015 with 1572 observations, covering five types of banks, namely city commercial banks (CCBs), foreign banks (FBs),[4] joint-stock commercial banks (JSCBs), rural commercial banks (RCBs), and state-owned commercial banks (SOCBs). Banks included in the sample have at least three consecutive years of data. This is by far the largest sample with the longest period of 21 years used to study banking competition in China. It contains extensive information on 19 CCBs, 30 FBs, 13 JSCBs, 28 RCBs, and 4 SOCBs. Table 5.1 reports the summary descriptive statistics of variables, which show significant variations in the variables across different banks and within each bank type. All variables are winsorized at cutoff values of 2% and 98% to reduce the effect of large outliers and alternative cutoff values of 1% and 99% do not alter out main conclusion. This chapter derives multiple measures to assess the level and evolution of competition in the Chinese banking sector using a more complete dataset on Chinese banks over a longer period of 1995–2015.

[4]Banks with more than 50% foreign ownership are classified as foreign banks.

Table 5.1 Summary descriptive statistics of variables (1995–2015)

	Full sample (Obs 1572)		CCB (Obs 816)		FB (Obs 257)		JSCB (Obs 248)		RCB (Obs 167)		SOCB (Obs 84)	
			Mean	Std. Dev.	Mean	Std. Dev.	Mean	Std. Dev.	Mean	Std. Dev.	Mean	Std. Dev.
Total asset	549.55	1788.26	88.46	140.52	41.37	51.37	856.58	1094.61	104.36	119.54	6562.13	4071.30
Total loan	286.89	946.28	38.72	60.62	19.38	23.98	442.54	555.68	49.02	49.46	3529.55	2081.41
Total deposit	339.01	1358.61	46.13	88.24	24.32	33.33	495.84	769.34	78.01	85.85	4202.82	4075.75
Equity	30.66	118.63	5.56	8.51	4.30	4.22	46.69	71.42	7.35	7.73	354.16	366.35
Total revenue	26.96	89.85	4.27	6.77	1.68	2.19	41.84	57.28	5.14	5.81	324.19	210.80
Total costs	17.38	59.05	2.72	4.35	1.19	1.50	26.43	34.49	3.18	3.83	210.88	144.09
ROA	1.26	0.70	1.32	0.67	0.95	0.82	1.16	0.60	1.67	0.51	1.09	0.60
Average cost	66.88	33.19	63.77	26.96	78.48	63.47	69.45	10.54	59.26	7.76	69.19	15.01
Loan/total assets	49.66	12.19	48.38	11.72	47.17	17.49	52.98	8.47	51.74	8.34	55.75	7.39
Nonearning assets/total assets	36.43	38.14	41.68	39.05	10.79	7.07	55.17	45.14	16.30	5.80	48.56	44.20
Short-term funding/ total fund	98.21	3.57	98.65	2.30	96.49	6.36	97.97	2.99	99.46	1.30	97.50	4.38
Non-interest income/total income	12.04	17.35	10.27	13.75	21.51	30.44	8.41	6.70	12.44	14.85	10.21	7.94
Equity/Total assets	8.28	7.40	6.64	3.16	18.18	12.94	5.10	2.88	7.61	2.05	4.61	3.74
Price of output	4.78	1.66	4.90	1.52	4.01	1.34	4.84	1.53	5.00	0.86	5.46	3.65

(continued)

Table 5.1 (continued)

	Full sample (Obs 1572)		CCB (Obs 816)		FB (Obs 257)		JSCB (Obs 248)		RCB (Obs 167)		SOCB (Obs 84)	
			Mean	Std. Dev.	Mean	Std. Dev.	Mean	Std. Dev.	Mean	Std. Dev.	Mean	Std. Dev.
Price of fund	2.29	1.46	2.29	1.09	1.98	1.02	2.48	1.27	2.04	0.61	3.20	4.29
Price of labour and physical capital	1.14	0.45	1.09	0.40	1.32	0.64	1.13	0.44	1.12	0.34	1.15	0.28

Note CCB: city commercial bank, FB: foreign bank, JSCB: Joint-stock commercial bank, RCB: rural commercial bank, SOCB: state-owned commercial bank. All variables are in RMB billion expect for ratio

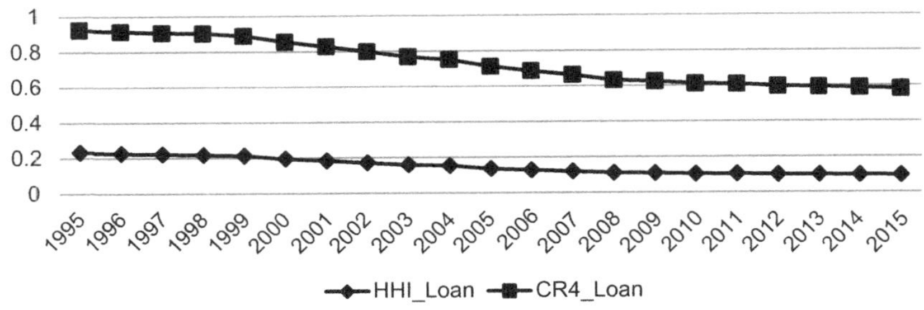

Fig. 5.1 Structural measure of market power in Chinese banking 1995–2015

5.4 Competition of the Chinese Banking Sector

5.4.1 Structural Measure of CR4 and HHI

HHI and CR4 are calculated in terms of total loans, total deposits, and total assets yearly over the period 1995–2015. As results are very similar, the following analysis is based on total loans only. As shown in Fig. 5.1, two structural measures consistently suggest rising competition in the banking market. The top 4-bank concentration ratio (CR4) in the loan market decreases steadily from a 92% in 1995 to 56% in 2015. HHI criteria to classify market concentration are as follows: a HHI index less than 0.01 for a highly competitive market, between 0.01 and 0.1 for an un-concentrated market, between 0.1 and 0.18 for a moderately concentrated market, and more than 0.18 for a highly concentrated market. Thus, our results suggest that the loan market was highly concentrated in 1995 with a HHI index of 0.2335, but became moderately concentrated in 2002 when the HHI index dropped to 0.1715. From 2012, the HHI index dropped 0.1, suggesting an un-concentrated market.

5.4.2 The Lerner Index of Market Power

A higher Lerner index is associated with a higher level of market power (a lower level of competition) in banking. The estimated Lerner index from the cost function in Eq. (5.3) is 0.35 over the sample period

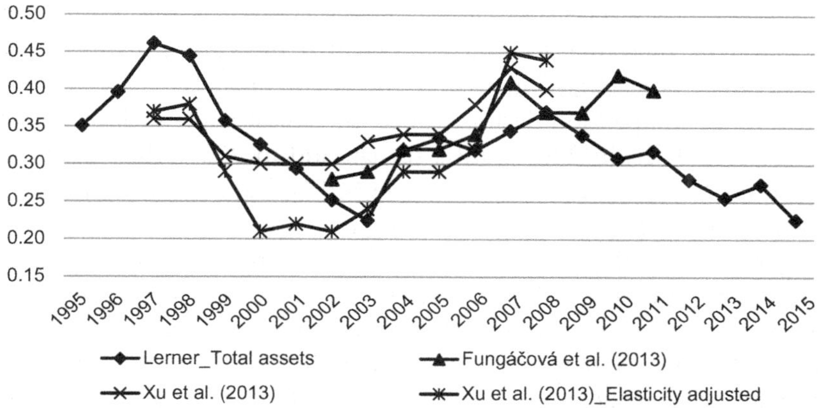

Fig. 5.2 Average Lerner index of Chinese banking (1995–2015)

1995–2015, with yearly average ranging from 0.24 to 0.49 when output is defined as total assets. When the output is defined as total loans, the estimated Lerner index is higher (0.46), ranging from 0.37 to 0.57, indicating a lower level of competition. These estimates are robust with the inclusion of the equity to total assets ratio as a control variable. The results suggest that market power is much stronger in the Chinese banking sector, compared to the advanced industrialized countries (Carbó et al. 2009; Berger et al. 2009) and other emerging economies (Fungáčová et al. 2010) where the mean Lerner index is generally less than 0.25. Our results indicate a low degree of competition in the Chinese banking sector, consistent with the mean Lerner index of 0.38 in Fungáčová et al. (2013) and 0.35 in Xu et al. (2013). Tang (2016) reports a much lower Lerner index of 0.18 over the period 2003–2011.

Figure 5.2 plots the estimated Lerner index along with the Lerner index by Fungáčová et al. (2013), Xu et al. (2013) for comparison purposes. The Lerner index increased from 0.35 to 0.46 during the first two years, suggesting a sharp drop in competition in the banking sector. The Lerner index declined from the peak level in 1998 to 0.22 in 2003, suggesting an increasing level of bank competition in China. The results are consistent with Xu et al. (2013) in which both the traditional Lerner index and the elasticity-adjusted Lerner index decreased during the period. From 2003, the Lerner index increased steadily up to 2008 and declined thereafter. Overall, we find that the Chinese banking sector became more competitive after the Asian financial crisis in 1998. The level of competition declined since the radical joint-stock ownership reform of SOCBs in 2003 until a turnaround in 2008 when the banking sector became more and more competitive. One may argue that it is less convincing to make general comments on the trend as the sample is smaller for the early years and changes in the sample composition may affect the Lerner index. As shown in Fig. 5.2, the trend is generally consistent with earlier studies that also document a decreasing competition in the Chinese banking sector during 2002–2008 and an increasing competition after the crisis (Fungáčová et al. 2013; Xu et al. 2013). After the 2008–2009 crisis, the Chinese authorities completed the overhaul of the SOCBs and started to reform CCBs and RCBs, with more and more CCBs and RCBs incorporated as joint-stock commercial banks. One of the main purposes is to increase banking competition and our results suggest that the latest banking reforms have played a positive and important role in achieving the policy goal. As such, we believe the overall trend reveals the full picture of the evaluation of banking competition in China.

Table 5.2 reports the mean Lerner indices by bank type over time. The analysis is based on the Lerner indices when output is defined as total assets, while the Lerner indices for output defined as total loans are also reported for comparison. Several interesting trends immediately emerge. Banks' market power varies with bank types. On average, RCBs are associated with the strongest market power and their average Lerner index is 0.42. Our explanation is that these newly restructured RCBs serve regional clients of small businesses and individuals that are overlooked by large banks, and these niche markets generally lack market pressures. Moreover, their borrowers are considered riskier and lack alternative financing sources, allowing RCBs to exercise more market power. SOCBs and CCBs both have a mean Lerner index of 0.35, indicating a rather high market power as well. The result for SOCBs is consistent with expectation. These four largest state-controlled banks dominate the Chinese banking sector as the main financing sources for the economy and they enjoy advantages arising from their extant large service networks and government protection, such as implicit

Table 5.2 Lerner index of Chinese banks by bank type (1995–2015)

		CCB		FB		JSCB		RCB		SOCB		All banks	
	Obs	Lerner total assets	Lerner loan	Lerner total assets	Lerner loan	Lerner total assets	Lerner loan	Lerner total assets	Lerner loan	Lerner total assets	Lerner loan	Lerner total assets	Lerner loan
1995	14	0.70	0.75			0.31	0.41			0.35	0.44	0.45	0.53
1996	14	0.67	0.72			0.40	0.49			0.32	0.42	0.46	0.54
1997	18	0.63	0.68	0.52	0.59	0.44	0.52			0.37	0.46	0.49	0.57
1998	21	0.43	0.51	0.64	0.70	0.46	0.54			0.33	0.43	0.46	0.54
1999	25	0.38	0.47	0.59	0.65	0.38	0.47			0.16	0.28	0.37	0.47
2000	27	0.31	0.42	0.49	0.58	0.33	0.43	0.55	0.62	0.26	0.37	0.39	0.48
2001	32	0.31	0.42	0.24	0.37	0.28	0.39	0.49	0.57	0.27	0.38	0.32	0.43
2002	40	0.25	0.37	0.13	0.28	0.26	0.38	0.41	0.50	0.33	0.43	0.27	0.39
2003	44	0.22	0.35	0.18	0.12	0.23	0.36	0.41	0.51	0.42	0.51	0.29	0.37
2004	50	0.33	0.45	0.24	0.37	0.25	0.38	0.61	0.68	0.41	0.51	0.37	0.48
2005	62	0.35	0.46	0.13	0.29	0.32	0.44	0.56	0.64	0.37	0.47	0.35	0.46
2006	80	0.33	0.45	0.12	0.28	0.31	0.43	0.47	0.56	0.34	0.45	0.31	0.44
2007	95	0.36	0.48	0.23	0.38	0.31	0.43	0.31	0.44	0.46	0.55	0.39	0.46
2008	98	0.39	0.51	0.35	0.47	0.31	0.43	0.33	0.46	0.45	0.54	0.37	0.50
2009	109	0.33	0.46	0.32	0.45	0.23	0.37	0.36	0.48	0.37	0.48	0.32	0.48
2010	122	0.30	0.43	0.29	0.42	0.28	0.41	0.40	0.51	0.40	0.51	0.33	0.45
2011	136	0.28	0.42	0.34	0.47	0.24	0.38	0.45	0.56	0.39	0.50	0.34	0.46
2012	142	0.24	0.39	0.32	0.45	0.15	0.32	0.41	0.52	0.37	0.49	0.30	0.47
2013	142	0.23	0.39	0.24	0.40	0.16	0.32	0.36	0.49	0.37	0.49	0.27	0.43
2014	142	0.25	0.40	0.32	0.46	0.17	0.34	0.33	0.47	0.37	0.49	0.29	0.43
2015	135	0.18	0.35	0.36	0.49	0.18	0.35	0.24	0.40	0.25	0.40	0.24	0.40
Average	1548	0.35	0.44	0.32	0.43	0.28	0.41	0.42	0.53	0.35	0.46	0.35	0.46

Note CCB: city commercial bank, FB: foreign bank, JSCB: joint-stock commercial bank, RCB: rural commercial bank, SOCB: state-owned commercial bank. A higher (lower) Lerner index is associated with an increase (decrease) in market power in banking government guarantee in the absence of a formal deposit insurance scheme.[5] These state-controlled banks have significant market power and enjoy monopolistic profits in the Chinese banking market. The mean Lerner index of CCBs is largely driven by high values in the early few years due to sample bias—only one CCB in 1995 and 1996 and three CCBs are included in the sample. When we exclude the first three years, the mean Lerner index becomes 0.30, suggesting a weaker market power enjoyed by CCBs, which is even lower than that of foreign banks. The Lerner index of FBs is 0.32, and their market power mainly stems from their niche market to serve foreign clients over much of the sample period. JSCBs have the least market power with a Lerner index of 0.28. Unlike SOCBs and CCBs that have enjoyed support and protection from the central and local governments, though less so more recently, and RCBs that have relatively clearly defined niche markets, JSCBs have no clearly defined niche markets and have to compete in the market. Thus, these banks are under more competition pressures and have less market power. The ranking of bank types in term of market power is RCBs, SOCBs, CCBs, FBs, and JSCBs. Our ranking of market power is slightly different from that of Fungáčová et al. (2013) in which CCBs have the highest market power, followed by Big Five banks and JSCBS, and foreign banks have the lowest market power. The main reasons for the difference are perhaps due to the differences in the sample period, the number of banks in the sample, and the classification of bank types. When considering the same sample period, 2002–2011, the rankings are generally consistent.

Figure 5.3 plots the average Lerner index by bank type,showing the evolution of the Lerner index of different types of banks over the past two decades. As more and more CCBs were included in the sample, the average Lerner index declined rapidly from more than 0.7 in 1995 with only one CCB in the sample (out of 26) to 0.22 in 2003. From 2003, the CCBs' Lerner index started to increase although the number of CCBs in the sample increased up to 55 in the sample by 2008. This provides strong evidence that the degree of banking competition

[5] The deposit insurance program was introduced in 2015—the last year of our sample period in China. Thus during our sample period, there is no formal deposit insurance program.

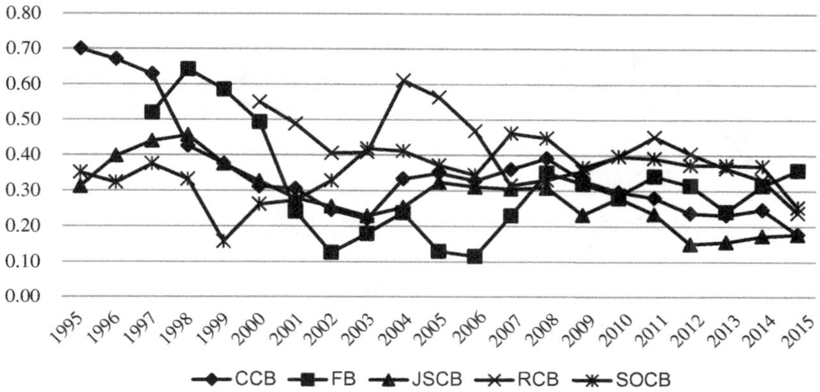

Fig. 5.3 Average Lerner index of the Chinese banking sector by bank type (1995–2015)

decreased during 2003–2008, which was not driven by the changes in the sample composition. In the post-crisis period, CCBs became more competitive with a steady decreasing Lerner index. The Lerner index of foreign banks exhibited a declining trend similar to that of CCBs up to 2002, and then fluctuated around a mean of 0.3 (with a slightly increasing trend) during the rest of the sample period.

The Lerner index of JSCBs fluctuated around a mean of 0.3 with a steady downward trend during the sample period, suggesting that the market power of JSCBs declined. In other words, JSCBs became more and more competitive. The Lerner index of RCBs declined in the first four years and increased in the fifth year with the same one RCB in the sample. With more and more RCBs included in the sample (21 RCBs in the sample in 2015), the average Lerner index declined sharply from 0.61 in 2004 to 0.31 in 2007 and fluctuated during the rest of the sample period. SOCBs was a balanced subsample and their average Lerner index fluctuated during the first half of the sample period and stayed stable during the second half of the sample period. Overall, the evolution of the market power of different types of banks supports our argument that the sample composition is not a major concern of driving the Lerner index and our estimates provide a fair view of the evolution of banking competition in China.

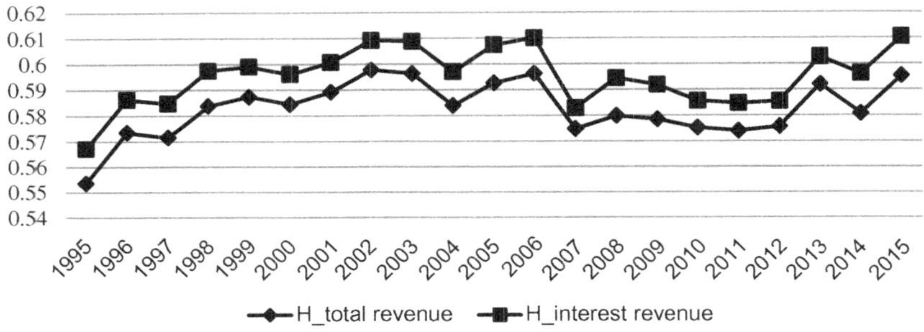

Fig. 5.4 *H*-statistics of Chinese banking sector (1995–2015)

5.4.3 The Panzar and Rosse (1987) *H*-Statistics

We obtain the *H*-statistics from estimating the unscaled revenue equation in Eq. (5.5) and the test for long-run equilibrium condition is also satisfied. For additional robustness check, we control for bank type, and the results are consistent. We also estimate the scaled revenue equation by adding total assets to control for the size effect on revenue and the results confirm an upward bias as discussed in Bikker et al. (2009, 2012). The extant literature commonly uses annual data to estimate the annual *H*-statistics in order to reveal the evolution of the banking competition condition. This approach does not suit our sample as annual samples are small in the first half of the sample period. Instead, we use the cross terms with year dummies to derive the time-varying *H*-statistics. The overall *H*-statistics is 0.58 when estimating the total revenue equation and 0.6 when estimating the interest income equation, suggesting that the Chinese banking industry features with monopolistic competition. Our results are slightly lower than those in Xu et al. (2013). Xu et al. (2013) use recursive least squares to estimate the scaled revenue equation and report an average *H*-statistics of 0.7, while they argue that their estimates of *H*-statistics are biased due to interest rate regulation in China.

Figure 5.4 plots the annual *H*-statistics estimated from the unscaled revenue equation using alternative revenue measures of total revenue and interest income over the sample period. The results suggest that the competition level of the Chinese banking industry increased slightly from 1995 up to 2002, then fluctuated for a few years and declined sharply in 2007. It remained stable and started to rise after 2012.

5.4.4 The Boone Indicator—the Profit Elasticity Approach

The Boone indicator of market power is obtained by estimating the relation between profitability and average cost in Eq. (5.7) using a panel fixed effect estimation approach with robust errors. Concerning the potential endogeneity issue as firm profitability and cost are jointly determined, we also employ the generalized method of moments (GMM) estimation approach where one-year lagged values of explanatory variables are treated as instruments. To estimate the time-varying Boone indicator over the sample period, we construct a dummy variable for each time period and include it in the cross terms with average costs in the estimation. The coefficient in each time period of the cross term is the Boone indicator. In all estimations, the coefficients for the Boone indicator from both panel regression and GMM estimation are negative and significant. For additional robustness check, we include a set of bank-specific control variables to capture the effects of differences in funding and asset structure across banks, including the ratio of customer deposits to the sum of total deposits and short-term funding, the ratio of loans to total assets, and the ratio of non-earning assets to total assets. The estimated Boone indicator from both panel regression and GMM estimation are not affected significantly and the trend remains consistent.

Figure 5.5 plots the annual Boone indicator of the Chinese banking industry over the sample period. We use the absolute value of the Boone indicator and the larger the value, the higher the degree of banking competition. The Boone indicators estimated from two different approaches are generally consistent in terms of magnitude and trend. It experienced fluctuations in the first few years and then declined sharply.

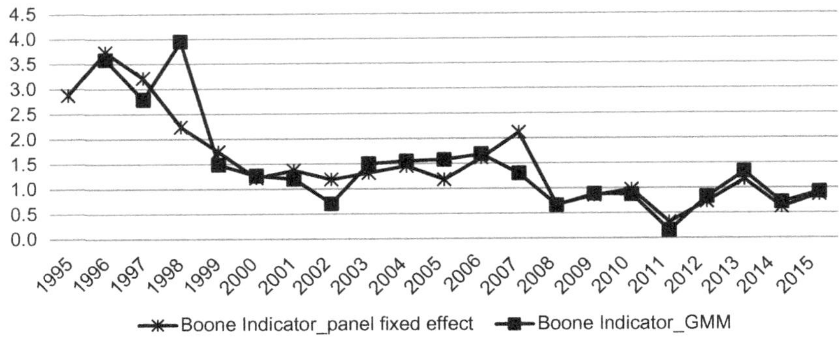

Fig. 5.5 Boone indicator of market power of Chinese banking sector (1995–2015). *Note* Boone indicator is negative and we plot its absolute value for convenient comparison

The downward trend stabilized in 2000 and increased slightly until a sudden drop during the 2008 crisis and a further drop in 2011, followed by a slight increase in the subsequent 4 years. Overall, the Boone indicator suggests that the degree of competition in the Chinese banking industry declined in the second half of the 1990s and remained relatively stable during the rest of the sample period.

5.4.5 A Comparison of Results from Different Measures of Competition

Having assessed the degree of competition of the Chinese banking industry using the structural and non-structural approaches, Table 5.3 summarizes the main trends of banking competition identified by different measures. The structural measures consistently suggest that the concentration level declined over the sample period, while, as the literature suggests, this does not necessarily imply more competition. The non-structural measures provide more detailed information on the evolution of banking competition with a mixed picture. Different measures do not show the same changes in the competition level during the first few years of the sample period (1995–1999): the Lerner index and the *H*-statistics indicate more competition, while the Boone indicator

Table 5.3 A comparison of competition measures

	Whole sample period	Sub-period			
Structural measure of concentration					
CR4	Decreasing				
HHI	Decreasing	1995–2001: Highly concentrated	2002–2011: Moderately concentrated		2012–2015 Un-concentrated
Non-structural measure of competition					
Lerner	Fluctuating, then increasing	1995–1997: Decreasing	1998–2003 C Increasing	2004–2008 Decreasing	2009–2015 Increasing
H-statistics	Stable, then increasing	1995–2006 Increasing		2007 Decreasing	2008-2012 stable, 2012–2015 Increasing
Boone indicator	Fluctuating and decreasing, stable since 1999	1995–1999: Decreasing	2000–2006 Slightly increasing	2006–2011 Decreasing	2012–2015 Increasing

Note Higher Lerner index indicates a lower level of competition; Higher *H*-Statistics indicates a higher level of competition; Boone indicator is negative, a higher absolute value of Boone indicator suggests a higher level of competition. Higher values of CR4 and HHI indicate a lower level of competition shows an opposite trend. However, different measures show a similar trend of competition from 2000 onwards. The *H*-statistics and the Boone indicator demonstrate more competition up to the global financial crisis in 2007, while the Lerner index indicates a similar trend up to 2003 followed by a drop up to 2007. A possible explanation is that the Lender index measures competition at the bank level and hence is more sensitive to changes in the competitiveness of individual banks than the Boone indicator and the *H*-statistics that estimate the respective coefficients at the industrial level. The turnaround point in the Lerner index was 2003 when radical SOCBs reform started. Government support during the reform provided SOCBs with more market power (reducing competition). The H-statistic captured this effect in 2004 but quickly vanished as shown in Fig. 5.4. All measures responded to the shock of the global financial crisis in 2008. After the crisis, the Boone indicator and the *H*-statistics indicate a stable level of competition, while the Lerner indicator suggests a steady rise in competition. From 2012, all measures consistently show a similar trend of rising competition in the Chinese banking industry.

Overall, the Lerner index and H-statistic are more consistent with each other, while the Boone indicator tends to give a different picture. The Boone indicator is theoretically superior to the other measures as discussed in Sect. 5.2. Although at the bank level the Boone indicator can be estimated, as proposed by Delis (2012), the empirical implementation of the local-maximum likelihood estimation to obtain bank-level marginal costs is time-consuming and not straightforward. The Lerner index has the advantage of measuring market power at the bank level and hence can better account for the heterogeneity in competition across banks, allowing for more comprehensive analysis compared to the other measures. This makes the Lerner index more attractive to researchers, especially for those who conduct bank-level analysis in a single-country study setting. A single-country study has the advantage of avoiding the complications or/and bias in regression due to country-specific factors suffered by cross-country studies. The research findings are of more policy relevance as single country study generally better accounts for the specialties of the country under consideration.

5.5 Conclusion

This chapter evaluates banking competition and depicts how the degree of competition evolves over the drastic banking reform in China during 1995–2015. The main findings are as follows. Despite different measures disagreeing with each other on the trend of banking competition before 2000, they tend to provide more consistent results from 2000. From 2000 onwards, with more comprehensive and radical banking reforms, the Chinese banking industry has steadily become more competitive, with a faster pace from 2012, suggesting a positive impact of banking reform on competition. Future research should focus on examining the drivers of banking competition and its potential impact on financial stability, regulation, financial innovation, and economic growth.

Despite criticisms, the bank-level measure of the Lerner index better accounts for heterogeneity in competition across banks than the other measures that focus more on competition at an aggregate industrial level. As to which measure(s) of competition is better remains an unsettled empirical issue and the choice of measure(s) large depends on the specific research questions, research goal, and data availability. We suggest the use of multiple measures that are complementary, together providing more detailed information on banking competition. In this regard, more research is needed to improve our understanding of the behavior of competition measures and develop more reliable measures.

References

Adams, R.M., and D.F. Amel. 2005. The Effects of Local Banking Market Structure on the Bank-lending Channel of Monetary Policy. Working Paper, Board of Governors of the Federal Reserve System.

Aftalion, F., and J.L. White. 1978. A Study of a Monetary System with a Pegged Discount Rate Under Different Market Structures. *Journal of Banking & Finance* 2: 351–354.

Allen, F., and D. Gale. 2004. Competition and Financial Stability. *Journal of Money, Credit, Banking* 36 (3): 453–480.

Angelini, P., and N. Cetorelli. 2003. The Effects of Regulatory Reform on Competition in the Banking Industry. *Journal of Money, Credit and Banking* 5: 663–684.

Bain, J.S. 1956. *Barriers to New Competition*. Cambridge, MA: Harvard University Press.

Bain, J.S. 1959. *Industrial Organization*. New York: Wiley.

Baumol, W., J. Panzar, and R. Willig. 1982. *Contestable Markets and the Theory of Industry Structure*. New York: Harcourt Brace Jovanovich.

Beck, T., A. Demirguc-Kunt, and R. Levine. 2006. Bank Concentration, Competition, and Crises: First Results. *Journal of Banking Finance* 30 (5): 1581–1603.

Beck, T., O. de Jonghe, and G. Schepens. 2013. Bank Competition and Stability: Cross-country Heterogeneity. *Journal of Financial Intermediation* 22: 218–244.

Berger, A.N., and T.H. Hannan. 1998. The Efficiency Cost of Market Power in the Banking Industry: A Test of the 'Quiet Life' and Related Hypotheses. *Review of Economics and Statistics* 8 (3): 454–465.

Berger, A.N., S.D. Bonime, D.M. Covitz, and D. Hancock. 2000. Why are bank Profits so Persistent? The Roles of Product Market Competition, Informational Opacity and Regional Macroeconomic Shocks. *Journal of Banking and Finance* 24: 1203–1235.

Berger, A., L.F. Klapper, and R. Turk-Ariss. 2009. Bank Competition and Financial Stability. *Journal of Financial Services Research* 35: 99–118.

Bikker, J.A. 2004. *Competition and Efficiency in a Unified European Banking Market*. Cheltenham: Edward Elgar.

Bikker, J.A., and K. Haaf. 2002. Competition, Concentration and Their Relationship: An Empirical Analysis of the Banking Industry. *Journal of Banking & Finance* 26: 2191–2214.

Bikker, J.A., S. Shaffer, and L. Spierdijk. 2009. Assessing Competition with the Panzar-Rosse Model: The Role of Scale, Costs, and Equilibrium. Utrecht School of Economics Discussion Paper Series No. 27.

Bikker, J.A., S. Shaffer, and L. Spierdijk. 2012. Assessing Competition with the Panzar-Rosse Model: The Role of Scale, Costs, and Equilibrium. *Review of Economics and Statistics* 94 (4): 1025–1044.

Boone, J. 2008. A New Way to Measure Competition. *Economic Journal* 118: 1245–1261.

Boone, J., Griffith, R. and Harrison R. 2005. Measuring Competition. AIM Research Working Paper 22-August-2005.

Bos, J.W.B., J.W. Kolari, and R.C.R. van Lamoen. 2013. Competition and Innovation: Evidence from Financial Services. *Journal of Banking & Finance* 37: 1590–1601.

Boyd, J.H., and G. De Nicolo. 2005. The Theory of Bank Risk Taking and Competition Revisited. *Journal of Finance* 60 (3): 1329–1343.

Bresnahan, T.F. 1982. The Oligopoly Solution Concept is Identified. *Economics Letters* 10: 87–92.

Bresnahan, T. F. 1989. Empirical Studies of Industries with Market Power. In *Handbook of industrial organization,* ed. R. Schmalensee and R.Willig, vol. 2, 1011–1057. Amsterdam: Elsevier.

Brissimis, S.N., M.D. Delis, and N.I. Papanikolaou. 2008. Exploring the Nexus Between Banking Sector Reform and Performance: Evidence From Newly Acceded EU Countries. *Journal of Banking & Finance* 32 (12): 2674–2683.

Carbó, S., D. Humphrey, J. Maudos, and P. Molyneux. 2009. Cross-Country Comparisons of Competition and Pricing Power in European Banking. *Journal of International Money and Finance* 28: 115–134.

Casu, B., and C. Girardone. 2006. Bank Competition, Concentration and Efficiency in the Single European Market. *The Manchester School* 74 (4): 441–468.

Cipollini, A., and F. Fiordelisi. 2012. Economic Value, Competition and Financial Distress in the European Banking System. *Journal of Banking & Finance* 36: 3101–3109.

Claessens, S., and L. Laeven. 2004. What Drives Bank Competition? Some International Evidence. *Journal of Money, Credit and Banking* 36 (3): 563–583.

Delis, M. 2012. Bank Competition, Financial Reform, and Institutions: The Importance of Being Development. *Journal of Development Economics* 92: 450–465.

Delis, M.D., and E.G. Tsionas. 2009. The Joint Estimation of Bank-Level Market Power and Efficiency. *Journal of Banking & Finance* 33: 1842–1850.

Demsetz, H. 1973. Industry Structure, Market Rivalry and Public Policy. *Journal of Law and Economics* 16 (1): 1–9.

De-Ramon, S., and M. Straughan. 2016. Measuring Competition in the UK Deposit-Taking Sector. Bank of England Working Paper No. 631.

Frame, W.S., and L.J. White. 2004. Empirical Studies of Financial Innovation: Lots of Talk, Little Action? *Journal of Economic Literature* 42 (1): 116–144.

Fernández de Guevara, J., J. Maudos, and F. Perez. 2005. Market Power in European Banking Sector. *Journal of Financial Services Research* 27: 109–137.

Fu, X., and S. Heffernan. 2009. The Effects of Reform on China's Bank Structure and Performance. *Journal of Banking & Finance* 33 (1): 39–52.

Fungáčová, Z., L. Solanko, and L. Weill. 2010. Market Power in the Russian Banking Industry. *International Economics* 124: 127–145.

Fungáčová, Z., P. Pessarossi, and L. Weill. 2013 Is Bank Competition Detrimental to Efficiency? Evidence from China? *China Economic Review* 27: 121–134.

Goddard, J., and J.O.S. Wilson. 2009. Competition in Banking: A Disequilibrium Approach. *Journal of Banking & Finance* 33: 2282–2292.

Goddard, J., P. Molyneux, and J.O.S. Wilson. 2004a. Dynamics of Growth and Profitability in Banking. *Journal of Money, Credit and Banking* 36: 1069–1090.

Goddard, J., P. Molyneux, and J.O.S. Wilson. 2004b. The Profitability of European Banks: A Cross-Sectional and Dynamic Panel Analysis. *The Manchester School* 72: 363–381.

Hakenes, H., and I. Schnabel. 2011. Bank Competition and Capital Regulation. *Economics Letters* 113: 256–258.

Hicks, J. 1935. Annual Survey of Economic Theory: The Theory of Monopoly. *Econometrica* 3: 1–20.

Iwata, G. 1974. Measurement of Conjectural Variations in Oligopoly. *Econometrica* 42: 947–966.

Keeley, M.C. 1990. Deposit Insurance, Risk, and Market Power in Banking. *The American Economic Review* 80 (5): 1183–1200.

Koetter, M., J.W. Kolari, and L. Spierdijk. 2012. Enjoying the Quiet Life Under Deregulation? Evidence from Adjusted Lerner Indices for U.S. Banks. *The Review of Economics and Statistics* 94 (2): 462–480.

Koetter, M., and T. Poghosyan. 2009. The Identification of Technology Regimes in Banking: Implications for the Market Power-Fragility Nexus. *Journal of Banking & Finance* 33 (8): 1413–1422.

Kumbhakar, S.C., S. Baardsen, and G. Lien. 2012. A New Method for Estimating Market Power with an Application to Norwegian Sawmilling. *Review of Industrial Organization* 40: 109–129.

Lau, L. 1982. On Identifying the Degree of Competitiveness from Industry Price and Output Data. *Economics Letters* 10: 93–99.

Lerner, A. 1934. The Concept of Monopoly and the Measurement of Monopoly Power. *Review of Economic Studies* 1: 157–175.

Liu, H., P. Molyneux, and J.O.S. Wilson. 2013. Competition and Stability in European Banking: A Regional Analysis. *Manchester School* 81 (2): 176–201.

Mason, E.S. 1957. *Economic Concentration and the Monopoly Problem.* Cambridge, MA: Harvard University Press.

Matthews, K., V. Murinde, and T. Zhao. 2007. Competitive Conditions Among the Major British Banks. *Journal of Banking & Finance* 31: 2025–2042.

Marcus, A.J. 1984. Deregulation and Bank Financial Policy. *Journal of Banking & Finance* 8 (4): 557–565.

Matsuoka, T. 2013. Sunspot Bank Runs in Competitive Versus Monopolistic Banking Systems. *Economic Letters* 118 (2): 247–249.

Maudos, J., and J. Fernández de Guevara. 2004. Factors Explaining the Interest Margin in the Banking Sectors of the European Union. *Journal of Banking & Finance* 28 (9): 2259–2281.

Maudos, J., and J. Fernández de Guevara. 2007. The Cost of Market Power in the European Banking Sectors: Social Welfare Loss vs. Inefficiency Cost. *Journal of Banking & Finance* 31 (7): 2103–2125.

Maudos, J., and L. Solís. 2011. Deregulation, Liberalization and Consolidation of the Mexican Banking System: Effects on Competition. *Journal of International Money and Finance* 30 (2): 337–353.

Mirzaei, A., and T. Moore. 2014. What are the Driving Forces of Bank Competition Across Different Income Groups? *Journal of International Financial Markets, Institutions and Money* 32 (2): 38–71.

Mueller, D.C. 1977. The Persistence of Profits Above the Norm. *Economica* 44: 369–380.

Mueller, D.C. 1986. *Profits in the Long Run.* Cambridge: Cambridge University Press.

Neven, D., and L.H. Röller. 1999. An Aggregate Structural Model of Competition in the European Banking Industry. *International Journal of Industrial Organisation* 17: 1059–1074.

Olley, S.G., and A. Pakes. 1996. The Dynamics of Productivity in the Telecommunications Industry. *Econometrica* 64: 1263–1297.

Olivero, M.P., Y. Li, and B.N. Jeon. 2011. Competition in Banking and the Lending Channel: Evidence from Bank-Level Data in Asia and Latin America. *Journal of Banking & Finance* 35 (3): 560–571.

Panzar, J.C., and J.N. Rosse. 1987. Testing for "monopoly" Equilibrium. *The Journal of Industrial Economics* 35: 443–456.

Rosenthal, R. 1980. A Model in Which an Increase in the Number of Sellers Leads to a Higher Price. *Econometrica* 48 (6): 1575–1579.

Rosse, J., and J. Panzar 1977. Chamberlin vs. Robinson: An Empirical Test for Monopoly Rents. Economic Discussion Papers, No. 90, Bell Laboratories.

Schaeck, K., and M. Cihák. 2010. Competition, Efficiency, and Soundness in Banking: An Industrial Organization Perspective. Discussion Paper 2010-68S, Tilburg University, Center for Economic Research.

Schaeck, K., and M. Cihák. 2012. Banking Competition and Capital Ratios. *European Financial Management* 18 (5): 836–866.

Schaeck, K., and M. Cihák. 2014. Competition, Efficiency, and Stability in Banking. *Financial Management* (Spring): 215–241.

Shaffer, S. 1982. A Nonstructural Test for Competition in Financial Markets. In *Proceedings of a Conference on Bank Structure and Competition*, 225–243, *Federal Reserve Bank of Chicago.*

Shaffer, S. 1983. Non-Structural Measures of Competition: Toward a Synthesis of Alternatives. *Economics Letters* 12: 349–353.

Shaffer, S. 1989. Regulatory Distortion of Competition. Federal Reserve Bank of Philadelphia Working Papers, 89–28.

Shaffer, S. 1993. A test of Competition in Canadian Banking. *Journal of Money, Credit and Banking* 25: 49–61.

Shaffer, S. 2004. Patterns of Competition in Banking. *Journal of Economics and Business* 56: 287–313.

Stiroh, K.J. 2000. Compositional Dynamics and the Performance of the US Banking Industry. Federal Reserve Bank of New York Staff Report No. 98.

Tang, 2016. The Impacts of Risk and Competition on Bank Profitability in China. *Journal of International Financial Markets, Institutions & Money* 40: 85–110.

Turk-Ariss, R. 2010. On the Implications of Market Power in Banking: Evidence from Developing Countries. *Journal of Banking & Finance* 34: 765–775.

Uchida, H., and Y. Tsutsui. 2005. Has competition in the Japanese banking sector improved? *Journal of Banking & Finance* 29: 419–439.

VanHoose, D. 1983. Monetary Policy Under Alternative Bank Market Structures. *Journal of Banking & Finance* 7: 383–404.

VanHoose, D. 1985. Bank Market Structure and Monetary Control. *Journal of Money, Credit and Banking* 17: 298–311.

Van Leuvensteijn, M., J. Bikker, A. van Rixtel, and C. Kok-Sørensen. 2011. A New Approach to Measuring Competition in the Loan Markets of the Euro Area. *Applied Economics* 43 (23): 3155–3167.

Vives, X. 2008. Innovation and Competitive Pressure. *The Journal of Industrial Economics* 56 (3): 419–469.

Weill, L. 2004. On the Relationship Between Competition and Efficiency in the EU Banking Sector. *Kredit und Kapital* 37 (3): 329–352.

Xu, B., A. van Rixtel, and M. van Leuvensteijn. 2013. Measuring Bank Competition in China: A Comparison of New Versus Conventional Approaches Applied to Loan Markets. BIS Working Papers No 422.

Zhao, T., B. Casu, and A. Ferrari. 2010. The Impact of Regulatory Reforms on Cost Structure, Ownership and Competition in Indian Banking. *Journal of Banking & Finance* 34: 246–254.

6

Shadow Banking in China

Preamble

[*Acknowledgement: the authors of this chapter are Chunxia Jiang, Shujie Yao, and Chunan Hu; Chunan Hu is PhD candidate of University of Nottingham China Campus, Ningbo, China*] Over the last few decades, the financial system has gone through enormous transformation due to a number of driving forces, such as globalization, financial liberalization, financial innovation, and technological advancement. Development in information and communication technologies has blurred the boundaries of different segments of the financial system. Both banks and non-bank institutions/intermediaries take advantage of arbitrage opportunities in information, regulation, price and taxation systems and engage in off-balance sheet activities for profit. Financial institutions have become more closely interconnected in a global network through financial derivatives and highly leveraged products. The disastrous global financial crisis in 2008–2009 showed the contagion effect among the financial systems in major developed economies, for which shadow banking activities have been considered by many scholars and authorities as one of the important causes for the crisis. Subsequently, the shadow banking system has become the centre of the governments' emergency policy in response to the crisis.

C. Jiang and S. Yao, *Chinese Banking Reform*, The Nottingham China Policy Institute Series, DOI 10.1007/978-3-319-63925-3_6

Shadow banking in China is still at the initial stage in terms of complexity, but its explosive growth in recent years has attracted a great deal of attention from researchers, practitioners, regulators, and policy makers. This chapter first introduces the concept of shadow banking and global development in Sect. 6.1. Section 6.2 provides a detailed account of shadow banking in China, followed by Sect. 6.3 that describes main product lines of shadow banking. Section 6.4 discusses risks associated with shadow banking and the regulatory framework to contain and control these risks. Section 6.5 concludes.

6.1 Shadow Banking and Its Development

6.1.1 Definition

The term shadow banking was coined by McCulley (2007)—the PIMCO analyst, referring to the proliferation of leveraged non-bank investment methods such as asset-backed securities and credit derivatives in the US financial market. These non-traditional banking activities have been described as a parallel banking system, near banks, and shadow finance system (IMF 2008; Roubini 2009). Shadow banking constitutes a set of unregulated or lightly regulated activities, markets, contracts, and institutions that operate outside of or partially intertwined with the traditional commercial banking sector. A key feature that differentiates shadow banking from traditional banking business is the breading down of the credit intermediation process that is sequentially carried out by a group of discrete entities (FSB 2011). Shadow banking may contain a single entity that intermediates funds between end-suppliers and end-borrowers, and/or a chain of multiple entities (FSB 2011; Pozsar et al. 2010).

Shadow banks perform functions, such as transformation of maturity, credit, and liquidity, and assume risks similar to traditional banks. Because they are not part of the formal banking sector, shadow banks have no access to safety-net facilities (e.g., the publicly guaranteed deposit insurance scheme) or support from central banks as lender of last resorts. Shadow banking business involves much more risks, but under different and lighter regulation and supervision, posing significant threats to financial stability. It has become an important issue in both advanced and emerging markets that face different challenges. In the United States and other advanced economies, shadow banking business involves multiple credit intermediation steps and complex linkages among shadow banks and/or between shadow banks with traditional banks. In emerging markets, these steps and linkages tend to be simpler, mainly involving finance, leasing, and factoring companies; investment and equity funds; insurance companies; pawnshops; and underground financial entities.

There is no agreed definition of shadow banking and it may vary across different countries or regions with different characteristics (FSB 2012). Literature frequently defines a shadow banking system from functional, institutional, and regulatory perspectives, while some scholars tend to combine functional and institutional perspectives. The functional perspective focuses on the role of shadow banking as financial intermediaries in transforming credit, maturity, and liquidity (Adrian and Ashcraft 2016). It is a market-funded credit intermediation system that transforms maturity and/or liquidity (Deloitte 2012) and channels deposit funds to investors (Claessens et al. 2013) through securitization and secured-funding mechanisms. It performs maturity transformation by financing longer-term financial assets using short-term (money-market) liabilities and outside banking social contract (Ricks 2010). Banks and non-bank financial institutions finance non-traditional and bank-like funding activities—so-called shadow banking funding activities, through noncore liabilities in forms such as securitization and collateral intermediation (IMF 2014).

The institutional perspective defines the shadow banking system in terms of instruments or markets. Shadow banks are levered-up financial intermediaries that have liabilities akin to bank deposits (McCulley 2007). Shadow banks are non-bank financial institutions but behave like banks, for example, they are highly leveraged and borrow short while lending and investing long in illiquid assets (Acharya et al. 2013) while they are under less regulation and not directly supported by government liquidity and credit enhancement. The shadow banking system integrates capital markets with money markets and uses money market funds to finance capital market lending via banks' on-balance sheet activities and other non-banking entities (Mehrling et al. 2013). Claessens and Ratnovski (2014) consider shadow banking as all financial activities except for traditional banking that requires private backstops of franchise value or public backstops of guarantees and safety net. Gorton and Metrick (2010) point out that "the shadow banking system is in fact a real banking system."

Focusing on the nature of the institutions and the strength of regulation, the regulatory perspective defines a shadow banking system as an unregulated or lightly regulated intermediation system without official safety protection but with potentially significant impact on financial stability. The shadow banking sector employs the "originate-to-distribute" business model that transfers banks' on-balance sheet regulated assets to unregulated off-balance sheets assets. Financial innovations, such as securitization vehicles, help banks evade relevant regulations.

Among different definitions, the most widely used one is proposed by the Financial Stability Board (FSB) that describes shadow banking as "credit intermediation involving entities and activities outside the regular banking system" (FSB 2014).[1] In a broad sense, shadow banking system includes all financial intermediaries other than traditional banks. In a narrow sense, shadow banking system refers to any institution or business that poses systemic risks due to maturity and liquidity transformation, high leverage, and regulatory arbitrage, excluding those entities not part of a credit intermediation chain or not prudentially consolidated into a banking group.

Although the definition of shadow banking system varies, there are commonly used criteria to distinguish shadow banking entities and activities from traditional banking institutions and services (Kodres 2013; Yan and Li 2014). The first criterion relates to maturity transformation function and shadow banks refer to non-banking entities that take short-term customer funds and make long-term investments. The second criterion relates to liquidity risk and shadow banks are those non-banking entities holding insufficient liquid assets and more likely

[1] FSB is an international body that monitors and makes recommendations about the global financial system. FSB was established in 2009 and its original charter was endorsed by the heads of state and government of the G20. On 28 January 2013, the FSB was established as a not-for-profit association under Swiss law with its seat in Basel, Switzerland. The FSB has assumed a key role in promoting international financial regulatory reform.

to experience liquidity problems or even a kind of bank run in case they are unable to fulfil customer demands for redemptions. The third criterion for identifying shadow banking activities relates to imperfect risk transfer. Debts and assets transfer through derivatives and other methods between the traditional banking sector and the shadow banking sector is usually associated with incomplete transfer of corresponding risks. The final criterion for spotting shadow banks is that non-banking entities have high leverage ratio similar to that of traditional banks. Shadow banks do not officially take deposits but finance their activities via other tools and financial instruments that accumulate large amounts of debt.

6.1.2 Relationship with Traditional Banking System

As a type of financial intermediary, shadow banking does not exist as an isolated financial system outside the traditional one, but it intertwines with and integrates into the financial systems through cross-ownership and financial interlinkages. Shadow banking significantly extends the banking sector and promotes the development and evolution of financial systems worldwide. Formal banking and shadow banking intertwine through both direct connections and indirect linkages. Direct connections occur when shadow banks participate in a banking intermediation and securitization chain, and indirect linkages happen when the two sectors share common counterparties or invest in similar assets; both induce contagion channels transmitting systemic risks among entities (FSB 2013).

These connections and linkages mainly arise from similar functions, tight operational relation, and assets holdings of similar characteristics. Both formal banks and shadow banks act as credit intermediaries channelling funds flowing from savers to borrowers with operational intersections over a wide range of business. Traditional banks offer the basic products such as credit and liquidity support, while they also actively engage in shadow banking business seeking costs savings and/or regulatory arbitrage opportunities. These linkages become channels for contagion effect and induce quick spread of risks from unregulated or lightly regulated shadow banking system to the regulated traditional banking sector.

Traditional banks' liabilities are mainly deposits, which are in turn a form of money. Shadow banks' debts are the personal money assets that are invested in money market funds by individuals. Shadow banking relies on traditional banks. For example, traditional banks' loan securitization provides shadow banks opportunities for investment, which has been a driving factor for rapid development of the shadow banking sector over the past decade. They permeate into each other and tend to converge across the structure of the financial system. The shadow banking system indeed is operated as formal banks' off-balance sheet businesses and/or purchases loans from banks for securitization (Yan and Li 2014).

Despite the convergence and permeation between traditional banking and shadow banking across the financing structure, money flow, and assets utilization, the shadow banking system and the regulated formal banking system differ. First, they differ in the mode of business conduct. Traditional banks are required to report all operations on one balance sheet, while shadow banks perform their financial intermediary activities across many interconnected markets and institutions. Traditional banks act as intermediaries to perform main functions in the markets, while shadow banks adopt market tools to replace traditional banks and perform liquidity and maturity transformation across institutions. In other words, shadow banks break down traditional banks' functions vertically into a chain that is integrated with markets. Shadow banks with a hybrid business mode have blurred the boundaries between different financial intermediaries in the markets (Yan and Li 2014). Second, traditional banking and shadow banking differ in regulatory requirements. Traditional banking is tightly regulated with strict entry and exit rules and detailed restrictions on certain banking activities from a micro-prudential perspective. The shadow banking system can evade regulations and in fact can take advantage of regulatory arbitrage opportunities. Third, traditional banking and shadow banking differ in daily operational models and support from governmental authorities. Traditional banks take out reserves and keep sufficient liquidity to meet daily operational needs and they have access to liquidity provided by the central bank. Depositors of traditional regulated banks are protected by a safety net, such as deposit insurance. Shadow banking entities tend to operate more aggressively to maximize profit and they are not under the protection of the government safety net (IMF 2014).

Shadow banking has a number of advantages and contributes to the proper functioning of financial markets. These advantages include liquidity generation, clearer loss absorbency process (investors bear losses in case of the default of non-banking institutions), and cost-reduction, thereby spurring economic growth by providing cheaper and widely available financial services. Shadow banking channels and products enhance funding sources and risk diversification for some credit-constrained sectors, investors, and other financial institutions and provide them with a wider range of tools for liquidity, maturity, and credit risk management. Alternative funding sources offered by shadow banks are especially helpful under the circumstance that the formal banking sector or financial market becomes temporarily impaired such as what occurred during the global financial crisis in 2008 (Yan and Li 2014; Ghosh et al. 2012; IMF 2014). Conversely, shadow banking also has certain disadvantages and poses threats to financial stability. Shadow banking encourages regulatory arbitrage, undermines market disciplines, generates uncertainties due to information opacity, and helps hide leverage, maturity transformation, and pro-cyclicality due to dependence on short-term wholesale funding (BBVA Research 2016). A well-developed non-bank sector is an essential part of a modern financial system and the shadow banking sector serves as a useful complement to the financial system. In India, non-bank financing firms are treated as a complementary way to allocate credit in nonurban areas as some banks with underdeveloped branching networks mainly focus on lending to the priority sectors.

6.1.3 The Status Quo and Driving Factors of Shadow Banking

Shadow banking is rapidly evolving and fluid with a higher level of information opacity relative to the traditional banking sector. Shadow banking activities and entities vary significantly across different regions and nations and the true size of the global shadow banking business is rather hard to estimate. FSB estimates are the most widely accepted measurement of shadow banking activities and its Global Shadow Banking Monitoring Report offers a systematic account of the size, composition, and trends of non-bank financial intermediation across the major global financial systems, covering about 80% of global GDP and 90% of global financial system assets.[2]

FSB defines the shadow banking system at two levels in terms of a broad measure and a narrow measure of shadow banking. Before the Global Shadow Banking Monitoring Report 2015, the FSB focused on the broadly defined shadow banking sector and its size was measured by the volume of total financial assets held by other financial intermediaries (OFIs), pension funds, and insurance companies.[3] Two broad measures of assets are employed—OFI for other financial institutions only and MUNFI (Monitoring Universe of Non-bank Financial Intermediation) that includes OFI, pension funds, and insurance companies. By the end of 2015, the global shadow banking assets of 21 jurisdictions[4] and the euro area was USD 151 trillion, accounting for 47% of total financial assets of financial intermediaries measured by MUNFI, and the corresponding figures for OFI were USD 94 trillion and 29%, respectively. The total banking sector assets was USD 133 trillion, accounting for 42% in 2015. In terms of the newly introduced narrow measure, after controlling for exchange rate, the shadow banking volume for 27 jurisdictions reached USD 34 trillion, accounting for 69% of GDP (FSB 2016).

As shown in Fig. 6.1, over the period 2002–2015, the shadow banking sector and the traditional banking sector show similar global trends. The share of banking assets and shadow banking assets in total financial

---

[2]Up to 2014, the report covers 20 individual non-euro area jurisdictions (namely Argentina, Australia, Brazil, Canada, Chile, China, Hong Kong, Indonesia, India, Japan, Korea, Mexico, Russia, Saudi Arabia, Singapore, Switzerland, Turkey, United Kingdom, United States, and South Africa) and the Eurozone (the euro area aggregate). Since 2015, the report covers 26 jurisdictions (including six individual euro area countries) and extends to 27 jurisdictions in 2017.

[3]The newly introduced narrow measure in 2015 may be subject to some degree of change in future reports.

[4]The 21 jurisdictions include Argentina, Australia, Brazil, Canada, Cayman Islands, Chile, China, Hong Kong, Indonesia, India, Japan, Korea, Mexico, Russia, Saudi Arabia, Singapore, Switzerland, Turkey, United Kingdom United States, and South Africa.

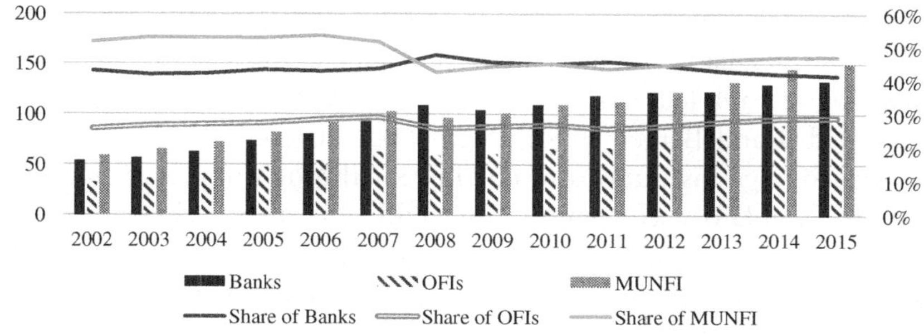

Fig. 6.1 The size of global banking and shadow banking (in USD trillion). *Note* OFI: other financial institutions; MUNFI: Monitoring Universe of Non-bank Financial Intermediation—the sum of OFI, pension funds, and insurance companies. *Data source* FSB 2016

assets are relatively stable. By the broad measure of MUNFI, the share of banking assets in total financial assets was lower than that of shadow banking assets until 2007, marginally higher in the following four years, and became lower again since 2012. The shadow banking sector appears to be more vulnerable to adverse shocks during the crisis time. By the narrow measure (OFIs), the share of shadow banking assets in total financial assets is stable over the sample period at around 30%.

6.1.4 Contributing Factors for Global Development of Shadow Banking

The development of the whole financial system offers opportunities for the shadow banking sector. The development of the shadow banking sector is strongly associated with the growth of institutional investors and the banking sector (IMF 2014). Despite the shadow banking sector varying significantly globally, extant literature indicates some common factors that have advanced shadow banking development, including regulatory arbitrage, financial innovation and technological advancement, and demand-side drivers.

Regulatory arbitrage is the most important driving factor for the development of shadow banking. Regulatory arbitrage refers to transactions or strategies designed to exploit differences or gaps within or between regulatory regimes (Gorton and Metrick 2010). The reserve and other regulatory requirements encourage the use of alternative financing to bank loans (Kanatas and Greenbaum 1982; Bernanke et al. 1991; Udell and Berger 1994; Duca 1992, 2016). Tight bank regulations encourage institutions to circumvent through non-bank intermediation. Regulatory constraints on banks' on-balance sheet activities, such as reserve requirements, encourage traditional banks to reduce on-balance activities and engage more in off-balance sheets activities. The latter is normally more profitable with no or less requirement on capital. Acharya et al. (2013) find evidence that liquidity-enhancing guarantees are structured to minimize regulatory reserves. Engaging in shadow banking activities, such as holding structured finance vehicles, banks can evade tight capital requirements to sustain higher leverage thereby boosting returns. Some lightly regulated tax havens and offshore financial centres give rise to the regulatory arbitrage opportunities, and shadow banking activities are interconnected both offshore and off balance sheet on a global scale. While regulations and reserve requirements imposed on the formal banking sector become more stringent after the 2008–2009 global financial crisis, regulation on shadow banking is still at its early stage, creating more regulatory arbitrage opportunities.

In advanced economies, the growth of securitization in Europe and the United States following the 1988 Basel Accord is a typical example of regulatory arbitrage. Banks have strong incentives to securitized low-quality loans in return for cash, which improve banks' liquidity position, and enable them to avoid high capital charge and take up more profitable investment opportunities. In the late 1980s, driven by regulatory arbitrage, collateralized debt obligations and structured investment vehicles emerged in the market. In emerging economies, shadow banking is largely motivated by restrictive regulations on banks. For instance, in 2010, the Chinese government tightened regulations (e.g., increasing reserve ratio) on the formal banking sector to slow down the conventional lending growth, which inspired the origination of off-balance sheet loans. Similarly, the rapid growth of special-purpose non-bank financial institutions in Mexico is encouraged by regulatory arbitrage and government support.

Financial innovation and technological advancement has facilitated and accelerated the growth of shadow banking. Financial innovation includes innovations of financial products, process of conducting business, and organizational forms. Prior to the 2008–2009 global financial crisis, a liberal and sanguine regulatory attitude towards financial innovations induced complex products and institutions in global financial markets in the absence of information and tools for proper risk management. It is argued that overconfidence about the riskiness of innovative financial products is one of the key factors causing the 2007 credit crisis in US (Boz and Mendoza 2010) and negative externalities are largely generated by innovations in the credit and money creation process (Turner 2012).

The application of technological advancement in the financial sector promotes financial innovations. Advanced and emerging economies choose to apply new financial technologies and advancements that fit their development stage. In the United States, the application of automated asset allocation algorithms and high-speed trading leads to movement of profit-seekers from equity markets to other markets such as bonds, currencies, and derivatives (Massoudi and Mackenzie 2013). In China, the newly developed shadow banking system has benefited significantly from financial technology platforms provided by Internet giant companies such as Alibaba and Tencent. Those platforms offer payments services and credit and transactions facilities to retail customers, competing directly with the formal banking sector.

On the supply side, a series of regulatory changes and financial innovations has broken up the competitive advantage of the traditional banking sector. On the demand side, since 2000, institutional investors (e.g., large corporations and financial intermediaries) have increased demand for safe, highly liquid financial instruments (Claessens et al. 2012). Meanwhile, as rapid economic development occurs in emerging markets, such as China and India, more and more individuals have become increasingly wealthy and they look for low-risk, high-return investment opportunities and channels. The formal banking sector became insufficient to meet the growing demand and banks turned to shadow banking channels, mainly securitization and collateral intermediation. Through securitization, banks fulfil corporations and the asset management industry's demand for safe and liquid assets to invest as well as large corporations' demand for liquidity management. Through securitization, banks can use securitized debt as collateral to boost repo funding. Collateral intermediation transfers illiquid assets such as mortgages into more fungible and liquid assets. An example is that dealer banks such as Lehman Brothers source collateral and hypothecate to other entities to obtain funding or support for other contracts. This process, however, increase the risks of pro-cyclicality and instability in the financial system.

Investors not only look for investment opportunities but also constantly look for higher-yielding assets—a search-for-yield effect. After the 2008–2009 global financial crisis, interest rates remain at a low level worldwide, while household and corporate savings are high, which makes the search-for-yield effect stronger. In emerging markets, the growth of pension funds and insurance companies has often come along with the growth of investment funds and other non-bank intermediaries (IMF 2014). In advanced economies, search-for-yield investment emerged around the mid-2000s and funds rapidly flow into hedge funds and private equity funds. In the euro area, investors facing low sovereign yields and ample liquidity in the financial market chase for higher returns with risky products (ECB 2006). Shadow banking prospers by supplying high-yielding products, especially when government bond yields are low (Jackson 2013; Caballero 2010; Goda and Lysandrou 2014).

6.2 Shadow Banking in China

6.2.1 Defining the Shadow Banking Sector in China

Taking into account China's specialities, the central bank considers the shadow banking sector as credit intermediation involving entities and activities that are outside the regular banking system but perform liquidity and credit transformation functions and could potentially be a source of systemic risk or regulatory arbitrage. In 2014, the State Council provided a more comprehensive definition that divides the shadow banking sector into three types of credit intermediaries: those without financial licenses and outside any regulatory regime, including innovative Internet financial companies and the third-party financial institutions; those without financial licenses and under insufficient regulations, such as financing guarantee companies and micro-credit companies; and those with financial licenses and under insufficient regulations, such as money market funds, asset securitization, and wealth management products (WMPs).

Shadow banking in China should be put into the context of its formal banking system that is dominated by a few large state-controlled banks under the guidance of the state. Shadow banks refer to non-bank financial institutions that participate in the shadow banking sector, including trust companies, brokerage firms, small lenders, and financial guarantors. Shadow banking activities also include formal banks' off balance sheet and informal bank lending that is motivated by regulatory arbitrage. Broadly speaking, shadow banking is a credit intermediary system that contains financial entities and businesses outside the traditional banking sector and shadow banking activities can be an independent credit activity carried out by shadow banks or a section of the credit chain that may involves formal regulated banks. This chapter employs this broad classification in the following analysis and discussion.

Due to insufficient disclosure requirements and variations in definition, assumptions, methodologies, and classifications of shadow banking activities, the estimate of the size of shadow banking in China by scholars varies significantly. As shown in Table 6.1, international scholars' estimates span from the lower end of RMB 4.6–12.5 trillion by Standard Chartered in 2013 accounting for 8% of GDP, to the higher end of more than RMB 60 trillion in 2016 by United Bank of Switzerland and Moody's, accounting for more than 80% of GDP. Domestic scholars' estimates are moderate between RMB 12.31 trillion in 2010 by Yan and Li (2014) to RMB 46 trillion in 2013 by a central bank report. The large variations in these estimates are largely due to differences in statistical methods, scopes, and the period.

According to the central bank's official Total Social Financing (TSF) statistics, non-bank credit, including entrusted and trust loans but excluding corporate bond and equity issuance, account for about

Table 6.1 Estimates of the size of shadow banking in China using different statistical methods and dimensions

Source	Estimated period	Size RMB trillion	Size USD trillion	% of GDP
International scholars and institutions				
Fung Global Institute	2012	22.5	3.6	43
	2013	30.1	4.8	53
	2014	32.2	5.2	51
Moody's	2012	29	4.65	55
	2013	37.7	6.2	66
	2014	45	7.3	71
	2015	53.4	8.2	79
	2016	64.5	9.3	87
United Bank of	20110630	10	1.5	24
Switzerland (UBS)	20121016	13.7–24.4	2.2–3.9	26–46
	2013	28.4–39.8	4.7–6.6	50–70
	2016	60–70	8.7–10.1	81–94
IMF	2012		2.5–3.3	30–40
	201403	19.9	3.3	35
JP Morgan	2012	36	5.8	69
	2013	46	7.5	81
Citi Research	2012	28	4.5	54
ANZ Bank	2012	15–17	2.4–2.7	29–33
Bank of America Merrill Lynch	201207	14.5	2.3	28
RBS	2012		4.7	57
Bangkok Bank	2012	36.4	6	70
Fitch ratings	2012	31.2	5	60
Standard & Poor's	2012	22.9	3.7	44.4
Deutsche Bank	201301	20	3.2	38
Standard Chartered	2013	4.6–12.5	0.7–2.1	8–22
Domestic scholars and institutions				
Guang Fa Securities	2012	30	4.8	57
HuaTai Securities	2012	25	4	48
Chinese Academy of	2012	20.5	3.3	40
Social Sciences (CASS)	2013	27	4.4	47
PBoC Report (Jin et al.	2012	35	4.7	67
2014)	2013	46.4	7.6	82
Yan and Li (2014)	2010	12.31	1.87	31
	2011	17.81	2.8	38
	2012	27.45	4.4	53
China International Capital corporation	2012	27	4.4	52

Source Various press release, regulatory authorities' websites, and research reports

11–25% of new financing flows over the period 2012–2016. According to the FSB report (2015a, b), as of the end of 2014, the estimated size of entrusted loans was around RMB 9.3 trillion (15% of GDP), assets managed by trust companies reached RMB 14 trillion (22% of GDP)—of which RMB 5.3 trillion (8% of GDP) was in the form of loans directly to non-financial firms—and as of the end of June 2014, the size of bank WMPs was RMB 12.7 trillion (around 22% of GDP and 10% of total banking deposits). The growth of a more recently emerged new form of intermediation—money market funds (MMFs)—as an alternative to bank WMPs almost tripled in 2014. As an alternative to trust company products, asset management services provided by securities and insurance companies emerged with estimated assets reached more than RMB 6 trillion as of the end of 2013 (11% of GDP). Despite extraordinary growth in the past few years, shadow banking remains substantially less important than formal banking in providing credit to the economy.

6.2.2 The Evolution and Driving Factors of Shadow Banking in China

In a constantly evolving financial system in China, shadow banking has developed rapidly after the crisis and a number of factors can be attributed to this development—some are similar to those driving the development of shadow banking globally and others are more specific to the Chinese context. This section looks into the drivers of shadow banking in China from the perspective of key market participants—financial intermediaries, investors, and borrowers.

Firstly, financial intermediaries take advantage of regulatory arbitrage opportunities, which push business away from the formal banking sector towards the shadow banking sector. Different from advanced economies such as the European Union and the United States where financial innovation and technologic advancement is one of the main drivers, shadow banking in China has arisen mainly to overcome tight regulations. Regulatory authorities keep making efforts to address emerging developments and associated risks, which however have catalyzed financial innovations and market adaptations to circumvent new regulations. Banks together with other financial intermediaries have created several innovative channels and products, such as WMPs, entrusted loans, loan-backed repurchase agreements with non-bank financial institutions, and other off-balance sheet activities. Banks also create products that have higher returns, which are not restricted by deposit reserve requirements and are not shown on their book to circumvent the regulatory supervision.

Although the authorities are well aware of the importance to liberalize the financial sector and have implemented a series of reforms to reduce state influences on the banking sector over the past three decades, Chinese banks still face tight regulation and government influences on lending decisions. Regulatory constraints include caps on bank lending volumes, conservative loan-to-deposit requirements (no more than 75%), reserve requirement, and an upper bound on the deposits rates, and the government also intervenes sectoral lending and new bank lending quota according to the overall economic status and loan growth. In 2008, the Chinese authorities released a RMB 4 trillion (USD $585 billion) stimulus package mainly via the banking sector (dominated by state-controlled banks), which boosted bank lending significantly with rising concerns over the quality of these new loans. The total credit to GDP ratio increased from 119% in 2008 to more than 140% in 2009. In response, the Chinese authorities significantly tightened credit controls, aiming at curbing overcapacity in certain sectors and reducing imbalances in the domestic economy.[5] On the other hand, most non-bank channels have lower capital and liquidity requirements and limits on loan or deposit rates and reserve requirement do not apply to non-bank institutions.

This renders non-bank channels some competitive advantages. Non-bank institutions and informal lending markets emerged to attract a larger share of savings by offering higher yields and investing in sectors

[5]The policy did keep the total credit to GDP ratio round 140% in the following two years, but since 2012, the total credit to GDP ratio has been growing much faster and reached 193% in 2015.

with strong demand for credit. This also creates regulatory arbitrage opportunities that encourage banks to engage in off-balance sheet shadow banking activities. It is argued that more than half to about two-thirds of shadow banking lending is effectively "bank loans in disguise" (Elliott et al. 2015; Sheng and Soon 2015). Formal banks are the key players of these transactions assuming most of the risks and taking corresponding rewards and the role of non-banks is to avoid regulatory constraints and costs. In 2013, the authorities tightened regulation on banks' off-balance sheet activities, and shadow banking activities started to move towards on-balance sheet interbank channels to circumvent regulations. As such, both banks and non-bank institutions take up the opportunities and shadow banking become flourishing.

Secondly, the strong growth of investor base and the search-for-yield effect fuelled the prosperity of shadow banking in China. Remarkable economic growth over the past three decades has significantly increased the wealthy population in China and as a result, the number of investors—both institutions and individuals—increased significantly. These investors look for new lucrative investment opportunities and search for high yield. While interest rates in the formal banking sector are not fully liberalized, the shadow banking sector is more flexible in setting interest rates. In such a dual track system with co-existence of policy rates and market rates within the financial system, investors are attracted by shadow banking channels and higher-yielding products. Individual deposits prefer investment tools such as WMPs, stocks, and other instruments, and corporate depositors have wider choices like the inter-bank market in additional to WMPs. These investment opportunities are more convenient and attractive over traditional bank deposits and funds flooded into the shadow banking sector.

Finally, borrowers' strong demand for credit is an impetus to the development of shadow banking that helps overcome market impediment. Rapid economic development requires continuous financing support. With an underdeveloped corporate bond market, the banking sector is the main funding source for most firms. Since 2012 the GDP growth and exports slowed down, many borrowers face cash flow problems and demand for more credit increased significantly (Yao 2015). In China, although private sector small and medium-sized enterprises

(SMEs) are more profitable and contribute to GDP growth increasingly more significantly, they have limited access to loans from the state-controlled formal banking sector. These firms are eager to obtain credit for development, but are overlooked by the formal banking sector. They largely rely on costly equity financing and have access to some small to medium-sized banks. The overall funding gap for private sector SMEs is substantial and they naturally turn to the shadow banking sector as alternative financing channels when such channels become available. These firms are willing to pay higher interest rates, providing shadow banks incentives to perform intermediation. On the other hand, some large firms with access to formal bank lending have incentives to turn to shadow banking channels because they may borrow at low rates due to cost savings from disintermediation. Moreover, other firms from certain industries (e.g., coal mining industry) or policy-sensitive industries (e.g., real estate sector with cumulated bubbles) are disfavoured by regulatory authorities and turn to the shadow banking sector where they may evade regulatory restrictions and borrow from banks.

6.2.3 Types of Shadow Banking in China

One way to classify the shadow banking system is by non-bank institutions' ultimate borrowers, which divide the sector into three parts (Pozsar 2010; Jin et al. 2014). The first part refers to entities that are most likely bank-dominated with resources to provide funding for the real economies and act as the middle part in the shadow banking chains. These entities siphon funds from channel intermediaries or capital pool (such as WMPs) to meet the financing demand of the real economies. These entities mainly conduct the following shadow banking business: entrusted loans, bankers' acceptances, interbank entrusted loan payments, trust loans, and financial leasing. The second part refers to entities providing the institutional service system for the market transactions to take place, mainly belonging to channel intermediaries and fund pools. These entities can trade directly in the market and connect to the market more closely. Their main activities involve banking WMPs, purchases of resale notes and beneficiary rights, private equity (PE) funds, non-loan trusts, and asset management for insurance and securities enterprises. The final part refers to entities that provide liquidity facilities using the derivatives and tools to mitigate credit risk and amplify transactional leverage, which is currently at the starting point in China.

Another way to classify the shadow banking system is by the regulation level, which divides the sector into three segments (Yan and Li 2014). Some financial institutions and their businesses are formally subject to three commissions' regulation and supervision, including banks' wealth management businesses, trust, fund and insurance, securities, and asset management business. Some other financial institutions are regulated by ministries, commissions, and local governments, including pawnshops, guarantee companies, financial leasing companies, private equity companies, and micro-loan companies. The final segment is unregulated credit intermediaries that engage in businesses such as private/informal lending, third-party wealth management, securitization, and repo.

According to the IMF approach (IMF 2014), the shadow banking system can be classified by the functions of financial intermediaries, which divide the sector into three types: commercial banks' off-balance sheet businesses (e.g., WMPs, entrusted loans, trust loans, undiscounted bankers' acceptancy), non-deposit financial institutions and products (e.g., trust companies, securitization), and informal finance (e.g., private/informal lending, pawnshops, microcredit companies, P2P online lending platforms).

6.2.4 Impact of Shadow Banking in China

At the macro level, shadow banking system affects the fiscal policies by alleviating financing constraints on local governments to support economic development. Under the dual taxation system, taxation income is shared between the central and local governments. The former wields more than half of total national fiscal income, which poses huge expenditure pressures on local governments that bear the majority of fiscal costs. Local governments have strong incentive to search or establish alternative financing channels and vehicles to solve the expenditure pressure and achieve fiscal freedom. Local governments aggressively raise debt via largely unregulated local governmental financing vehicles (LGFVs) to support local economic development. Subsequently, the central government tightened regulations to restrict bank lending to local governments (and their financing vehicles), while shadow banking channels enable them to bypass these restrictions. Consequently, some local governments have no sufficient fiscal income or resources to serve their debts, posing significant default risks. Shadow banking an also affect industrial policies that are implemented by governments in favour of specific industries in terms of entry standards, financing and investment mechanisms, preferential tax policies, and the like. Some policy-restricted sectors are able to circumvent the regulatory constraints and obtain finance through shadow banking channels and products, thereby realizing growth opportunities. The downside effect of shadow banking at the macro level is that investing massive funding in local governmental financing vehicles with insufficient sources for repayment or in industries with excessive capacity inevitably accumulates systemic risks detrimental to sustainable economic development.

Financial intermediation through non-bank channels can have significant impact on the development of the financial system (European Central Bank ; FSB 2015a; Pozsar 2010). Shadow banking, as an important supplement, has far-reaching influences on the financial system at all fronts—banking industry, capital markets, financial stability, and regulation. Shadow banking introduces competition to the financial sector and expects to improve efficiency of capital allocation. Shadow banking challenges the business model of the formal banking sector that has been dependent on interest margin as the main source of profits, which may influence the direction of future banking reform. Shadow banking as the intersection of financial intermediaries and different financial market creates a stimulus for capital market development by widening the channels and products (e.g., money market funds and other informal/network lending platforms).

The downside effect of shadow banking on the financial system is greater potential for financial instability. Shadow banking inherently operates at higher risks (market, credit, and maturity or liquidity risks) and poses systemic risk to the formal banking sector through their direct and indirect interconnections. Shadow banks' overreliance on the formal banking system for funding particularly makes the financial system fragile. As a node of financial markets, shadow banking can synchronize different markets and magnify financial risks. Furthermore, exploring regulatory arbitrage opportunities for profit, the shadow banking system may weaken the effectiveness of micro-prudential regulations, such as the Basel capital accords. These downside effects are not necessarily the consequence of shadow banking credit activities but the opacity of these activities (Sheng and Soon 2015). Under properly designed regulatory framework and effective prudential mechanisms to control potential risks, the healthy development of shadow banking as a supplement to the traditional financial system will contribute to economic development.

6.3 Main Products of Shadow Banking in China

The expansion of shadow banking in China stands out especially in trust loans, entrusted loans, undiscounted bankers' acceptance, and bank WMPs that together account for more than 50% of the shadow banking system (IMF 2014). The three core shadow banking products—entrusted loans, trust loans, and undiscounted bankers' acceptance—hold a large share in shadow banking by the broad definition (Moody's 2016). Trust companies are the main non-bank intermediation channels, while entrusted loans represent a unique form of intermediation in China. WMPs have been constantly increasing at a pace of nearly twofold per annum from RMB 2.9 trillion in 2012 to 21.6 trillion RMB in 2015 accounting for 16% and 40% of the shadow banking sector activities (by the board term definition) of the same year, respectively (Moody's 2016). WMPs are a key funding source for the non-bank sector. This section focuses on three core shadow banking products and bank WMPs, while briefly introducing other institutions and channels.

6.3.1 Trust Loans

Trust companies are legal entities that conduct custody and fiduciary obligations and tend to benefit from regulatory or tax arbitrage (Yao 2015), the second largest financial sector in China by total assets, next to the banking industry (Li 2014). Trust companies in China have a special financial operational license that allows them to participate in the businesses that the formal banking sector and financial markets cannot reach. They may engage in a variety of money market businesses, capital market businesses, and alternative investments such as lending, asset management, real estate investment, and private equity investment. Through these business channels, the trust companies can help other financial institutions (including commercial banks) to participate in the business areas that they usually are not permitted to run independently. For example, trust companies are able to offer loans to some restricted or risky sectors such as real estate. Acting only in trust for their principals, there would be less due diligence on trust lending compared with bank lending or capital market. Shadow banking lending in China is largely through trust companies.

The trust sector has experienced several dramatic booms and busts since the early 1990s and the years 2007 and 2014 witness two noticeable momentums. Before 2007, trust companies were called trust investment companies and concentrated on credit extension to the private sector. Under light local governments' regulation, the trust sector was one of main financing channels for long-term, high-risk real estate and infrastructure projects. After sudden deterioration in assets quality in the early 1990s, the sector faced tight regulations to address problematic assets by enhancing risk management. In 2007, the trust sector was restructured and consolidated with the number of trust companies dropping from about 2000 in the 1990s to 54. After the global financial crisis, the assets managed by trust companies increased tenfold and reached RMB 10.91 trillion as of the end of 2013.

In 2014, facing economic downturn and intensified competition, the trust sector stopped rapid growth and entered into a transitional stage with structural changes in main businesses, under the guidance from CBRC. During this transitional period, the trust sector has achieved initial success with increasingly rational business structure, strengthened non-discretionary business and investment function, enhanced management capability, and continuously matched supply and demand of funds. As shown in Fig. 6.2, the assets of the trust sector was RMB 1.22 trillion in 2008. Following rapid expansion at an average rate of more than 50%,

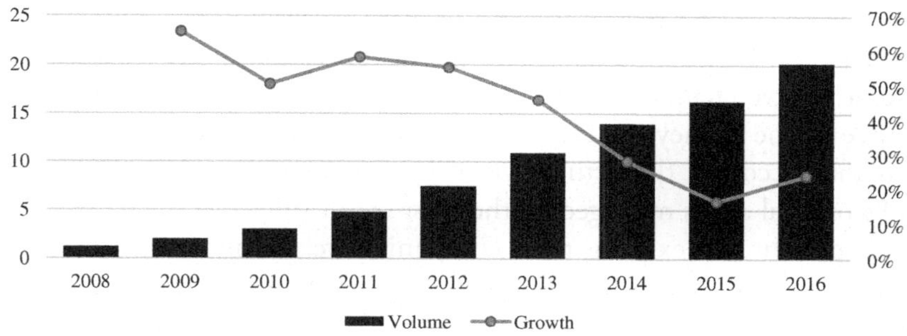

Fig. 6.2 Size and growth rate of trust asset over 2008–2016 (in RMB trillion and %). *Source* China Trustee Association

the trust asset increased 10 times to more than RMB 14 trillion in 2014, and since then the growth rate has slowed down to around 20% with total trust asset reaching more than RMB 20 trillion in 2016. By the end of 2016, trust funds were channelled mainly to industrial and commercial sectors, financial institutions, bond investments, the real estate sector, and fundamental industries such as manufacturing, energy, and transportation and construction. The share of loans in asset managed by the trust sector was 35% and the corresponding figure for securities held to maturity and securities ready for sale is 27% and 15%, respectively.

The trust sector and the banking sector cooperate closely and they are intertwined through ownership and business operations. It is common practice for banks to hold controlling shares in trust companies. In this bank-trust cooperation model, banks make loans to or investments in trust companies in exchange for their products as WMPs, and trust companies release high-yield loans to small or risky borrowers who normally have limited access to bank credits. This cooperation model enables formal banks to "outsource" part of lending business and remove these loans from their balance sheets, effectively avoiding regulatory requirements. In 2009 and 2010, bank-trust cooperation loans accounted for more than half of total assets managed by the trust sector. In 2010, to improve regulatory transparency, CBRC strengthened disclosure requirements relating to information and data of bank-trust cooperation products, which slowed down the growth rate of bank-trust cooperation products from 54.61% in 2010 to 27.18% in 2012, and further to 23.51% by the end of 2016, according to China Trustee Association. However, a new bank-trust cooperation mode emerged that uses a passive channel between banks and trust companies to make the source of the money appear from this channel instead of banks. Taking this into account, the actual size of bank-trust cooperation may reach 70% of total assets managed by the trust sector (Green et al. 2014).

At present, 68 existing trust companies are mainly owned by state-owned enterprises (SOEs), local governments, and banks, and these owners have strong incentives to protect their trust companies from bankruptcy. However, the trust sector's lending mainly focuses on policy restriction and risky segments of the economy. When economic growth slows down or policy changes, these assets are the first group to be affected as seen in several recent default cases from 2013. With poor capitalization, a small default rate may lead trust companies to fail (Cui et al. 2014), which may be contagious and affect the banking sector due to their close connection. It is important to understand and control risks associated with trust products thereby preventing potential systemic risks.

6.3.2 Bank Wealth Management Products (WMPs)

WMPs are investment vehicles comprising mainly of closed-end funds that are non-redeemable prior to maturity (Perry and Weltewitz 2015). WMPs can be issued by a variety of financial institutions, such as banks, securities and insurance firms, and trust companies (known as trust beneficiary rights). Since 2004, commercial banks started WMPs business as a means of competing with foreign banks and WMPs by banks account for a large portion of the shadow banking sector. In the post-crisis era, negative real deposit rates made alternative investments with higher returns like WMPs increasingly attractive. Banks issue WMPs targeting high net worth individuals, institutional investors, and private banking clients, while other financial institutions such as trust companies and securities and insurance firms can also become their clients (Li 2014).

WMPs are backed up by three main types of underlying assets: the securitized bank loans through a trust company, the securitized loans through another bank or shadow banking institutions, and new loans bought by banks from the corporate sector and repackaged into their products (Yao 2015). The packing process of WMPs can be very complicated involving more than one bank or other financial institutions using reverse repos. The final issuers of WMPs may only disclose the underlying assets as interbank assets that are in fact normal bank loans. Through repacking, bank loans with high risks are treated as low-risk interbank assets in the final step. The issue becomes even more complicated when many banks engage in a fund/asset pool to issue WMPs (Li 2014). Various money market instruments, such as interbank notes, bonds, credit assets, and other products, are pooled together and against this fund/asset pool, banks issue WMPs to raise funds from different customers. Sometimes, issuing banks may offer to buy back the WMPs from other banks to improve their liquidity. As this process give rise to a number of serious issues, such as liquidity problems, maturity mismatches, and insufficient information on risk features of the underlying assets, CBRC banned such businesses in 2013, leading to significant decline in transaction volume. According to CBRC, outstanding WMPs issued by banking institutions reached RMB 29.1 trillion, accounting for 39% of GDP at the year end of 2016. Under the tightened regulatory environment, the number of WMPs issued in 2016 slowed down. According to PY Standard's report (a research institute focusing on WMPs), as of the end of 2016, there were 452 commercial banks with issuance of 125,730 WMPs, increased by 11%—just a quarter of the corresponding figure of 44.01% in 2015.

WMPs are usually of short maturity as shown in Fig. 6.3. During 2006–2007, more than 60% of WMPs took more than 6 months to mature. After the crisis, with tightening regulation on shadow banking and WMPs (e.g., Circular on Further Reinforcing Issues Related to Risk Management of WM Business of Commercial Banks issued by CBRC), the maturity of WMPs became shorter. By 2016, about 80% of WMPs matured in 3–6 months and 49% of WMPs matured in 1–3 months.

As shown in Fig. 6.4, the market share of state-controlled banks and JSCBs in WMPs tends to decline, while that of CCBs increases. In 2016, city commercial banks had the largest share in the WMPs market at 37.5%, followed by joint-stock commercial banks at 22%, and

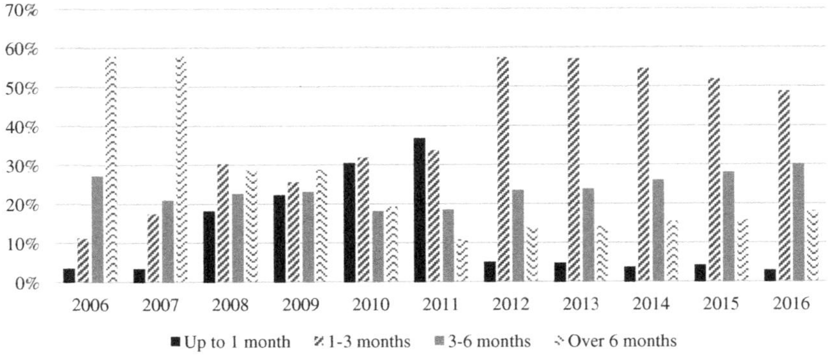

Fig. 6.3 Market shares of bank-issued WMPs with different maturity (in percentages). *Source* Data from Hwabao Securities (Hwabao Securities 2007–2017)

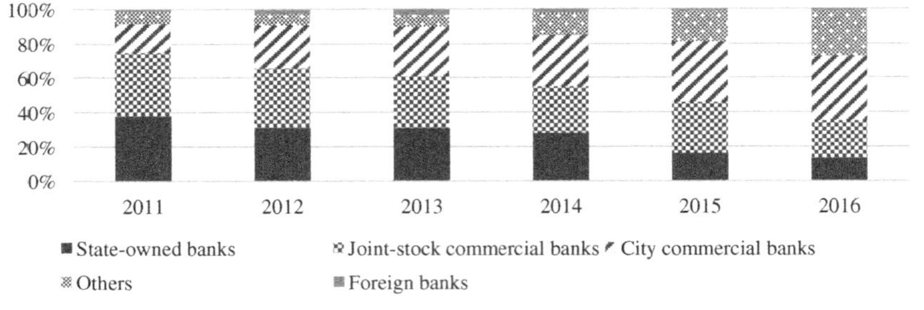

Fig. 6.4 Market shares of WMPs by the ownership of issuers. *Source* Data from Hwabao Securities 2012–2017

state-controlled banks at 13%, and the corresponding figures in 2011 were 17%, 37%, and 38%, respectively.

Bank-issued WMPs can be in the form of guaranteed principal or non-guaranteed and principle-guaranteed products can be further divided into fixed return or floating return. The share of bank-issued WMPs without guarantee on either the rate of return or principal increased dramatically after the crisis from less than 17% in 2006 to 64% in 2016. Overall, after the dramatic change during the crisis, the share of WMPs with different types of guarantees remains stable for the rest of sample period (as shown in Fig. 6.5).

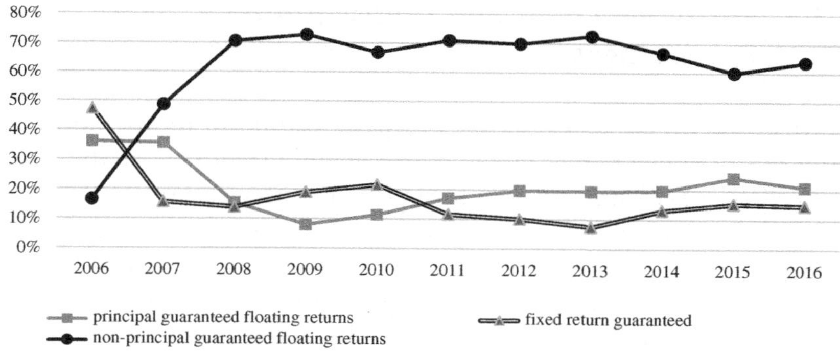

Fig. 6.5 Bank-issued WMPs by types of guarantees. *Source* Data from Hwabao Securities (Hwabao Securities 2017)

A large proportion of individual investors is unaware of the risks associated with WMPs and believes bank-issued WMPs (sold at banks' counters) as safe investment tools implicitly guaranteed by the government. Individual investors practically view WMPs as "quasi" bank fixed deposits and (wrongly) assume banks would bear all the risks of default. As investors significantly underestimate the underlying risks of WMPs, banks are able to cover losses from old WMPs by issuing new WMPs, cumulating unreported NPLs and credit losses (Yao 2015). As the underlying assets of interbank assets (e.g., WMPs), are not at as same level of scrutiny and monitoring as other on-balance sheet assets, interbank assets can help hide the potential credit risks of WMPs within the banking system. Banks' WMPs are kept on the liability side both on and off the balance sheet. The principal payment of those on-balance sheet WMPs are guaranteed with underlying assets—mostly deposits, treasury bonds, and interbank loan assets—while off-balance sheet WMPs are not guaranteed with underlying assets mainly coming from other financial institutions, such as trust companies and microcredit companies (He 2016). In theory, only off-balance sheet WMPs are shadow banking assets, since on-balance sheet WMPs are covered by NPL provisions. In practice, the lack of clarity and discipline of property rights is the key issue in the shadow banking system in China (Li 2014; Sheng and Soon 2015; Zhu and Conrad 2014). The credit risks should be clear to financial institutions or investors to avoid an endogenous "opaque box" of inherent risks.

6.3.3 Entrusted Loans and Undiscounted Bankers' Acceptances

Entrusted loans are loans between firms agreed on in terms and conditions with banks or finance companies mainly standing for the lender to facilitate payments and monitoring. Banks receive fees in return for their services and entrusted loans are off-balance sheet activities for banks. As only banks and trust companies are allowed to release loans to non-financial corporations, since 1996, non-financial firms and securities and insurance companies embarked on an entrusted loans business, which became a major interbank asset. Bigger firms normally have easy access to likely cheaper funding and can use entrusted loans to provide credit support for their subsidiaries or to lend to smaller partners or firms for profit. Certain sectors subject to strict regulations have high demand for entrusted loans, especially in recent years.

The banker's acceptance bill is another important tool for commercial banks to conduct shadow banking activities. Banker's acceptance is a short-term debt instrument issued and guaranteed by commercial banks. Issuing these types of off-balance sheet quasi-loans to target companies, banks can evade the loan to deposit ratio limit, raise fee income, and require firms to deposit a proportion of total amount of banker's acceptance as guarantee. The sum of entrusted loans and undiscounted banker's acceptance bills is an important indicator for interbank assets of shadow banking business.

The classification of these interbank assets as shadow banking assets is in line with the substance over form principle. These interbank assets are essentially loans between non-bank entities (governments, corporate, or individuals) or between commercial banks and non-bank entities, although these assets are traded between banks under repurchase agreements (repo) in interbank markets. Moreover, these interbank assets are frequently repackaged into WMPs by banks, brokers, and targeted asset management companies. According to the central bank statistics, the size of total social financing (stock) reached RMB 155.99 trillion in 2016 at a growth rate of 12.8%, of which entrusted loans (stock) amounted to RMB 13.2 trillion at a growth rate of 19.8% and undiscounted banker's acceptance bills reached RMB 3.9 trillion with a decreasing rate of 33.4%. In terms of annual flow, as shown in Table 6.2, the size of entrusted loans has been rising since 2007, while that of the undiscounted banker's acceptance bills starts to shrink since 2012.

6.3.4 Other Instruments and Institutions in the Shadow Banking Sector

Except for the aforementioned mainstream tools, there are other types of shadow banking activities in the informal financial sector. From 2008, micro-credit companies have been legalized and governmental authorities started to grant a license to such firms as part of financial deepening and finance inclusion reform. These companies mainly extend microcredit loans to micro- and small enterprises and SMEs and the size of micro-credit loans business expanded rapidly (PBoC 2014). Pawnshops, as a type of financial intermediaries, have a long history in China. They initially served individual residents borrowing

Table 6.2 Entrusted loans and undiscounted bankers' acceptances (billion RMB)

Year	Total Social Financing (TSF) flow	Entrusted loans	% of TSF	Undiscounted bankers' acceptances	% of TSF
2002	2011	18	1	−70	−4
2003	3411	60	2	201	6
2004	2863	312	11	−29	−1
2005	3001	196	7	2	0
2006	4270	270	6	150	4
2007	5966	337	6	670	11
2008	6980	426	6	106	2
2009	13910	678	5	461	3
2010	14019	875	6	2335	17
2011	12829	1296	10	1027	8
2012	15763	1284	8	1050	7
2013	17317	2547	15	776	5
2014	16413	2507	15	−129	−1
2015	15294	1591	10	−1057	−7
2016	17802	2185	12	−1953	11

Source The central bank

for immediate cash flow requests or social use, while now they mainly focus on supporting SMEs with largely self-financed loans. These small-sized shadow banking institutions may pose contagion risks locally or regionally because of poor loan quality and/or illegal deposit taking. To support the rising private economy, which has been largely overlooked by the formal banking sector, the informal lending market has prospered especially in Zhejiang, Guangdong, and Fujian provinces. There are four main practices in the private lending market, including mutual financing among individuals at low interest rates, credit lending at relatively higher interest rates between private enterprises, informal underground banking and illegal fundraising, and internal financing of enterprises.

New forms of intermediation with similar economic functions have also emerged. For example, as a substitute for bank WMPs, money market funds through Internet providers are available in the interbank market. Asset management services provided by securities and insurance companies have been growing since 2012 as an alternative to trust companies' products, largely due to the tightening regulations on trust products but relaxed regulations on securities firms from 2009 and insurance companies from 2012. With the development of information technologies, P2P lending via Internet credit platforms has grown rapidly since 2006. As a result of frequent occurrence of default events or fraud in the P2P market, regulatory measures have been taken to regulate P2P lending platforms in recent years, especially from 2016.

6.4 Risks and Regulatory Framework

6.4.1 Risks

Risks of the shadow banking system in advanced and emerging economies are different, depending on the systematic importance of the shadow banking sector in the nation's overall financial market. In particular, it depends on the size, type, complexity, and riskiness of shadow banking activities, degree of connection between shadow banking and the regulated banking sector, and the regulatory strengths and conditions.

The likelihood of systemic risk transmission is high in China. As discussed in the previous section, shadow banking activities are linked and intertwined with the formal banking system through a complicated system of interconnections. In China, the bank-dominated financial system makes these interconnections even stronger as banks play a significant role in both sectors. Commercial banks are the main parts in the shadow banking chain or the supporters providing explicit or implicit help for shadow banking vehicles to perform maturity or liquidity transformation. The close interconnections are likely to worsen the pro-cyclical building up of leverage and assets price bubbles. Moreover, even indirect linkages via common holdings of assets and derivative positions, banks can be exposed to common concentration risks in the financial markets. As such, the default of an institution in the shadow banking sector may have significant repercussions on the financial sector as a whole. For example, in 2014 a WMP—"Credit Equals Gold #1"—failed to repay upon maturity as a result of legal problems and the suspension of the underlying enterprise called Zhenfu Energy Group. The WMP was issued by the China Credit Trust Company and sold by the largest state-controlled bank—the Industrial and Commercial Bank of China (ICBC) from 2011. Although not the issuer, ICBC was under pressure from investors and potential damage to reputation and paid back the principals in full.

Institutional risk is higher in shadow banking channels compared with the traditional financial sector because market failures in shadow banking channels and products are harder to control (Schwarcz 2017). Performing similar functions as the formal banks and facing competition from formal banks, shadow banks adopt riskier business practices for maintaining market niches and earning higher returns. However, shadow banking channels have no access to public backstops in case of market failures and thus are more vulnerable to default risks and major difficulties. Defaults of individual WMPs and closures of trust companies are more likely to precede the systematic collapse (Perry and Weltewitz 2015).

The shadow banking sector may increase liquidity risks of the formal banking sector. The shadow banking system extract deposits from depositors in the traditional banks to WMPs. Although liquidity risk currently is manageable and under control, in some areas with growing private lending it may cause regional problems. Moreover, when any regulatory changes benefiting deposit-taking institutions in the formal sector occur, shadow banking channels may face liquidity squeezing given their high dependence on short term funding.

Finally, maturity mismatch is more serious in the shadow banking sector, posing risks and challenges in two particular ways. Shadow banking lenders lack access to interbank markets and liquidity-supporting instruments and tend to use shorter-term and more complex funding instruments to finance the long-term projects. For instance, WMPs are frequently used by banks and trust companies to gather short-term funds (usually with less than 6 months' maturity) and issue longer-term trust loans. On the other hand, borrowers in the shadow banking market lack alternative financing sources. When the regulatory authorities tighten the supervision on off-balance sheet activities of formal banks, it becomes harder for borrowers to roll over their loans, which may lead to serious interruptions in business operations and even cause bankruptcies especially for small and medium-sized borrowers.

6.4.2 Regulatory Framework

The FSB has proposed fundamental framework guidelines for the regulatory authorities worldwide to regulate shadow banking. Currently there are three regulatory models: the sector-based model, the integrated regulation model, and twin-peaks model, which are typically adopted in the United States, the United Kingdom and Australia, respectively. Proper prudential regulations are essential for the health development of the shadow banking sector. Currently, the regulatory framework in China is sector-based, and in principle, the approving bodies of shadow banking operations are responsible for regulating these operations. In practice, however, shadow banking institutions act as the intersection among several segments of the financial market and the cross-sector nature makes regulation much harder and less effective. Regulatory arbitrage undermines the effectiveness of macro-prudential regulation and increases the likelihood of systemic risk. In the short term, China needs to continuously improve the sector-based regulatory framework and enhance information transparency. In the long term, a more comprehensive integrated or twin-peaks model is needed. The current regulatory system for the shadow banking sector focuses on three aspects: the arrangement of supervision powers and clear provisions for responsibilities, guidelines on transparency rules governing shadow banking statistics and information policy, and regulations for specific institutions and products.

A variety of regulatory bodies oversees the shadow banking sector in China and the systemic risk-monitoring framework consists of two tiers.[6] The first tier comprises the State Council and the Financial Crisis Response Group. The State Council is the highest administrative office, responsible for organizing discussions at the ministerial level among the central bank and regulatory agencies through the inter-agency committee and coordination on the technical level. The central bank and other regulatory agencies report directly to the State Council. The Financial Crisis Response Group is an important inter-agency body of the first layers in charge of the financial sector as a whole. Members are representatives from the central bank, the State Administration of Foreign Exchange, the National Development and Reform Commission, the Ministry of Finance, CBRC, CIRC, and CSRC. The Financial Crisis Response Group organizes regular meetings to discuss systemic risks and make policy decisions on the shadow banking sector. The second tier consists of agencies responsible for risk monitoring and analysis within their respective sectors. The central bank is directly led by the State Council, responsible for formulating and implementing monetary policies, guarding against and eliminating financial risks, and maintaining financial stability. The central bank governs relevant regulatory bodies including CBRC for banking regulation and supervision, CSRC for regulating capital markets, and CIRC for insurance

[6]For example, seven regulatory bodies oversee guarantee enterprises, including the central bank, CBRC, National Development and Reform Commission, Ministry of Finance, Ministry of Commerce, Ministry of Industry and Information Technology, and State Administration for Industry and Commerce (Yan and Li 2014).

activities, respectively. This layer also has an inter-department coordinating agency—the Financial Regulatory Coordination Joint Ministerial Committee (JMC)—and members include the governor of the central bank as the chair of this committee, and the chairs of the CBRC, CSRC, CIRC, State Administration of Foreign Exchange, and, as necessary, the ministers of the National Development and Reform Commission and the Ministry of Finance. The aim of this coordinating body is to enhance regular inter-agency coordination and information sharing among relevant sector regulators, not to alter the configuration of decision-making functions of its member agencies. Relevant regulatory agencies cooperate closely and form an integrated supervisory system to deal with practical issues, while overseeing the shadow banking sector and the financial stability. For example, to assess the overall risks of the financial system, relevant agencies have established a financial stability report steering group to prepare the Financial Stability Report (FSB 2015b). The coordination among regulatory agencies facilitates more effective identification and communication of individual agencies' view toward different shadow banking vehicles.

To enhance the sectors-based regulatory framework and cooperation, in January 2014, the State Council issued the Circular No. 107 that sets out more detailed guidance on the institutional structure of shadow banking regulation in China. It is an entity-based approach to clarify and attribute regulatory responsibilities among different sector regulators with their assigned legal mandates (Huang 2015). Under this regulatory framework, shadow banking entities are clearly categorized and shadow banking activities are regulated separately by respective sector regulators. The central bank is the general regulator responsible for assessing the risks of the non-bank financial sector as a crucial part of overall financial stability. CBRC, CSRC, and CIRC are responsible for regulating and supervising shadow banking activities/products carried out by banks and trust companies, securities firms, and insurance companies, respectively. Local governments are in charge of regulating certain shadow banking entities (e.g., financing guarantee companies) under a uniformed set of rules promulgated by the relevant departments of the central government. However, given the highly innovative nature of shadow banking activities, some newly innovated shadow banking vehicles may not fall into any one sector regulator's scope but into multiple sector regulators' scope. While more research and regulatory efforts are underway to find solutions, the central bank, in collaboration with other relevant authorities, assumes the responsibility. For example, the central bank regulates shadow banking activities, such as cross-sector WMPs, securitization by non-financial institutions, Internet finance businesses, and other innovative shadow banking entities and products.

Authorities have also taken several measures to enhance data collection and risk assessment. To build up monitoring capabilities, the scope of data collection is extended with improved accuracy. While the Total Social Financing (TSF) indices issued by the central bank become an important indicator for the shadow banking activities, CBRC, along with CSRC and CIRC, collect data on WMPs in terms of duration, maturity, types of investments, remaining products, and nature of clients. The inter-regulator coordination had also facilitated data sharing by constructing an overall statistical framework for non-bank financial institutions.

Risk-management framework includes the identification, assessment, control, and monitoring of risk and it is an important part of the regulatory system for maintaining financial stability. At present, the risk assessment of the shadow banking sector is conducted on a sectoral basis by relevant regulatory agencies. A great deal of granular data is collected for assessing risks from the non-financial and non-bank sectors, which is mainly for widely used risk monitoring and factual reports rather than for system-wide analytical exercises. To improve risk management, the central bank has launched the Financial Stability Bureau responsible for systemic risk analysis. The central bank has also constructed a systemic risk index that capture risks in five areas—macroeconomic condition and markets, banking, securities, insurance, and quasi-financial institutions—for which responsibilities are organized according to individual agency's mandate. While institutional framework has taken shape, further improvement in risk monitoring and assessment system should enlarge its coverage of other non-bank financial intermediation and provide more comprehensive account of the whole shadow banking sector.

Over the past decade, regulatory authorities have taken a number of prompt policy measures and regulatory actions in respond to rapidly developing and innovative shadow banking activities. Table 6.3

Table 6.3 Regulations on shadow banking (2005–2016)

No.	*Time*	*Tittle and Information*
1	20050924	(a): 银监会:《商业银行个人理财业务管理暂行办法》 (银监会令(2005)2号)CBRC: Interim Measures Concerning Managing Personal Financial Management Services of Commercial Banks (No. (2005)2 of the CBRC); (b) 《商业银行个人理财业务风险管理指引》 (银监发(2005) 63号). The Guidelines for Risk Management of Commercial Banks' Wealth Management Business for Individuals (No. (2005)63 of the CBRC)
2	20051107	银监会:《金融机构信贷资产证券化试点监督管理办法》(银监会令(2005)3号). CBRC: The Measures for Supervising and Administrating the Pilot ABS by Financial Institutions (No. (2005)3 of the CBRC)
3	20070512	银监会:《关于调整商业银行代客境外理财业务境外投资范围的通知》(银监发(2007) 114号). CBPC: Circular on Revising the Scope of Overseas Investment for Overseas WM Services on Behalf of Customers of Commercial Banks (No. (2007)114 of the CBRC)
4	20080508	中国人民银行和银监会:关于小额贷款公司试点的指导意见 银监发 (2008) 23号. PBOC and CBRC: jointly issued the Guidelines on Pilots of Small Loan Companies (No. (2008)23 of CBRC)
5	20080824	中国人民银行:关于村镇银行、贷款公司、农村资金互助社、小额贷款公司有关政策的通知 (银发(2008)137号). PBOC: issued the Circular on Relevant Policies of Village and Town Banks, Loan Companies, Rural Credit Unions, and Small Loan Companies (No. (2008)137 of PBOC)
6	200905	证监会:《证券公司企业资产证券化业务试点指引 (试行)》. CSRC: issued the Guidance on Enterprise Asset Securitization Business Pilot of Securities Firm (Trial Implementation).
7	20090706	银监会:《关于进一步规范商业银行个人理财业务投资管理有关的问题的通知》 (银监发(2009)65号). CBRC: Circular on Further Standardizing Issues Related to Individual WM Business and Investment Management of Commercial Banks (No. (2009) 65 of the CBRC)
8	2006–2010	银监会:信托公司管理办法修订和信托公司集合资金信托计划管理办法. CBRC: Measures for the Management of Trust Companies and Measures for the Management of the Collective Trust Schemes of Trust Companies ("the two new regulations") were revised
9	20100812	银监会:关于规范银信理财合作业务有关事项的通知 银监发(2010)72号. CBRC: Notice on Regulating Relevant Matters concerning the Wealth Management Cooperation between Banks and Trust Companies (No. (2010) 72 of CBRC)

(continued)

Table 6.3 (continued)

No.	*Time*	*Tittle and Information*
10	20100824	银监会:《信托公司净资本管理办法》(银监会令(2010)第五号). CBRC: the Administrative Measures on Net Capital of Trust Companies (No.5 of Order of CBRC)
11	20110120	关于进一步规范银信理财合作业务的通知 (银监发 (2011) 7号). CBRC: Notice on Further Regulating the Wealth Management Cooperation between Banks and Trust Companies (No. (2011) 7 of the CBRC)
12	20110127	银监会:《信托工资净资本计算标准有关事项的通知》(银监发 (2011)11号). CBRC: the supporting Circular on Issues Concerning Promulgation of the Criteria on Computation of Net Capital of Trust Companies No.(2011) 11 of CBRC)
13	20110223	人力资源保障部、银监会、证监会和保监会联合发布:《企业年金基金管理办法》. MOHRSS, CBRC, CSRC and CIRC: Revised Measures for the Management of Enterprise Annuity Funds
14	20110826	中国人民银行:下调金融机构人民币贷款和存款基准利. PBoC: Notice to broaden the base for calculating banks' required reserve ratios by including banks' margin deposits.
15	20110828	银监会:商业银行理财产品销售管理办法 (银监会令 (2011) 5号). CBRC: Administrative Measures on Sales of Wealth Management Products by Commercial Banks (Order No. (2011) 5 of China Banking Regulatory Commission)
16	20120926	证监会:基金管理公司特定客户资产管理业务试点办法 (证监会令 (2012) 83号). CSRC: promulgated the Trial Measures for Fund Management Companies to Provide Asset Management Services for Specific Clients (No. (2011) 83 of CSRC)
17	20110930	银监会:关于进一步加强商业银行理财业务风险管理有关问题的通知 (银监发 (2011) 91号). Circular on Further Reinforcing Issues Related to Risk Management of WM Business of Commercial Banks (No. (2011)91 of the CBRC)
18	20120221	银监会:关于信托公司票据信托业务等有关事项的通知 (银监办发 (2012) 70号). Notice on Bill Trusts and Other Related Issues by Trust Companies (No. (2012) 70 of the CBRC)
19	201210	证监会: (a) 证券公司客户资产管理业务管理办法. CSRC: the Measures for the Administration of the on Client Asset Management Business of Securities Firms; (b) 证券公司集合资产管理业务实施细则. Detailed Rules for the Implementation of the Collective Asset Management Business of Securities Firms; (c) 证券公司定向资产管理业务实施细则. Detailed Implementation Rules for Client-Specific Asset Management Business of Securities Firms

(continued)

Table 6.3 (continued)

No.	*Time*	*Tittle and Information*
20	20121029	证监会:证券投资基金管理公司子公司管理暂行规定 (证监会公告〔2012〕32号). CSRC: promulgated the Tentative Provisions for the Administration of the Subsidiaries of Securities Investment Fund Management Companies. (No. (2012)32 of the CSRC)
21	20121228	第十届全国人民代表大会常务委员会:证券投资基金法修订通过. The standing committee of the people's congress: The Law on Securities Investment Funds issued at the end of 2012 first brought private funds into China's regulatory framework.
22	20130325	银监会: 《关于规范商业银行理财业务投资运作有关问题的通知文号》(银监发(2013)8号). CBRC: Notice of the China Banking Regulatory Commission on Relevant Issues Concerning Regulating the Investment Operation of Wealth Management Business of Commercial Banks (No. (2013)8 of the CBRC)
23	20130719	中国证券业协会: 发布《关于规范证券公司与银行合作开展定向资产管理业务有关事项的通知》. Securities Association of China (SAC): officially issued the Notice on Matters Relevant to Regulating Cooperation between Securities Firms and Banks in Engaging in Client-Specific Asset Management Business.
24	20130218	证监会:《资产管理机构开展公募证券投资基金管理业务暂行规定》(证监会公告〔2013〕10号). CSRC: the Interim Provisions on the Management of Publicly Offered Securities Investment Funds by Asset Management Institutions (Announcement No. (2013) 10 of the CSRC)
25	20130315	证监会:《证券公司资产证券化业务管理规定》(证监会公告(2013)16号). CSRC: issued the Regulations on Management of Asset Securitization Business of Securities Firms (No. (2013) 16 of the CSRC)
26	20130308	银监会:《关于2013年商业银行理财业务监管工作的意见》(银监办发(2013)70号). CBRC: Guiding opinions of regulatory supervision on Wealth management business of commercial banks of 2013 (No. (2013) 70 of the CBRC)
27	201401	国务院: 关于加强影子银行监管有关问题的通知 (国办发(2013) 107号). State Council: Notice of the State Council on Further Reinforcing the Regulation of Shadow Banking (No. (2013)107 of the State Council)

(continued)

Table 6.3 (continued)

No.	*Time*	*Tittle and Information*
28	20140126	人民银行: 关于商业银行理财产品进入银行间债券市场有关事项的通知(银市场(2014)1号). PBOC: Notice of the Financial Market Department of the People's Bank of China on Issues concerning the Entry of Wealth Management Products of Commercial Banks into the Interbank Bond Market (No.(2014)1 of Market department in PBoC)
29	20140212	中国证券业协会:关于进一步规范证券公司资产管理业务有关事项的补充通知(中证协发〔2014〕33号). The Securities Association of China: Supplementary Notice on Matters Related to Further Standardizing Corporate Asset Management Business of Securities Companies (No. (2014) 33 of the SAC)
30	20140219	银监会:关于2014年银行理财业务监管工作的指导意见(银监办发(2014)39号). CBRC: Guiding opinions of regulatory supervision on Wealth management business of commercial banks (2014) (No. (2014) 39 of the CBRC)
31	20140408	银监会:关于信托公司风险监管的指导意见 (银监办发(2014) 99号). CBRC: Guiding Opinions of the General Office of the China Banking Regulatory Commission on the Risk Supervision of Trust Companies (No. (2014) 99 of the General Office of the CBRC)
32	20140424	中国人民银行,中国银行业监督管理委员会,中国证券监督管理委员会,中国保险监督管理委员会,国家外汇管理局:关于规范金融机构同业业务的通知 (银发(2014)127号). PBoC, CBRC, CSRC, CIRC, State Administration of Foreign Exchange: Notice on Regulating the Interbank Business of Financial Institutions (No. (2014) 127 of PBOC)
33	20140505	保监会:关于保险资金投资集合资金信托计划有关事项的通知 保监发〔2014〕38号. CIRC: Notice on Matters concerning the Investments in Collective Fund Trust Plans with Insurance Funds (No. 38 (2014) of the CIRC)
34	20140508	银监会办公厅:关于规范商业银行同业业务治理的通知 (银监办发(2014)140号). the General Office of CBRC: Notice on regulating interbank businesses of commercial banks (No. (2014) 140 of the general office of CBRC)
35	20140714	银监会: 关于完善银行业务组织管理体系有关事项的通知 银监发 2014(35)号. CBRC: Notification on issues about improving organizational management system of businesses in commercial banks (No. (2014) 35 of CBRC)

(continued)

Table 6.3 (continued)

No.	*Time*	*Tittle and Information*
36	20140722	中国人民银行上海分行:关于加强银行业金融机构人民币同业银行结算账户管理的通知(上海银发(2014)183号). PBoC Shanghai Branch: Notice on Strengthening the Administration of RMB Interbank Settlement Accounts of Banking Financial Institutions (No. (2014)183 of the Shanghai Branch of the PBoC)
37	20140810	国务院:《关于加快发展现代保险服务业的若干意见》国发(2014)29号. State Council: Several Opinions on Accelerating the Development of the Modern Insurance Service Industry (No. (2014) 29 of the State Council)
38	20140912	中国银监会办公厅、财政部办公厅、人民银行办公厅: 关于加强商业银行存款偏离度管理有关事项的通知(银监办发(2014)236号). the General Office of CBRC, the General Office of the Ministry of Finance and the General Office of PBoC: Matters concerning Strengthening the Administration of Deposit Deviation Degree of Commercial Banks (No. (2014) 236 of the General Office of the CBRC).
39	20141017	保监会: 关于试行《保险资产风险五级分类指引》的通知. CIRC: Notice on Trial Implementation of guidelines to five levels of classification for risks of Insurance assets
40	20141121	中国人民银行关于下调金融机构人民币贷款及存款基准利率并进一步推进利率市场化改革的通知 (银发(2014)348号). PBoC: Notice on Lowering the RMB Benchmark Loan and Deposit Interest Rates for Financial Institutions and Further Promoting the Interest Rate Liberation Reform (No. (2014) 348 of the People's Bank of China)
41	20141204	保监会:印发《保险集团并表监管指引》的通知 (保监发〔2014〕96号). CIRC: Notice on Guidance of Consolidated Supervision on Insurance groups No. (2014) 96 of the CIRC
42	20141210	银监会,财政部:信托业保障基金管理办法 (银监发 (2014) 50号). CBRC and the Ministry of Finance: Administrative measures of the Trust funds. (No. (2014) 50 of CBRC)
43	20141212	保监会:关于保险资金投资创业投资基金有关事项的通知 (保监发〔2014〕101号). CIRC: Notice on Matters concerning the Investment of Insurance Funds in Venture Capital Funds (No. (2014) 101 of the CIRC)
44	20141227	中国人民银行: 关于存款口径调整后存款准备金政策和利率管理政策有关事项的通知 (银发(2014)387号), PBoC: Notice on Matters concerning the Deposit Reserve Policy and Interest Rate Management Policy after the Adjustments of Deposit Indicators (No. (2014) 387 of the People's Bank of China)

(continued)

Table 6.3 (continued)

No.	*Time*	*Tittle and Information*
45	20150217	国务院: 宣布存款保险制度将于5月1日正式实施 (国务院令第660号), State Council: The Deposit Insurance Regulation, as adopted at the 67th executive meeting of the State Council on October 29, 2014, is hereby issued, and shall come into force on May 1, 2015. Order (No. (2015) 660 of the State Council)
46	20150225	银监会办公厅:关于做好信托业保障基金筹集和管理等有关具体事项的通知 (银监办发(2015)32号), CBRC: Notice of the CBRC General Office on Specific Issues Concerning Properly Dealing with the Raising and Management of Trust Guarantee Fund (No. (2015) 32 of General Office of the CBRC)
47	20150410	保监会:关于印发《保险工资资金运用信息披露准则第2号:风险责任人》的通知 (保监发〔2015〕42号), CIRC: Notice on Issuing the Standards for the Disclosure of Capital Use Information by Insurance Companies No. 2: the Persons Responsible for the Risks (No. 42 (2015) of the CIRC)
48	20150410	银监会: 下发《信托公司条例(征求意见稿)》, CBRC: Issue Consultation Paper of Trust Company regulations (Drafting for comments)
49	20150605	银监会:下发《信托公司行政许可事项实施办法》(银监会令(2015)5号), CBRC: The Measures for the Implementation of Administrative Licensing Matters Concerning Trust companies (No. (2015) 5 of Order of the CBRC)
50	20150709	保监会:《关于保险资产管理产品参与融资融券债券收益权业务有关的问题的通知》(保监资金〔2015〕114号), CIRC: Notice on Issues concerning the Participation of Insurance Asset Management Products in the Business of Right to Yields on Claims of Margin Trading and Short Selling (No. (2015) 114 of the CIRC)
51	20151023	中国人民银行: 决定从2015.10.24起,对商业银行和农村合作金融机构等不再设置存款利率浮动上限,并抓紧完善利率的市场化形成和调控机制, PBoC: From 24th October 2015, abolish floating limits on interest rates on deposits and improve interest rate liberalization and regulatory mechanism.
52	20151203	保监会:关于加强保险公司资产配置审慎性监管有关事项的通知 (保监资金〔2015〕219号), CIRC: Notice on Matters concerning Strengthening the Prudential Supervision of Insurance Companies' Assets Allocation (No. (2015) 219 of the CIRC)

(continued)

Table 6.3 (continued)

No.	*Time*	*Tittle and Information*
53	20151216	中国信托业协会:《信托公司行业评级指引(试行)》正式发布, China Trustee Association: Issuance of guidelines for rating in the industry for trust companies
54	20151229	中国人民银行:提出将对商业银行的考核升级为宏观审慎评估体系(MPA), PBOC: Improve the assessment framework on commercial banks into Macro Prudential Assessment
55	20160318	银监会办公厅:《关于进一步加强信托公司风险监管工作的意见》(银监办发(2016)58号), General Office of CBRC: Further Reinforcing Issues Related to Risk Supervision of Trust companies (No. (2016) 58 of General Office of CBRC)
56	20160415	中国基金业协会:关于发布《私募投资基金募集行为管理办法》的通知, Notice of the Asset Management Association of China on Issuing the Measures for the Administration of the Fundraising of Privately Offered Investment Funds
57	20160428	银监会办公厅:《关于规范银行业金融机构信贷资产收益权转让业务的通知》(银监办发(2016)82号), General office of CBRC: Notice on regulating transferring transactions of Right to Yields on Credit Assets in Banking Financial Institutions (No. 28 (2016) CBRC)
58	20160504	保监会:《保险公司资金运用信息披露准则第4号:大额未上市股权和大额不动产投资》(保监发〔2016〕36号), CIRC: the Standards for the Disclosure of Capital Use Information by Insurance Companies No. 4: Large-amount unlisted shares and real estate investment (No. (2016) 36 of the CIRC)
59	20160616	证监会:修订并公布《证券公司风险控制指标计算标准规定》(证监会公告(2016)10号), CSRC: Provisions on the Calculation Basis for Risk Control Indicators of Securities Companies (No. (2016) 10 of CSRC)
60	20160622	保监会:《关于加强组合类保险资产管理产品业务监管的通知》(保监资金〔2016〕104号), CIRC: the Notice on Stepping up the Business Administration of Portfolio Insurance Assets Management Products (No. 104 (2016) of CIRC)
61	20160706	银监会:《商业银行理财业务监督管理办法(征求意见稿)》公开征求意见, CBRC: The Measures for Supervising and Administrating Wealth Management Business in Commercial banks (Drafting for comments)
62	20160829	银行业理财登记托管中心有限公司正式成立, Banking Wealth Management Registration trusteeship limited company was established

(continued)

Table 6.3 (continued)

No.	*Time*	*Tittle and Information*
63	20160927	银监会:《银行业金融机构全面风险管理指引》的通知 (银监发(2016)44号), CBRC: Issuing the Guidelines on the Integrated Risk Management of Banking Financial Institutions (No. (2016) 44 of CBRC)
64	20161123	银监会:《商业银行表外业务风险管理指引(修订征求意见稿)》, CBRC: Notice on Issuing the Guidelines for the Management of Off-Balance-Sheet Business Risks of Commercial Banks (Revised drafting for comments)
65	20161219	人民银行:表外理财业务正式纳入广义信贷考核, PBoC: Off-balance sheet Wealth Management Businesses are officially include in MPA

Note PBoC: People's Bank of China (the central bank); CBRC: China Banking Regulatory Commission; CSRC: China Securities Regulatory Commission; CIRC: China Insurance Regulatory Commission

Wsummarizes regulations on shadow banking from 2005 to 2016. The sectoral-based regulatory framework may induce sectoral arbitrage, calling for a more comprehensive and integrated regulatory framework with effective inter-agency coordination to keep up with the changing shadow banking sector. Such a framework should combine a macro-prudential framework for the measurement and management of systemic risks with micro-prudential mechanisms for shadow banks, which requires higher level of coordination across financial authorities and governmental agencies. Short-term regulations on the shadow banking system should focus on information disclosure mechanisms to reduce information asymmetry, mechanisms for controlling contagion effect between the formal banking sector and shadow banks, early warning and responding mechanisms to proactively address potential risks and crises, effective liquidity regulations, and building up a risk culture to enhance investors' risk awareness (Yan and Li 2014; FSB 2015b). In the long run, the regulatory framework on the shadow banking system should promote financial development and financial innovations to better support the real economy, as well as properly balance between regulatory supervision and the development of the financial sector. Cooperative supervision and a data-sharing system under a unified statistical framework are the key toward a highly developed macro-prudential framework and micro-prudential regulatory mechanisms in the future (Yan and Li 2014; He 2016).

6.5 Conclusion

Despite rapid development in the past decade, the shadow banking sector in China is still at an initial stage in terms of disintermediation and the adoption of innovative instruments such as securitization and derivatives. The overall complexity and riskiness of shadow banks is lower than those of advanced economies. The size of the Chinese shadow banking sector is small relative to GDP compared with that of developed countries, but the growth rate of the shadow banking sector is faster.

As a double-edged sword, shadow banking in China has promoted financial deepening and economic development by providing alternative financing channels and innovative products. It also poses systemic risk to the financial system and even challenges macroeconomic stability due to its close interconnections with the formal banking sector. Having experienced rapid and somewhat bumpy expansion, the main challenge for future development is how to shape the shadow banking sector as a healthy supplement to the financial system. It requires an integrated and comprehensive macro-prudential regulatory framework and effective micro-prudential mechanisms to control and mitigate various risks, which ensures the shadow banking sector positively contributing to economic development.

References

Acharya, V.V., Khandwala, H., and Sabri Öncü, T. 2013. The Growth of a Shadow Banking System in Emerging Markets: Evidence from India. *Journal of International Money and Finance* 39, 207–230.

Adrian, T., and Ashcraft, A.B. 2016. Shadow Banking: A Review of the Literature. In *Banking Crises* 282–315. UK: Palgrave Macmillan.

BBVA Research. 2016. Financial Regulation Outlook.

Bernanke, B.S., C.S. Lown, and B.M. Friedman. 1991. The Credit Crunch. *Brookings Papers on Economic Activity* 1991 (2): 205–247.

Boz, E., and Mendoza, E. 2010. Financial Innovation, The Discovery of Risk, and the U.S. Credit Crisis. (IMF Working Papers 10/164), International Monetary Fund. Available from: https://www.imf.org/external/pubs/ft/wp/2010/wp10164.pdf. Accessed 30 Mar 2017.

Caballero, R.J. 2010. *The "other" Imbalance and the Financial Crisis* (No. w15636). National Bureau of Economic Research.

Claessens, S., M.A. Kose, and M.E. Terrones. 2012. How Do Business and Financial Cycles Interact? *Journal of International Economics* 87 (1): 178–190.

Claessens, S., Pozsar, Z., Ratnovski, L., and Singh, M. 2013. 4.3 Shadow Banking: Economics and Policy Priorities. *Post-Crisis Banking Regulation*, 135.

Claessens, S., and Ratnovski, L. 2014. What is Shadow Banking? (IMF Working Paper WP/14/25), IMF.

Cui, D., Gao, B., Kapurand, A.S., Wu, W., Tian, T., and Tai, K. 2014. *The Coming Trust Defaults*. Bank of America Merrill Lynch.

Deloitte. 2012. *2012 China Banking Industry Top Ten Trends and Outlook: Enhancing Capital Management, Meeting New Challenges*. Deloitte China Financial Services Industry Center of Excellence Report.

Duca, John V. 1992. U.S. Business Credit Sources, Demand Deposits, and the Missing Money. *Journal of Banking and Finance* 16 (3): 567–83.

Duca, J.V. 2016. How Capital Regulation and Other Factors Drive the Role of Shadow Banking in Funding Short-term Business Credit. *Journal of Banking & Finance* 69: S10–S24.

Elliott, D., Kroeber, A., and Qiao, Y. 2015. Shadow Banking in China: A Primer. Research paper, The Brookings Institution.

European Central Bank (ECB). 2006. *Financial Stability Review*. Frankfurt: European Central Bank.

FSB. 2011–2014, 2015a, 2016. *Global Shadow Banking Monitoring Report*. Financial Stability Board.

FSB. 2015b. *Peer Review of China*. Financial Stability Board.

Ghosh, S., I. Gonzalez del Mazo, and İ. Ötker-Robe. 2012. Chasing the Shadows: How Significant is Shadow Banking in Emerging Markets? *World Bank-Economic Premise* 88: 1–7.

Goda, Thomas, and Photis Lysandrou. 2014. The Contribution of Wealth Concentration to the Subprime Crisis: A Quantitative Estimation. *Cambridge Journal of Economics* 38 (2): 301–327.

Gorton, G., and A. Metrick. 2010. Regulating the Shadow Banking System. *Brookings Papers on Economic Activity* 2010 (2): 261–297.

Green, S., Li, W., and Shen, Lan. 2014. Your Map of the Expanding Credit Universe. Standard Chartered Global Research.

He, D. 2016. *Financial Security in China: Situation Analysis and System Design*. Singapore: Springer.

Huang, R.H. 2015. The Regulation of Shadow Banking in China: International and Comparative Perspectives. *Banking & Finance Law Review* 30 (3): 481.

Hwabao Securities. 2007–2017. *The Annual Report of Financial Products in China*.

IMF. 2014. *Global Financial Stability Report moving from liquidity- to growth-driven markets*. International Monetary Fund. Available from: http://www.imf.org/external/pubs/FT/GFSR/2014/01/pdf/text.pdf. Accessed 25 Mar 2017.

IMF. 2008. *Global Financial Stability Report.*

Jackson, P., 2013. Shadow Banking and New Lending Channels–Past and Future. In *SUERF 50th Anniversary Volume Chapters*, 377–414.

Jin, L., Liu, C., and Zhou, Y. 2014. The Banking System in the Shadow of Sun: To Measure the Scale and the Risk of the Shadow Banking System in China. In *China International Conference in Finance.*

Kanatas, George, and Stuart I. Greenbaum. 1982. Bank Reserve Requirements and Monetary Aggregates. *Journal of Banking & Finance* 6 (4): 507–520.

Kodres, L.E. 2013. What is Shadow Banking? *Finance & Development* 50 (2).

Li, T. 2014. Shadow Banking in China: Expanding Scale, Evolving Structure. *Journal of Financial Economic Policy* 6 (3): 198–211.

Massoudi, A., and M. MacKenzie. 2013. In Search of a Fast Buck. *Financial Times* 20: 11.

McCulley, P. 2007. *Teton Reflections. Global Central Bank Focus Series*, PIMCO, August/ September.

Mehrling, P., Pozsar, Z., Sweeney, J., and Neilson, D.H. 2013. *Bagehot was a Shadow Banker: Shadow Banking, Central Banking, and the Future of Global Finance.* Available from: https://papers.ssrn.com/sol3/papers.cfm?abstract_id=2232016).

Moody's. 2016. *Quarterly China Shadow Banking Monitoring Report.* Moody's Investor Service.

PBoC (People's Bank of China). 2014. *China Financial Stability Report 2014.*

Perry, E., and Weltewitz, F. 2015. Wealth Management Products in China. *RBA Bulletin*: 59–68.

Pozsar, Z., Adrian, T., Ashcraft, A., and Boesky, H. 2010. *Federal Reserve Bank of New York Staff Reports Shadow Banking.*

Ricks, M. 2010. Shadow Banking and Financial Regulation. Columbia Law and Economics Working Paper No. 370.

Roubini, N. 2009. Mother of All Carry Trades Faces an Inevitable Bust. *Financial Times.*

Schwarcz, S.L., 2017. Shadow Banking and Regulation in China and Other Developing Countries (November 16, 2016). *Working Paper*, Duke Law School Public Law & Legal Theory Series 2017–2018.

Sheng, A., and Soon, N.C. 2015. Bringing Shadow Banking into the Light: Opportunity for Financial Reform in China. Fung Global Institute Asian Perspectives Global Issues (FGI report).

Turner, A. 2012. Securitization, Shadow Banking and the Value of Financial Innovation. In *The Rostov Lecture on International Affairs, SAIS, Johns Hopkins University*, April, 19.

Udell, G.F., and Berger, A.N. 1994. Did Risk-Based Capital Allocate Bank Credit and Cause a Credit Crunch in the U.S.? *Journal of Money, Credit and Banking* 26 (3): 585–628.

Yan, Q., and Li, J. 2014. *Research of China Shadow Banking Supervision*. China Renmin University Press.

Yao, W. 2015. Shadow Banking with Chinese Characteristics. In *Shadow Banking in China: An Opportunity for Financial Reform*, eds. A. Sheng and N.C. Soon, 83–132. Wiley, Chichester, UK.

Zhu, N., and Conrad, J. 2014. The People's Republic of China Knowledge Work on Shadow Banking—Trust Funds and Wealth Management Products. Consultant's Report for Asian Development Bank. Available from: http://www.adb.org/sites/default/files/project-document/80950/shadow-banking-trust-funds-and-wmps-prc.pdf. Accessed 21 Apr 2017.

7
Internet Finance in China

Preamble

[*Acknowledgement: the authors of this chapter are Chunxia Jiang, Shujie Yao, and Chunan Hu; Chunan Hu is PhD candidate of University of Nottingham China Campus, Ningbo, China*] In the past decade, the financial services industry has changed significantly, especially after the 2008 global financial crisis. The emergence of FinTech has been enabled by a "perfect storm" of rising customer expectations for services, increased access to VC funding, reduced barriers to entry, and accelerated technological advancements (Capgemini 2017). The dramatic rise of FinTech opens up a revolutionary means of financing and global FinTech investment continues to grow; it reached $15 billion by mid-August 2016 (BI Intelligence 2016). More than 80% of global financial services companies consider their business at risk and plan to increase FinTech partnerships with tech companies to avoid losing revenue to innovators (PWC 2017). As mainstream financial institutions adopt new business models and emerging technologies, FinTech and the financial industry become more integrated. The influence of FinTech on the markets is growing with significant long-term potential.

In China, the industry, termed Internet finance, grows at a galloping pace. According to an index developed by Peking University, the industry

C. Jiang and S. Yao, *Chinese Banking Reform*, The Nottingham China Policy Institute Series, DOI 10.1007/978-3-319-63925-3_7

grew almost four times over the year to December 2015 and the market size reached USD $1.8 trillion (RMB 12.4 trillion). This chapter starts by introducing the definition of Internet finance in Sect. 7.1. Section 7.2 explores the forces shaping the Internet finance sector and Sect. 7.3 describes major practices of Internet finance in China. Section 7.4 discusses the theoretical framework, challenges and regulation, and Sect. 7.5 concludes.

7.1 Definition and Status Quo

Despite rapid worldwide expansion, there has been no widely accepted definition for Internet finance from the industry or academia. Generally speaking, Internet finance is a new type of financial business mode that combines the functions of financing, payment, and information processing via Internet and mobile communications technologies, covering all forms of financial transactions and organizations. The Financial Stability Report of China (2014) considers Internet finance, in a broad sense, as financial services provided by Internet companies through a non-financial institution platform and Internet services provided by financial institutions, and in a more narrow sense, as financial services provided by Internet companies based on Internet technologies. "The Guiding Opinions on Promoting the Healthy Development of Internet Finance" issued by the People's Bank of China in 2015 (hereinafter the "Guiding Opinions 2015") defines Internet finance as a new form of financial services (such as financing, payment, investment, and intermediary services) provided through online channels by financial institutions and Internet enterprises using Internet technologies and information and communication technologies rather than through traditional financial institutions such as banks. Xie et al. (2016) suggest that the concept of Internet finance covers all financial activities and institutional structures under the influence of Internet including both exchanges totally following Walrasian equilibrium (without the presence of financial intermediaries and markets) and traditional financial intermediaries and markets such as commercial banks, securities firms, insurance companies, and stock exchanges.

The rapid development of Internet finance in China has several characteristics. Financial services through Internet channels are largely promoted by technological advancement, including the adoption of mega data, cloud computing, social media, and search engines, which facilitate gathering information about customer behavior and credit investigation. Internet helps the two parties—surplus units and deficit units—to find each other directly and strike a deal online to fulfil their needs for investing and financing. Internet finance efficiently allocates financial resources using direct transactions in a simplified transaction environment at low costs. The third-party payment institutions have become increasingly important in supporting Internet finance activities. However, the core function of financial system in allocating financial resources to serve the real economy remains unchanged in Internet finance (Xie et al. 2016). Internet finance has significant implication on risk-taking, financial stability, and externalities in the real economy.

Since its emergence in the 1990s, Internet finance in China has gone through three main stages. The first stage is the online banking period during 1990–2003 when banks started to offer online banking services as supplement to services provided at branches. Internet finance was dominated by large traditional financial institutions such as banks. The pace of development was slow for two reasons. The first reason is the requirement for large-scale investment in infrastructure (i.e., hardware and system) for conducting financial activities via Internet. The second reason is that the financial sector was undergoing major reforms—the commercialization reform in the mid-1990s and the modernization reform from the early twenty-first century.

The second stage began in 2004 when online peer to peer (P2P) lending platforms and the third-party payment platforms emerged. During this stage, the integration of Internet and finance moved up from a technological support level to a financial business model level. AliPay was launched in 2004, followed by CreditEase in the following year. A milestone event was that the announcement by the country's central bank—People's Bank of China—to issue payment licenses in 2011. Since then, the third-party payment services—one of the representative forms of Internet finance—have been under regulators' oversight. The main achievement is to lay down (regulatory and technological) foundations for the future development of Internet finance.

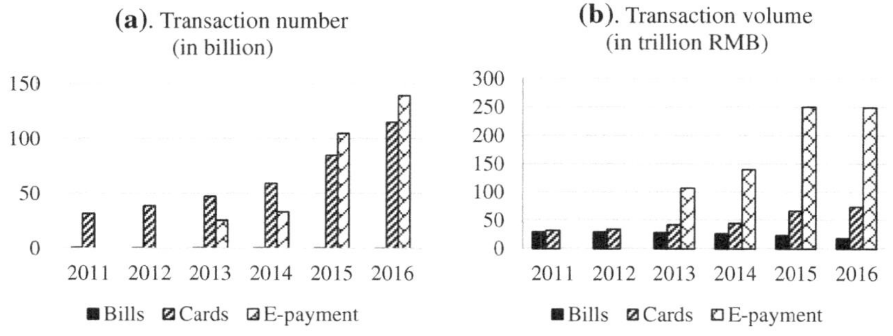

Fig. 7.1 Transaction number and volume by non-cash payment channels (2011–2016). *Source* People's Bank of China (2011–2016)

The third stage started in 2012 with rapid growth of financial activities online and explosive development in the Internet finance industry. The year 2013 is regarded as "Year One" of the Internet finance era with a bunch of landmark events, including the launch of the first licensed Internet insurance companies Zhong An Online, an online sales platform for money market funds; Yu'ebao by Alibaba's Ant Financial Services; and WeChatPay, which facilitates money transfer between the users of a mobile messaging app, WeChat, and payments with offline participating retailers. Meanwhile, banks and securities companies also overhauled their business model and built online platforms. These developments have opened a new era of Internet finance in China under a unique mode (Financial Stability Report, 2014).

Figure 7.1a depicts the total number of transactions by three main non-cash payment channels, namely bills, cards, and E-payment. The number of various bill transactions is very low, that of card transactions increase steadily. Since ePayment emerged in 2013, the number of transactions soars rapidly, surpassing that of card transactions in 2015. As shown in Fig. 7.1b, the transaction volume of bills is stable with a slightly decreasing trend, while that of cards increases steadily. The transaction volume of ePayment takes the leading position since its emergence in 2013 with a sharp rising trend up to 2015 but no further expansion in 2016. Figures 7.1a and 7.1b clearly mark the new phase of the payment industry that shifts from traditional cash and bill payment channels to card and electronic payment channels.

As of the end of 2015, the overall market size of Internet finance reached RMB 12–15 trillion, accounting for nearly 20% of GDP in that year. The number of users reached more than half a billion—ranked the top of the world (McKinsey 2016). Third-party payments and online lending are the two most widely used Internet finance services. The third-party payments was dominated by two key players, AliPay and WeChatPay, with more than 270 million and 200 million active users respectively and the transaction volume was more than RMB 10 trillion, surpassing the global Internet finance leaders (the United States and the European Union). Online lending includes P2P lending platforms and online micro credit. By the end of 2015, the volume of P2P lending reached RMB 875 billion (iResearch 2016). CreditEase, launched in 2006, is one of the first P2P firms in the world. Its spinoff, Yirendai, was listed on the New York Stock Exchange at the end of 2015 and now is the largest P2P firm in the world. CreditEase gradually develops and provides full financial services from inclusive finance to wealth management products and services. All in all, after the rapid expansion in the past decade, currently, the most significant segments of Internet finance in China are network banking, third-party payment, and P2P lending. The rapid development of Internet finance has significant impacts on many areas in China not limited to the traditional financial sector.

7.2 The Development of Internet Finance

7.2.1 The Forces Driving the Development of Internet Finance

Internet finance in China has experienced explosive expansion, thanks to a number of internal and external factors, such as government endorsement, open and friendly regulatory environment, the advancement of information and Internet technologies, and the distorted and inefficient financial system.

The financial authorities exert a strong pushing force on the development of Internet finance in China. Government endorsement provides the Internet finance industry an open and supportive environment and encourages the integration of Internet technology in the financial sector. Government officials and relevant authorities, such as the central bank—the People's Bank of China—explicitly expressed positive attitude towards the development of Internet finance by high-tech companies. The Chinese Premier Li Keqiang highlighted the role of Internet finance in the Report on the Work of the Government (2015) by stating that "Internet-based finance has swiftly increased to prominence ... to encourage the healthy development of Internet finance." During Davos World Economic Forum in 2015, Premier Li further expressed government's support for start-ups and technology innovations. The initiative of establishing an inclusive financial system by the central bank greatly stimulated the development of Internet finance. The government embracement induces regulators to take a light and friendly regulatory approach to Internet finance in contrast to the highly regulated traditional financial sector. For instance, major non-financial Internet firms and social media platforms, such as Alibaba and Tecent, are encouraged and granted licenses to offer financial services.

The Internet technology advancement in big data, social networks, search engines, and cloud computing offers a new way with extraordinary potential to conduct financial activities, not only merely providing technical support but also a playing field for financial innovations. Over the past decades, the Internet has had strong influences on many industries ranging from telecommunication, journalism, publishing to retail, television, film, and education sectors. Among others, the financial sector is one of the most affected industries, as Xie and Zou (2013) argued that the numerical nature of financial products and financial activities make their movement easily depicted on the Internet as a movement of a series of continuous figures. Moreover, the digitalization of information provides convenient and low-cost access to information, facilitating the conduct of Internet finance business. Currently, nearly 70% of societal information has been digitized and digitized information will be the mainstream channel in providing information in the future induced by increasingly popular sensing devices and technologies (McKinsey Global Institute 2011). The digitalization is transforming the way that customers access financial products and services. Furthermore, the application of big data information technology and

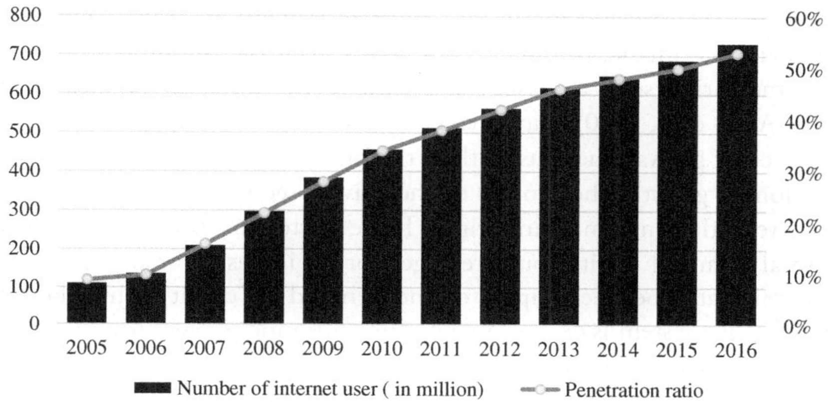

Fig. 7.2 Internet users and Internet penetration in China. *Data sources* National Bureau of Statistics, China Internet Network Information Center

advanced risk-management techniques to financial products and transactions mitigates the asymmetric information problem and lowers transaction cost, as well as greatly promotes Internet finance. More importantly, with improvement in Internet infrastructure and policy supports, China now has the world's largest online population with more than 700 million Internet users. Internet has become an integrated part of modern lifestyle with strong influences in virtually every aspect. Figure 7.2 shows the number and penetration rate of Internet users. As of June 2016, the number of Internet users was 710 million, and the Internet penetration rate increased steadily by 12 percentage points over four years from about 40% in 2012 to 52% in 2016. Mobile phone has become the most important device for Internet access with 656 million mobile Internet users, accounting for 92.5% of all the Internet users in 2016 (CNNIC 2016).

The distorted and inefficient Chinese financial system creates opportunities for Internet finance. China's financial system is dominated by the banking sector, which, in turn, is dominated by a few large state-owned commercial banks. Due to historical government protection and regulatory constraints, formal finance from the banking sector has favored the state sector with massive resources converging to the central government and state-owned industries. A large segment of small- and medium-sized private enterprises and rural residents are usually not qualified and are unable to obtain bank loans from the traditional financial intermediaries, such as banks, and turn to the informal finance channels. Allen et al. (2005) find evidence that despite the fact that the private sector grows much faster than the others and provides most of the economy's growth, the growth of the private sector is largely supported by alternative informal financing. Those customers overlooked by the formal financial institutions are eager for an inclusive financial system. The mismatch between supply of and demand for credit within the formal finance system is exacerbated by the economic restructuring to adapt to the "new normal" economy after the global financial crisis in 2008–2009. Conversely, the traditional financial markets offer institutional and individual investors limited investment opportunities due to a combination of various factors, such as interest rate ceilings on deposits, poor performance of the stock markets, the risky housing market with cumulated bubbles as well as restrictive policy on property purchases, and congested equity financing through the initial public offerings (IPOs) under the current management system. There is an increasing demand for lucrative investment opportunities from investors including private households owing to income growth. In short, the traditional formal financial system becomes partially dysfunctional in effectively channeling funds from investors to sectors demanding capital for development. Internet finance came into play to fulfill the gap and non-conventional financial institutions thrive by establishing their own network/platforms for selling financial products.

The prevalence and success of Internet finance in China is not simply driven by technological advancement, but largely driven by the demand for a brand-new financial business model to fill in the gap that traditional financial institutions fail to serve. The key successful factor of Internet finance in China is the integration of finance, customers' need, and Internet technology. The Internet finance business model is embraced by key participating parties. Internet companies, represented by two well-developed e-commerce businesses of Alibaba and Jingdong, take advantage of the success in the firms' main business segments and extend their business spectrum into the financial sector via Internet finance. This move is not only passively motivated by the need for better serving Internet companies' main businesses but also motivated by the long-term high profitability from guaranteed interest rate spreads in the banking industry. The traditional financial institutions, on the other hand, have also proactively expanded their online business and major large banks now offer online financial products similar to Yu'E Bao, as well as e-commerce services. Some banks even developed P2P online lending platforms and crowdfunding platforms. Internet finance essentially concentrates on the process of financial disintermediation and presents a brand-new business model that effectively satisfies the credit demands of individuals and small and medium-sized enterprises (SMEs).

7.2.2 An Overview of Internet Finance Activities

Internet finance activities evolve rapidly in response to various forces, such as demand condition, regulatory environment, cybersecurity issues, and increasingly blurring boundaries between different financial activities. In addition, financial innovations induce new forms of Internet finance activities, contributing to the rapid expansion and complexity of the Internet finance market. Participants of Internet finance include Internet companies, investment companies, commercial banks, and other financial institutions. There are different ways to classify different types of Internet finance activities. Based on the mode of business conduct, Internet finance can be classified into financing activities (e.g., P2P lending, crowdfunding, and e-commerce micro credit loans), financial services activities (e.g., third-party payment, mobile payment, and mobile wealth management terminal), and traditional financial activities via online platforms by financial institutions (e.g., Internet banking, Internet securities, and Internet insurance) (Rui and Liu 2014). By the functions of financial activities, Internet finance activities can be classified into two broad types: activities based on intermediation function (e.g., online banking services, crowdfunding, e-commerce micro-credit loans, P2P lending) and activities based on services functions (e.g., Internet banks, Internet securities, Internet insurance, Internet wealth management, third-party payment, and other online investment consulting companies) (National Bureau of Statistics, 2015). In

Table 7.1 The forms of Internet finance based on business mode

	Forms	Typical institutions
Financial services	Third-party payment	Alipay, Tenpay, 99 Bills, YeePay
	Third-party consulting platform	WDZJ, Hexun, P2PEye
	Vertical search platform	Rong360, Haodai, Andaike
	Online financial supermarket	91FinSupermarket, service platform for FinTech by Beijing Software and information services exchange
Financing	e-commerce micro credit loans	Ali Microcredit, JD Microcredit, Suning Microcredit
	P2P lending	Lufax, Renrendai, PPdai, YRD
	Crowdfunding	Demohour, Dreamore, Tmeng, Angel Crunch
Online platform	Traditional services	Major financial institutions, new online banks, mobile banks, telebanks, online securities, online insurance
	Innovative services	Online-only and direct banks, such as MyBank, Suning Bank, and direct banks of Minsheng Bank and Bank of Beijing; network insurance companies, such as Zhong'an online property insurance; network funds such as Yu'e Bao, funds market of Tencent, online Taobao stores selling funds, and wealth management platform of Baidu, Inc.
	Financial e-commerce	Banking business including self-built platforms (Shanrong service of China Construction Bank) and cooperation platforms (WeChat bank of China Merchants Bank; securities business, including self-built platforms (online stores of Guotai Junan Securities) and cooperation platforms(online store of Founder Securities on Tmall; insurance including self-built platforms of large insurance enterprises and cooperation platforms of small- and medium-sized insurance firms such as Taobao Insurance.

Source National Bureau of Statistics of China, 2015

terms of three core pillars of Internet finance, activities can be classified into those offering payment systems (e.g., third-party payment), those gathering and processing information (e.g., big-data finance) and those allocating resources (e.g., P2P lending and crowdfunding) (Xie and Zou 2013; Zhou 2014). For regulatory purposes, the "Guiding Opinions 2015" issued by the People's Bank of China in 2015 divides Internet finance into the following different types: Internet payment business, online lending (P2P lending and online microfinance), Internet trust and Internet consumer finance, equity crowd-funding, online fund sales, and Internet insurance business. Table 7.1 summarizes the forms of Internet finance based on business mode with illustrative examples of institutions, which shows a variety of existing and new institutions engaging in different Internet finance activities.

7.3 Major Practices in Internet Finance

The previous section illustrates different types of Internet finance in terms of business mode, financial function, core pillar, and regulatory division. In this section, we take an alternative approach to grouping major practices of Internet finance into three categories, namely the internetization of traditional finance, the emergence of innovative Internet financial institutions, and Internet financial infrastructure. We use typical examples of each category to illustrate basic information and operation condition of Internet finance practices. In particular, the banking sector is taken as the example to illustrate the internetization of traditional financial activities, covering internetization of traditional banking services, network banks, and financial e-commerce; Internet financing channels of P2P network lending and crowdfunding are used to discuss the emerging Internet financial institutions; and mobile and third-party payments are examples to present the development of Internet financial infrastructure.

7.3.1 The Internetization of Traditional Finance

In the process of the internetization of traditional financial activities, innovative inter-industry expansion takes the lead. On the one hand, traditional financial institutions cooperate with Internet companies and launch the e-commerce and financial service platforms to support retail sales and fund transfer and financing activities for better serving their clients. The Internet banking sector, also known as network banking, incudes the Shanrong e-commerce platform of China Construction Bank (CCB), the e-Mall of Bank of Communications (BOCOM), the online mall of China Merchants Bank, and the online banking arm of Huaxia Bank for wholesale customers (Stability Report, 2014). In the Internet insurance sector in November 2013, Taikang Life Insurance, the fourth largest life insurer in China, signed a deal with Taobao to sell insurance policies to Taobao's online sellers. Taikang Online is the first network insurance company launched and operated by conventional insurance institution. This move marks the beginning of the integration of financial enterprises and Internet companies in exploring the online insurance market. As to security institutions, 18 out of 23 listed securities companies have already started online securities trading. For example, Haitong Securities Company cooperates with 91JingRong to improve its network securities platform, e Haitongcai (Boao Review Internet Finance Research Institute BRIFI 2016). Different from the traditional business activities for which the main profit source is margins between purchase and sale prices of the goods and services, e-commerce and financial service platforms help to diversify traditional financial institutions' profit sources into payment and settlement, financing for firms and consumers, credit card installment, guarantee, and other services. On the other hand, Internet enterprises launched professional online financial institutions that have no physical outlets and conduct all business online. Alibaba, Tencent, C-Trip, PingAn, and another five companies established the Zhong An online Property Insurance that only conducts Internet-related business and sells insurance products on its own website and third-party e-commerce platforms. Zhong An, in partnership with Ping An, launched the first O2O cooperative auto insurance, Bao Biao auto insurance, on 6 November 2015. The internetization in the traditional fund industry is typically represented by Yu'E Bao by Alibaba. With gradual interest rate liberalization and operational integration, vertical search engines (e.g., 91Jingrong and Rong360) were established, leading to significant reductions in costs of searching information across a wide range of financial products and sales channels. Moreover, Internet currency, an innovative Internet financial product supported by the Blockchain technology, has great potential for future development.

The Internet banking sector is the mainstay of Internet finance. Online banking, mobile banking, and telephone banking of conventional banking services are early forms of Internet banking and widely adopted by commercial banks. Direct banks, network banks, and e-malls are three new types of Internet banking (Boao Review Internet Finance Research Institute 2016). Direct banks include the division of traditional banks (e.g., Direct bank of China Minsheng Bank and Orange Bank of PingAn Bank) and online-only banks with independent licenses. Bank of Beijing opened the first direct bank in 2013, while Baixin Bank is the first online-only direct bank with independent legal qualification under cooperation between Baidu Inc. and China CITIC Bank Corp. Direct banks appeared in the late 1980s and become popular in the United States and Europe. According to Analysys (2016), as of the end of 2015, there were 57 direct banks, of which more than 80% are owned joint-stock and city commercial banks. More than 60% offer wealth investment products and deposit products, and more than 80% offer monetary fund management. Twenty-one percent of direct banks act as a new platform for Internet investment and financing services. No doubt, the mushrooming direct banking sector has a great potential and is an important channel for traditional banks to extend their service boundaries into Internet finance. For the success of direct banking, innovation, customer-centric, and efficiency are the three imperatives (Deloitte 2015). A direct bank is more than just online banking. The key difference is that online banking serves existing customers, while direct banking reaches out for new customers, mostly young people who are proficient at Internet and related technologies. The appearance of direct banking is a result of market competition, while their rapid development further intensifies the completion. The business model of direct banking is innovatively different from the traditional one by offering standardized products and services to a specific customer segment while realizing cost advantages. Direct banking operates under a flatter organizational structure with a substantially leaned process compared to the traditional approach and avoids the conventional top-down operation

Table 7.2 Five online-only wholly private-funded banks in China (July 2016)

Name	Founder
Webank	Tencent: holding 30% of shares, Baiyeyuan (20%), Liye (20%) and seven other shareholders (30%)
Wenzhou Minshang Bank	Chint Electric (29%), Zhejiang Huafon Spandex (20%) and 11 other enterprises
Kincheng Bank of Tianjin	Huabei 20 percent, Maigou (18%), and 14 other enterprises
Mybank	Ant Financial Group (30%), Shanghai Fosun Hi-tech Group (25%), Universal Agriculture Group (18%), Jinrun Capital (16%) and two other shareholders (11%)
Shanghai HuaRui Bank	JuneYao (30%), Metersbonwe (15%) and 10 other shareholders (55%)

Source Individual banks' websites

approach, thereby achieving a high level of operation and process efficiency. Direct banks are customer-centric and have response mechanisms to rapidly changing customer needs. Products are designed to meet customer needs and processes are designed to fit the product requirements.

Online-only banks operate their business through Internet, which is separated from the traditional institutions. In 2014, China sped up financial liberalization and launched a pilot project to establish five entirely privately owned online-only banks aiming at improving credit availability to small businesses. Tencent, one of the top Internet companies in China, launched the first private online-only bank, WeBank, in Jan 2015, promising "lower costs for and delivering practical benefits to small clients, while forcing traditional financial institutions to accelerate reforms." Subsequently, Wenzhou Minshang Bank, Kincheng Bank of Tianjin, Mybank, and Shanghai Huarui Bank were launched. Table 7.2 shows the founders and their share in the five private online-only banks.

Online-only banking is growing. Webank's report shows that since micro-lending products and Webank App launched in May 2015, its integrated service system focused on inclusive financial products and now have more than 6 million clients with a nonperforming loan (NPL) ratio around 0.3%. In March 2016, Mybank's total credit value reached RMB 45 billion serving more than 800,000 SMEs that are mostly small merchants on Alibaba's e-commerce platform. Ninety-eight percent are short-term micro-loans of less than RMB 50,000 with a typical repayment cycle within three months. The number of micro-loans granted by MyBank is about 40,000–50,000 daily and the NPL ratio is around 1.67%, which is lower than that of the traditional banks by 0.67 percentage points (BRIFI 2016). One of the online-only banks' key competences is low costs, which drives traditional banks to invest more in their online and mobile banking. However, cost advantage of online-only banks comes at the price of not having physical branches. According to Accenture Survey (2014, 2016), 87% of consumers will use branches with human interaction in the future and only 39% of consumers in the 18–34 age group would consider a bank with no physical branches. Thus, online-only banks are a supplement to but not a substitute for the traditional banking system.

The main players in network banking include commercial banks' online branches for online banking and new entrances of online-only banks. Online branches are an extension of traditional business to supplement functions of the physical branches of commercial banks (Nath et al. 2001). An example is U-BANK8, which is a network bank of China Merchants Bank offering financial support for SMEs. According to iResearch (2014, 2015), online banking is an oligopolistic market, dominated by ICBC, ABC, BOC, and CCB, which collectively accounted for 77% of the market shares of the personal online banking services in 2013. The transaction volume of online banking increased four times in five years from RMB 326 trillion in 2009 to RMB 1304 trillion in 2014, with the highest growth rate of 40% in 2014. As a result of competition from the rapid development of related industries such as mobile and third-party payment, the growth rate of online banking slowed down after 2014.

e-malls include online e-commerce platforms and e-malls for credit cards that are either owned and operated by commercial banks, are independent legal entities, or are cooperative operations between commercial banks and Internet companies. According to iResearch (2015), self-owned e-commerce platforms include Shanrong Business (善融商务) of CCB, Jiaobohui (交博汇) of Bank of Communications, E-Shangguanjia (E商管家) of Agricultural Bank of China, and Rong-e-Gou (融e购)

of Industrial and Commercial Bank of China. e-malls for credit cards include e-mall of China Merchant Bank, Minsheng Mall, Card Mall of PingAn Bank, and Ecitic Mall of China CITIC Bank. Seven main e-commerce platforms/malls for credit cards of the Chinese commercial banks steadily increased from 2012 to 2014 in terms of coverage of Users. Self-owned e-commerce platforms such as Shanrong Business of CCB, developed rapidly with more than one million users per month, while the user coverage of e-malls for credit cards (e.g., Card Mall of PingAn Bank (PAB)) is much lower.

There are four types of e-commerce banking, namely self-owned e-commerce platforms, e-malls for credit cards, cooperative platforms between commercial banks and Internet companies (e.g., WeChat Bank of China Merchant bank), and e-commerce platforms with independent legal qualification (e.g., Minsheng e-commerce). The first two types of e-commerce platforms are the mainstream e-commerce banking platforms, which started earlier than the latter two.

7.3.2 The Emergence of Innovative Internet Financial Institutions

P2P network lending, crowdfunding, and Internet consumer finance are three main types among innovative emerging Internet financial institutions. This section focuses on the first two as the Internet consumer finance sector in China is still at its nascent stage. As a supplement of traditional financial institutions, P2P lending platforms directly match borrowers and lenders to satisfy micro business and individuals' needs for financing and investing. For borrowers, the large amount of financing need can be divided into small portions and thus receive funding from a large group of lenders; while for lenders, the diversified loan portfolio helps them to reduce individual risks. Internet-based technologies help mitigate information asymmetry problems and lower transaction costs during the whole process. As such, online P2P lending platforms enable borrowers to benefit from reliable and convenient low-cost financing and lenders have higher returns than the bank deposits. The main functions of P2P lending platforms are information provision, evaluation, and other related necessary services to facilitate financing transactions. In practice, P2P lending platforms provide a wide range of services that include, but are not limited to releasing credit demand information, credit investigation, investment consulting, recovery of overdue loans, and other value-added services. The main source of profit is service fees rather than the interest margin between the borrowing and lending rates.

The launch of PPdai in 2007 marked the beginning of Internet P2P lending platforms in China. The time-consuming, lengthy, and rigid procedures of normal bank loans opened great opportunities for the subsequent explosive growth of P2P lending, making China the largest and the most dynamic P2P lending market in the world. P2P lending platforms offer simplified procedures, more transparency, quick decisions, and better interest rates. According to authority's report, as of the end of November 2015 there were 2612 P2P platforms running normally, brokering more than 400 billion yuan (USD 61.7 billion) of loans in total (www.gov.cn). The geographical distribution of P2P lending platforms mirrors the development level of Internet finance that provinces ranked top five are Guangdong, Beijing, Shandong, Zhejiang, and Shanghai (P2Peye 2015). The top 10 P2P platforms in 2015 in terms of transaction volume were Honling Capital, Lufax, PPmoney, Xinhehui, Weidai, Eloancn, Lianjia, Jinxin99, Niwodai, and Touna, according to Mingin data from Haitong Securities (2015).

P2P network lending in China has a number of unique characteristics (Xie et al. 2016; BRIFI 2016). First, the information disclosure system is not adequate for the needs of credit assessment and many promotional activities are offline, making the protection for financial consumers increasingly important. Second, Chinse investors prefer fixed payment schemes and P2P lending platforms always allocate a certain proportion of the revenue to the pool as the principal of investors. Third, some platforms that adopt the "professional lenders and debt transaction" model tend to actively matching borrowers and investors, which may easily lead to capital pool. In brief, the mode of P2P online lending in China is more similar to private loans on the Internet platform with excessive development causing risk events (BRIFI 2016). Consequently, P2P business is of relatively high risk.

With rapid expansion but lack of appropriate regulations and poor risk management, the associated risks (i.e., incredible acts of fraud and misuse of lenders' fund) escalated quickly, leading to hundreds of platforms collapsing, growing financial risks, and even potential social unrest. According to the China Banking Regulatory Commission (CBRC), as of the end of June 2016, there were 1778 troubled P2P platforms, accounting for 43.1% of the total.

Crowdfunding is a new way of raising money through donations or investments from multiple individuals to finance projects or ventures proposed by businesses or other organizations based on an online platform. Crowdfunding emerged after the 2008 global financial crisis. When entrepreneurs and early-stage small enterprises were faced with difficulties in raising funds from traditional banks, they started to look for capital elsewhere. Through an online crowdfunding platform, entrepreneurs can raise external financing from the "crowd"—every participant only provides a very small amount—instead of soliciting a small group of sophisticated investors (Belleflamme et al. 2014). The process of crowdfunding involves three parties: project initiators who have ideas but no fund to bring it into reality, supporters who are interested in the ideas or the return from the project and provide funds to initiators, and the crowdfunding platforms that connect the other two parties (Liu 2015). Depending on the form of return required by funders, crowdfunding can be classified into four types: (1) donation-based crowdfunding where contributions go towards a charitable cause; (2) loan-based crowdfunding where investors are repaid for their investment over a period of time; (3) reward-based where participants are given incentives (e.g., a tangible item or service) in return for their funds; and (4) equity-based crowdfunding where participants are given equity shares in the company in return for donations.

Crowdfunding was introduced into China in July 2011 by Demohour, which set up the first crowdfunding platform. Its subsequent development has gone through two main phases: initial emerging phase during 2011–2013 and rapid expansionary phase since 2013 onwards, as illustrated in Table 7.3. Restricted by the Securities Act that the number of investors cannot exceed 200, crowdfunding is mainly restricted to charitable donation of some innovative art projects and

Table 7.3 Development of online crowdfunding in China

	Time	Event
Phase 1	July 2011	Launch of first crowdfunding platform: Demohour
	November 2011	Launch of first equity-based crowdfunding platform: Angelcrunch
	March 2012	Launch of first vertical crowdfunding platform: Tmeng
	October 2012	Make.V sell its initial shares on Taobao due to violation of regulations on public financing
Phase 2	December 2013	Taobao launched its crowdfunding platform: Hi.Taobao
	July 2014	JD launched its crowdfunding platform
	March 2015	JD launched its private equity financing platform: JD Dongjia
	April 2015	Suning launched its crowdfunding platform
	November 2015	Antsdaq, equity-based crowdfunding under Ant Financial was launched
	April 2016	Baidu launched its crowdfunding platform named Baidubaizhong
	June 2016	MiC Finance was launched by Mi covering crowdfunding services
	October 2016	Netease lauched its crowdfunding platform: Netease Sanshi

Source Analysys, Zhongchoujia

does not cover the financing mode for SMEs. For example, Demohour, the largest crowdfunding website in the country, limits crowdfunding projects to technology, design, film and video, music, publishing, games, and photography for which film and video is at the top, and rewards must be relevant to the project; they cannot be in the form of equity stake, bond, interest returns, or cash returns of any kind. Other crowdfunding websites, such as Dreamore, Tmeng, Jue.so, and Emie, adopt similar rules (World Bank 2013). As of the end of 2013, there were only about 16 crowdfunding companies, but crowdfunding began to boom after 2014. The transaction volume rocketed from RMB 4.3 billion in 2013 to RMB 19.6 billion in 2014 and reached RMB 98.9 billion in 2015 (Liu 2015). RMB 11.4 billion (USD $1.7 billion) was raised through crowdfunding platforms in 2015, an increase of more than 400% compared to 2014 (Word Bank 2013). By the end of 2015, there were 283 crowdfunding platforms that funded 49,242 projects, of which 69% were reward-based crowdfunding; donation-based and equity-based crowdfunding each accounted for about 15% of projects (Erdenebileg 2016). Despite remarkable growth, crowdfunding in China remains a relatively nascent industry, but with enormous potential for growth. By 2025, China's crowdfunding is estimated to reach USE $50 billion, accounting for 52% of the world's total (World Bank 2013).

7.3.3 Internet Financial Infrastructure

Internet financial infrastructure, dominated by mobile and Internet payment, along with third-party depository, big data, and credit management systems, are the foundations to support sound development of Internet finance. In August 2015, Fuioupay cooperated with CCB Shanghai Branch to set up a third-party depository system, Jinzhanghu 3.0, for online P2P lending. Through this system, the financing activities on P2P lending platforms can be testified, significantly improving the operational order in the P2P lending market. Big data also entered into Internet financial market and focus on marketing and risk management. For example, Ant's micro-loans adopt big data-based analysis of target consumers' fragmentation behavior to control the risks and credit limits. As to the credit rating system, competing with the largest personal credit rating system in PBOC, Sesame Credit Management Company, Tencent Credit Management Company, and six other institutions started the marketization of the credit management system.

The third-party payment platform is the main premise of Internet financial infrastructure. It is a separate operating agency acting as intermediary and provides secure guarantee and technological support for two trading parties under the supervision of banks and government business-management agencies. Third-party payment can be divided into three categories: payment gateway services dominated by the major commercial banks (e.g., UnionPay) with advantages in financial backgrounds, non-independent payment instruments (e.g., Alipay) based on large-scale business to consumer, consumer to consumer websites, and independent payment platforms and terminals (e.g., 99Bill, Kyifu, and Lakala).

Third-party payment is the earliest, largest, and most developed segment in China's Internet finance market, providing the basis upon which many Internet finance applications are built and compete for customers' affinity and loyalty. The beginning of third-party payment in China started with Capital e-commerce in March 1999, the first third-party payment firm in the country, which was jointly founded by Beijing Municipal Government, the People's Bank of China, the Ministry of Information, and the National Domestic Commercial Bureau. The third-party payment sector expanded gradually with IPS founded in Shanghai in 2000 and Union Pay in 2002. Noticeably, in 2005, Alipay was launched, international online payments giant PayPal entered the Chinese market, and subsequently small payment companies sprang up rapidly. In May 2011, the People's Bank of China issued the first batch of payment licenses to third-party payment firms and new big players entered the market, such as WeChat Payment, which launched in 2013. As of 10 April 2015, there were 270 licensed companies. The most concentrated location is Beijing with 58 companies (Research in China 2015).

Figure 7.3 shows that the volume of two main methods of third-party payment—online and mobile payment—has experienced a dramatic increase in the last few years, especially since 2013. The total transaction volume for third-party online payments was RMB 900 million in 2001, increasing to RMB 2.2 trillion a decade later in 2011, and continued to flourish, hitting RMB 11.9 trillion in 2015. The third-party mobile

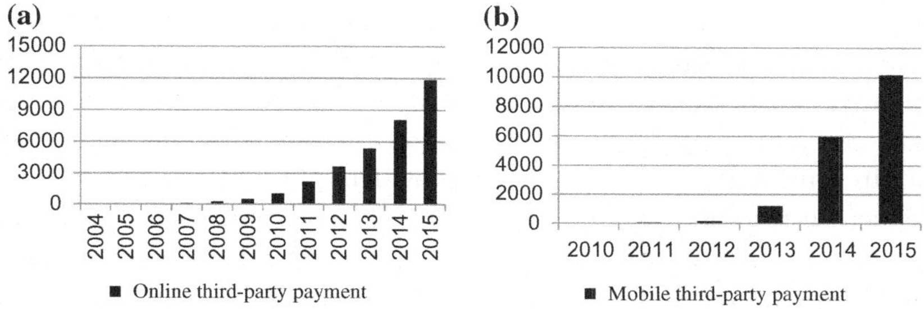

Fig. 7.3 Volume of online and mobile third-party payment (in billion RMB). *Source* iResearch

Table 7.4 Transaction structure of online third-party payment

Year	Online consumption (%)	Online topping-up (%)	B2B e-commerce (%)	Funds (%)	Others (%)
2005	48	27	9		16
2006	46	27	8		19
2007	56	26	7		11
2008	59	19	5		17
2009	63	15	3		19
2010	60	13	3		24
2011	58	9	5		28
2012	57	9	4		30
2013	43	7	3	18	29
2014	42	7	7	15	29
2015	32	6	5	20	37

Source iResearch

payment market rapidly gained momentum after 2013. Gross merchandise volume (GMV) was RMB 80 billion in 2011 and increased to RMB 10,171 billion in 2015. The sector is dominated by large companies and first movers, such as Alipay and WeChat Wallet services.

Table 7.4 reports the share of online third-party payment for different purposes. Traditional purposes, such as online consumption, online topping-up, and B2B e-commerce have been declining. The main reasons are twofold. First, payment in the traditional sector, such as traveling, moves from personal computers to mobile terminals. Second, innovative finanical products, such as online wealth management (included in others) and fund sales via online third-party payment, which occupy more than half of the current market, grow quickly.

In 2015, the People's Bank of China announced new regulations for online payment firms taking effect on 1 July 2016, which is part of the initiatives taken by the Chinese authorities to enhance legislation to regulate the rapidly growing Internet finance sector. The new regulations require third-party online payment providers to verify the real name of the account holder for all user accounts and to categorize all accounts into three types based on security requirements with each category capped with a maximum annual payments threshold. While aiming at reducing financial risk and protecting consumers, the new regulations make online payment increasingly complex for consumers, which arguably creates barriers to innovations and is in favor of traditional banks. There is no doubt that the new regulations bring important changes to online payments businesses requiring careful and strategic considerations on the implementation of the new compliance procedures.

7.4 Theoretical Framework and Regulation

7.4.1 Theoretical Framework

The primary function of the financial system is to channel funds from surplus units to deficit units, which is vital for saving and investment and ultimately for economic growth. Financial intermediation bridges the gap between borrowers and lenders and transforms the funds' characteristics, such as size, maturity, and risk. Mishkin (1995) put forward two main reasons for the existence of financial intermediaries—transaction costs and asymmetric information problems. Transaction costs refer to time and costs spent on matching borrowers with lenders and legal fees. Asymmetric information problems refer to unequal distribution of information between borrowers and lenders. Financial intermediaries have cost advantage in monitoring (i.e., banks to monitor credit risks) and collecting information due to economies of scale. They also have expertise to process information and alleviate information-related problems such as adverse selection and moral hazard problems. Financial intermediation can transform liquidity and enable economic agents to smooth consumption (Casu et al. 2006). The traditional financial system allocates resources through indirect financing via the banking sector and direct financing through capital markets and a well-functioning financial system efficiently channels funds towards the most productive sectors thereby promoting economic growth.

However, the traditional financial system is faced with higher costs and risk taking, resulting in increasingly frequent financial crises that generate huge direct costs to banks and indirect costs to the society. The development of a series of Internet-based technologies can effectively lower transaction costs and reduce asymmetric information problems because some complicated tasks such as client screening, risk evaluation and sharing, and maturity matching are substantially simplified. Traditional financial intermediaries' cost advantage comes from economies of scale and economies of scope, while Internet finance beats traditional intermediaries by having the additional advantage of the network effects. Network effects refer to the increases in the value of a connection to a network with the size of the network, and the Internet is the largest network on earth (Economides and Himmelberg 1995). Internet finance facilitates direct finance and accelerates the disintermediation process, challenging the theoretical fundamentals of financial intermediation. Xie et al. (2016) argue that the Internet itself can be defined as a financial market where investors and borrowers resolve the problem of matching maturity and risk-return profiles online and evolving gradually toward a Walrasian general equilibrium.

The financial sector has shifted from the traditional way to a new business model—Internet finance. The latter promotes inclusive finance by offering a variety of financial services to a wide range of customers, helps SMEs with financing, and enhances the safety of informal financing. Internet technology advancement (in the digitization of information, computing capacity, and the availability of telecommunications technologies, e.g., high-speed Wi-Fi networks) and financial innovations have brought fundamental changes in Internet finance. The boundaries between different segments within the financial sector become blurred and the integration and co-operation between the financial sector and non-financial sectors are deepening. The economies of size and network effects (Economides and Himmelberg 1995) enable Internet finance fast growth potential and the ability to develop competitive advantages (Varian 2003). The growing tendency of disintermediation requires changes in the forms of financial transactions and institutions. Alternatively, Internet finance as a new business model does not change the functions of the financial market or the intrinsic properties of financial contracts (Xie et al. 2016). Internet finance performs primary resource allocation functions through an improved process that exchanges commodities, services, and assets with clearance and settlement services; that separates equity interests and large-scale fundraising; that offers channels for transfer of economic resources over time and space; that facilitates risk control and management; that produces and releases pricing information and promotes decentralization of policy making; and that mitigates information asymmetry (Bodie and Merton 2000). Internet finance, instead of a replacement for the traditional finance industry, is an efficient supplementary extension that promotes inclusive finance and financial deepening.

The development of Internet finance challenges the theoretical fundamentals of the financial sector, calling for research to develop a more comprehensive theoretical framework that accommodates new developments in Internet finance. Early attempts by Xie and Zou (2013) focuses on three pillars of Internet finance—payment, information processing, and resource allocation. Technological advancement results in fundamental changes in payment and information processing, which in turn has significant implications for the efficiency of resource allocation. Theoretical research lags behind the real world development and more studies are needed to broaden our view and deepen our understanding of the rapidly growing Internet finance industry.

7.4.2 Risks and Challenges

The future development of Internet finance in China faces a number of challenges—*customer base and long-tail risk.* Internet finance extends the boundaries of transactions and services to a large group of individuals who are not covered by the traditional finance industry, and these individuals—mostly seniors and less-educated citizens—are referred to as the long-tail part (Mckinsey 2016). These individuals have been used to guarantees that are implicitly backed by the government in traditional finance. They can be easily attracted by financial products with a "high rate of return" during the transaction process as they are usually unable to identify the underlying risks. With the development of Internet finance, individual and collective irrationality becomes more likely, which may cause contagion effects in the money market when things go wrong and pose threats to the stability of the financial system. As such, long-tail risk becomes a unique risk for Internet finance, particularly relevant to the P2P online platforms, Internet fund trading, online insurance, and online trust companies. How to effectively educate those individuals of the long-tail part and develop a risk culture among market participants as well as how to control and manage the long-tail risk is a challenge for regulators and firms. It requires a professional, knowledge-based, mandatory, and durable regulatory system with firms' support and cooperation.

Information technology risk. Internet finance depends on information technologies and a sound management scheme for Information Technology (IT) risk is critical. IT is the great enabler of Internet finance, while it also presents a pervasive, potentially high-impact risk. IT risk refers to the risk of unexpected losses caused by a wide range of IT-related issues, such as hacking attacks, hardware failure, system crash, computer viruses, and deficient internal control. These issues may lead to data loss and personal information/identity leakage, which induce online financial fraud. McKinsey (2016) classifies IT risk into three categories: data risk stemmed from errors in data processing, platform-based risk caused by inferior management of hardware devices, networks, operating systems, databases, middleware or operations systems, and physical environmental risk due to earthquakes, thunderstorms, and equipment failures in core engine rooms. The occurrences of IT-related events not only lead to direct costs, but also undermine customers' confidence and weaken customer preference to Internet finance. How to control and manage IT risk is another challenge for the development of Internet finance, especially as cyber-crime becomes more and more sophisticated. Regulatory authorities and firms may take measures such as off-site operation and on-site inspections and employ advanced risk-management techniques/models in risk measurement, ratings, and other risk control practices.

Regulation. The prosperity of Internet finance initially takes place under a largely unregulated environment. In the recognition of risks, especially after wide spread losses in the P2P market, authorities embarked on regulations for Internet finance activities. The newly issued regulations address potential risks in the Internet finance sector to enhance macro-financial stability. After a series of regulations are issued, the regulatory environment will become more sophisticated and industry players need to adapt and comply with new rules quickly, which presents a challenge to the development of Internet finance in the short term. In the long term, the challenge is to develop a more comprehensive and sophisticated regulatory framework that promotes and supports the healthy development of Internet finance, taking account of its complex and unique features. The right way to approach Internet finance sector regulation and supervision is to design an effective and flexible regulatory framework. This framework should be capable of dealing with financial innovations and systemic risks in Internet finance through measures addressing IT risks and cybersecurity, allowing for effective coordination between various authorities and agencies, creating an environment that promotes self-regulation and consumers protection.

Other challenges. With the development of Internet finance, homogeneous competition and controversial evaluation of certain financial innovations are the other two challenges (Zheng 2014). Homogeneous competition may induce higher risk taking and jeopardize financial stability. On one hand, when new types of products appear, similar institutions will copy the innovative products and even design a more optimal one in order to gain market shares. These institutions are more likely to launch high-yield products associated with the high level of credit risk, liquidity risk, and market risk, which lead to the unhealthy development of online financial trading and impair the interests of Internet financial enterprises and consumers. On the other hand, controversy exists among a variety of regulatory commissions in some countries and regions in the evaluation of some innovative products through Internet, such as bitcoin. The uncertain consequences of the assessment and attitude from authorities towards this type of financial innovation will have an important effect on the Internet financial ecology and business models. These challenges need to be dealt with care for healthy and prosperous development of Internet finance.

7.4.3 Regulation

In an efficient financial market, rational participants' self-interested behaviors realize market equilibrium automatically through the "invisible hand" (price), and the "laissez-faire" argument against regulation is more appealing. However, Internet finance cannot completely eliminate market failures, justifying regulation. In theory, as an extension of the financial system, Internet finance should be under the umbrella of existing regulations and apply risk-management tools to control various financial risks.[1] In practice, due to a number of factors, regulations have not kept up with the unprecedented boom in Internet finance in China in recent years and there has been a legal vacuum. For instance, Internet finance has the distinct features, such as rapid innovations and blurring boundaries between different segments within Internet finance or between the financial sector and non-financial sectors, which make the market more complex and volatile. The existing regulations may not be applicable or less straightforward, which induces regulatory arbitrage that is actually argued to partially contribute to the rapid development of Internet finance. Moreover, the simplified transaction procedure and the availability of a wider range of feasible transactions may induce irrational behavior. Individual behavior may not meet the rational expectations hypothesis as behavioral finance suggests and it is important to control excessive speculative behaviors by restricting markets or products access to qualified users.

Properly designed regulations focusing on Internet finance are vital to safeguard customer interest, build a healthy environment for financial innovations, and ultimately the sound development of Internet finance. As such, the development of Internet finance has necessitated the reconsideration of even the basic principles of financial regulation. A broad reconsideration of the regulation and supervision of financial institutions is needed to balance the quest for financial stability with the imperatives of the development of Internet finance.

Since 2010, the Chinese authorities issued a series of regulations to tighten the regulatory environment of Internet finance. Key regulatory measures broadly fall into two types: financial business conduct

[1] Recent regulatory moves in the United States are going in this direction. For example, in December 2016, a key US regulator—the Office of the Comptroller of the Currency—announced to regulate Fintech firms more like traditional lenders and chartered Fintech would be formally subjected to federal banking rules. Fintech refers to financial technology that is an industry in which companies use new technology and innovation to offer financial services competing with traditional financial institutions and intermediaries.

regulation and prudential regulation. Financial business conduct regulation is to protect consumers and supervise all firms to ensure that their businesses across financial services and markets are conducted in a way that safeguard the interests of all participants. It is about how firms conduct businesses, relating to information disclosure, fair business practices, competence, honesty and integrity of financial institutions, and the like. Financial business conduct regulation relates to the monitoring and supervision of financial institutions. Due to information asymmetries and agency problems, consumers are not in a position to judge the soundness of financial institutions and have higher monitoring costs, and firms may take the information advantage to fraud. For instance, Shumi Fund in Zhejiang exaggeratedly promoted their Internet wealth management products and Tiantian Fund in Shanghai advertised false yields of its Internet financial products. Both received notice of administrative violation from relevant CBRC branches.

Prudential regulation is concerned with the safety and soundness in the financial services sector, covering all firms that manage significant risks involved in their business, such as banks and other deposit takers, insurance companies, and large investment banks. These regulations ensure that the business of the firms is carried on in a healthy way and minimizes the contagion effect that the failure of one firm may spread to other similar firms. Prudential regulations aim at reducing excessive risk taking and the risk of financial crisis and thus to avoid adverse effects on financial stability and negative externalities to the economy and society. Internet finance involves all major financial risks. For example, credit risk existing in the P2P network lending and when Internet financial institutions perform the function of maturity transformation during credit intermediation process, they are faced with liquidity risk.

The Chinese authorities also lay down institutional groundwork for Internet finance regulation. On 18 July 2015, the "Guiding Opinions on Promoting the Healthy Development of Internet Finance of Cross-border E-Commerce" (hereinafter "Guiding Opinion") was jointly issued by 10 central government agencies and industry regulators, namely the People's Bank of China, the Ministry of Industry and Information Technology, the Ministry of Public Security, the Ministry of Finance, the State Administration for Industry and Commerce, the Legislative Affairs Office of the State Council, the China Banking Regulatory Commission, the China Securities Regulatory Commission, the China Insurance Regulatory Commission, and the China Internet Information Technology Office. This is the most comprehensive regulation on Internet finance in China. The Guiding Opinions divide various Internet finance operations into six types: Internet payment, Internet loans, equity crowdfunding, Internet sale of funds, Internet insurance, and Internet trust and consumer finance. Each falls under the jurisdiction of a government agency as a specialized and focused regulator. The People's Bank of China overseas online payment; the CRBC is in charge of Internet loans and Internet trust and consumer finance; the China Securities Regulatory Commission (CSRC) supervises funds selling and equity crowdfunding; and the China Insurance Regulatory Commission (CIRC) is responsible for Internet insurance. Firms with mixed operations in Internet financial activities are subject to regulations corresponding to the detailed products and risks.

The primary principle of the regulatory framework in China is "separate operation, separate supervision" with the ultimate regulatory power highly concentrated in the central government. Thus, the effective and timely coordination among different regulator bodies and authorities with clearly defined responsibilities is essential for the implementation of the new regulations. In Internet finance, mixed operations of various financial activities emerge rapidly and trading of financial products, banking services, securities, funds, and insurance can be conducted on the same Internet platform. For instance, Yu'E Bao is a typical example consisting of third-party payment and money market funds, presenting a challenge for regulatory authorities. As a response, in August 2013, the People's Bank of China with support of the State Council, established a "financial supervisory coordination leading group" to coordinate cross-financial products and cross-marketing financial innovations.

Table 7.5 lists the main regulations and laws on Internet finance since 2010, issued by authorities and agencies, including the People's Bank of China regulatory bodies (CBRC, CSRC, CIRC), and relevant government ministries. As government tightens the grip on Internet finance and these new regulations, laws, and rules will have far-reaching effects not only on Internet finance but also the related sectors. To regulate online

Table 7.5 Summary of main regulations and laws about Internet finance from 2010 to 2016

No.	Time	Tittle and information
1	20100901	人民银行:《非金融机构支付服务管理办法》(〔2010第 2号) [100901]. People's Bank of China: administrative measures for the payment services provided by non-financial institutions (Order No. 2 [2010] of the People's Bank of China)
2	20101201	人民银行:《非金融机构支付服务管理办法实施细则》(中国人民银行公告〔2010〕第17 号)[101201]. People's Bank of China: detailed rules for the implementation of the administrative measures for the payment services provided by non-financial institutions (Announcement No. 17 [2010] of the People's Bank of China)
3	20110616	人民银行:《非金融机构支付服务业务系统检测认证管理规定》[110616]. People's Bank of China: provisions on the administration of testing and certification of the payment service business system of non-financial institutions (No. 14 [2011])
4	20110823	银监会办公厅:《关于人人贷有关风险提示的通知》(银监办发[2011] 254 号)[110823]. The General Office of China Banking Regulatory Commission: notice of the General Office of China Banking Regulatory Commission on warning of risks associated with peer-to-peer lending ((No. 254 [2011] of the General Office of China Banking Regulatory Commission, August 23, 2011)
5	20120105	人民银行:《支付机构互联网支付业务管理办法(征求意见稿)》[120105]. People's Bank of China: administrative measures for the Internet payment services of payment institutions (Draft for Comments)
6	20120308	中国人民银行关于印发《支付机构反洗钱和反恐怖融资管理办法》的通知(银发[2012]54 号)[120308][失效]. People's Bank of China: notice of the People's Bank of China on issuing the guidelines against money laundering and terrorist financing through payment and clearing organizations (No. 54 [2012] of the People's Bank of China) [Expired]
7	20121101	人民银行:《支付机构预付卡业务管理办法》[121101]. People's Bank of China: the administrative measures for prepaid card business of payment institutions (No. 12 [2012])
8	20130307	支付清算协会:关于印发《支付机构互联网支付业务风险防范指引》的通知[130307]. Payment and Clearing Association of China: Guidelines of risk prevention of Internet payment services of payment institutions
9	20130607	人民银行:《支付机构客户备付金存管办法》(中国人民银行公告[2013]第6 号)[130607]. People's Bank of China: Measures for the custody of clients' reserves of payment institutions (Announcement of the People's Bank of China (No. 6 [2013]))

(continued)

Table 7.5 (continued)

No.	Time	Tittle and information
10	20130705	人民银行:《银行卡收单业务管理办法》[130705]. People's Bank of China: the administrative measures on bank card acquiring business (No. 9 [2013])
11	20131203	中国人民银行、工业和信息化部、中国银行业监督管理委员会、中国证券监督管理委员会、中国保险监督管理委员会《关于防范比特币风险的通知》(银发(2013)289 号)[131203]. People's Bank of China, Ministry of Industry and Information Technology, China Banking Regulatory Commission, China Securities Regulatory Commission, China Insurance Regulatory Commission: the notification on preventing Bitcoin risk (No. 289 [2013])
12	201312	国务院办公厅《国务院办公厅关于加强影子银行监管有关问题的通知》(国办发〔2013〕107号). The General Office of State Council: the "notice on strengthening regulation of shadow banks and related issues" ("the 107th text")
13	20140314	中国人民银行支付结算司:《关于暂停支付宝公司线下条码(二维码)支付等业务意见的函》[140314](附:推动创新 规范服务——央行有关负责人回应当前互联网金融监管热点话题[140324]). People's Bank of China: moratorium on offline QR code payment and other business of Alipay company
14	20140318	人民银行:《关于手机支付业务发展的指导意见全文及起草说明》[140318]. People's Bank of China: guidelines and drafting note of the development of mobile payment services
15	20140325	最高人民法院、最高人民检察院、公安部关于办理非法集资刑事案件适用法律若干问题的意见(公通字(2014)16 号)[140325]. Opinions of the Supreme People's Court, the Supreme People's Procuratorate and the Ministry of Public Security on several issues concerning the application of law in the handling of illegal fund-raising criminal cases (No. 16 [2014])
16	20140403	银监会、人民银行:《关于加强商业银行与第三方支付机构合作业务管理的通知》(银监发〔2014〕10 号)[140403]. China Banking Regulatory Commission and People's Bank of China: notice on strengthening the administration of cooperative business between commercial banks and third-party payment institutions (No. 10 [2014] of the China Banking Regulatory Commission)
17	20140415	中国保险监督管理委员会对《关于规范人身保险公司经营互联网保险有关问题的通知(征求意见稿)》公开征求意见[140415]. China Insurance Regulatory Commission: notice on regulating the Internet insurance business of life insurance companies (Draft for Comments)

(continued)

Table 7.5 (continued)

No.	Time	Tittle and information
18	20141218	中国证券业协会:《私募股权众筹融资管理办法(试行)(征求意见稿)》及起草说明(中证协发(2014)236 号)[141218]. China Securities Regulatory Commission (CSRC): the administrative measures for private equity crowdfunding (Draft)
19	20150712	中国证券监督管理委员会:《关于加强证券公司信息系统外部接入管理的通知》(证监办发〔2015〕35号). CSRC: the notice on strengthening the management of external access to the information system of the securities companies
20	20150718	中国人民银行、工业和信息化部、公安部、财政部、工商总局、法制办、银监会、证监会、保监会、国家互联网信息办公室:《关于促进互联网金融健康发展的指导意见》(银发〔2015〕221号)[150718]. People's Bank of China, Ministry of Industry and Information Technology, Ministry of Public Security, Ministry of Finance, State Administration for Industry and Commerce, Legislative Affairs Office of the State Council, China Banking Regulatory Commission, China Securities Regulatory Commission, China Insurance Regulatory Commission and State Internet Information Office: the guiding opinions on promoting the healthy development of Internet finance (No. 221 [2015])
21	20150722	中国保监会:《互联网保险业务监管暂行办法》(保监发(2015)69号). China Insurance Regulatory Commission: notice of the China Insurance Regulatory Commission on issuing the interim measures for the supervision of the Internet insurance business (No. 69 [2015] of the China Insurance Regulatory Commission)
22	20150731	人民银行:《非银行支付机构网络支付业务管理办法(征求意见稿)》[150731]. People's Bank of China: administrative measures for the online payment business of non-banking payment institutions (Draft for Comments)
23	20150803	中国证监会办公厅: 关于对通过互联网开展股权融资活动的机构进行专项检查的通知 (证监办发[2015]44号). Notice of the General Office of the China Securities Regulatory Commission on conducting special inspections of institutions engaging in equity financing via the Internet (No. 44 [2015] of the General Office of the China Securities Regulatory Commission)
24	20150806	最高人民法院:《关于审理民间借贷案件适用法律若干问题的规定》(法释〔2015〕18 号)[150901]. Supreme People's Court: the provisions of the Supreme People's Court on several issues concerning the application of law in the trial of private lending cases (No. 18 [2015] of the Supreme People's Court)

(continued)

Table 7.5 (continued)

No.	Time	Tittle and information
25	20151228	银监会:《网络借贷信息中介机构业务活动管理暂行办法(征求意见稿)》. China Banking Regulatory Commission: interim measures for administration of business activities of Internet lending information intermediary agencies (Draft for Comments)
26	20151228	中国人民银行公告《非银行支付机构网络支付业务管理办法》(2015)第43号. Announcement No. 43 [2015] of the People's Bank of China—administrative measures for the online payment business of non-banking payment institutions
27	20160119	中国保监会《关于加强互联网平台保证保险业务管理的通知》(保监产险〔2016〕6号). Notice of the China Insurance Regulatory Commission on strengthening the administration of the guarantee insurance business on Internet platforms (No. 6 [2016] of the China Insurance Regulatory Commission)
28	20160204	国务院《关于进一步做好防范和处置非法集资工作的意见》国发〔2015〕59号. The State Council: guidance on improving prevention and management of illegal fund raising No. 59 (2015) of the State Council
29	20160320	中国人民银行、银监会《关于加大对新消费领域金融支持的指导意见》. The Central Bank and China Banking Regulatory Commission: guidance on efforts to increase financial support for new consumer sectors
30	20160419	中国人民银行 《非银行支付机构分类评级管理办法》. People's Bank of China—administrative measures for credit rating of non-banking payment institutions
31	20160527	中国人民银行:征信业务管理办法(草稿). People's Bank of China—administrative measures for credit investigation
32	201608	中国人民银行和银监会支付清算协会《条码支付业务规范征求意见稿》. Payment and Clearing Association: regulations for QR code payment business (Draft for comments)
33	20160824	银监会、工业和信息化部、公安部、国家互联网信息办公室联合发布《网络借贷信息中介机构业务活动管理暂行办法》. China Banking Regulatory Commission, Ministry of Industry and Information Technology, Ministry of Public Security and State Internet Information Office: interim measures for administration of business activities of Internet Lending information intermediary agencies
34	20161013	国务院办公厅《关于印发互联网金融风险专项整治工作实施方案的通知》. The General office of State Council: notice of the General Office of the State Council on issuing the implementation plan for special rectification on risks in Internet finance

(continued)

Table 7.5 (continued)

No.	Time	Tittle and information
35	20161013	中国人民银行等十四个部门发布《非银行支付机构风险专项整治工作实施方案》. The People's Bank of China and other 13 departments: the implementing scheme of special rectification of risks of non-banking payment institutions; 中国人民银行等十七个部门发布《通过互联网开展资产管理及跨界从事金融业务风险专项整治工作实施方案》. The People's Bank of China together with other 16 departments: the implementing scheme of special rectification of risks in making assets management on the Internet and doing financial business on a cross-over basis; 工商总局等十七个部门下发《开展互联网金融广告及以投资理财名义从事金融活动风险专项整治工作实施方案》. The State Administration for Industry and Commerce together with other 16 departments: the implementing scheme of special rectification of risks in making Internet finance advertisement and doing financial business in the name of investment and wealth management; 中国证监会等十五个部门发布《股权众筹风险专项整治工作实施方案》. The China Securities Regulatory Commission and other 14 departments: implementing scheme of special rectification of risks concerning equity-based crowdfunding; 中国保监会等十五个部门制发《互联网保险风险专项整治工作实施方案》. The China Insurance Regulatory Commission and other 14 departments: implementing scheme of special rectification of risks concerning Internet-based insurance; 中国银监会等十五个部门下发《P2P网络借贷风险专项整治工作实施方案》. The China Banking Regulatory Commission together with other 14 institutions: the implementing scheme of special rectification of risks concerning online peer-to-peer (P2P) lending.
36	20161028	中国互联网金融协会:《互联网金融信息披露个体网络借贷(T/NIFA 1—2016)》和《中国互联网金融协会信息披露自律管理规范》. National Internet finance association of China (NIFA): Internet finance information disclosure P2P lending and self-regulatory measures for information disclosure of NIFA

insurance companies, in April 2014, CIRC released the "Notice on Regulating the Internet Insurance Business of Life Insurance Companies" and in July 2015 officially issued the "Interim Measures for the Supervision of the Internet Insurance Business" taking effect on 1 October 2015. To regulate mobile and third-party payment activities, the People's

Bank of China issued a series of regulations since 2010.[2] For instance, following the two announcements on administrative measures for payment services provided by non-financial institutions in 2010, the "Notice of the Guidelines against Money Laundering and Terrorist Financing" was issued in March 2012, and more recently, the "Administrative Measures for credit Rating of Non-Banking Payment Institutions" was released in April 2016. Online lending is a rapidly expanding segment of Internet finance with high risks, attracting considerable regulatory attention. In November 2011, for the first time, CBRC issued the "Notice on Warning of Risks Associated with Peer-to-Peer lending." In August 2015, China's Supreme People's Court clarified the rights and obligations of debtors, creditors, and the platforms regarding operational problems during the P2P lending transactions in the "Provisions on Several Issues concerning the Application of Law in the Trial of Private Lending Cases." In December 2015, "Interim Measures for Administration of Business Activities of Internet Lending Information Intermediary Agencies" was released specifically for clarifying the bottom line for the financial activities on the P2P platform and controlling credit risks in P2P network loans. This crucial file prohibits the P2P lending platforms from running self-financing, cash pooling, guarantee, and nine other types of business. Similar to banks that under Basel III capital accord need to provide for capital loss reserves and assets against credit risk, P2P platforms are required to allocate part of their revenue to risk reserve pools. On 17 August 2016, four government agencies—CBRC, Ministry of Industry and Information Technology (MIIT), Ministry of Public Security (MPS) and the Cyberspace Administration of China (CAC)—jointly issued the "Interim Measures for Administration of the Business Activities of Network-based Lending Information Intermediary Agencies" with immediate effect. Under the new rules, P2P platforms are not allowed to take public deposits, create asset pools, provide any forms of guarantee for lenders, sell wealth-management products, issue asset-backed securities, and P2P firms have to use

[2]Detailed regulations and laws are available on the official website of the Payment and Clearing Association of China.

third-party banks as custodians for investors' funds. The aim is to clean up the market environment and protect investors' interests through improved risk control measures including information disclosure and credit rating.

7.5 Conclusion

The development of Internet finance in China is driven by some general factors as in other countries, such as increasing customer expectations for more personalized services in the digital era and technological advancements such as big data and blockchain. The pace of the development, however, has been accelerated by China-specific factors, such as government's endorsement to support finance inclusion, and a friendly regulatory environment to promote financial deepening. More importantly, the distorted and inefficient financial system has offered great opportunities for the development of the Internet finance industry. Internet finance simplifies the transaction process and lowers financing costs while responding to market demand more quickly, flexibly, and efficiently via the online platforms. These appealing features have popularized Internet finance and the sector has been growing at exponential rates, involving a variety of innovative financial institutions offering a wide range of innovative products through a number of innovative channels and platforms. Supplementary to traditional finance, Internet finance has a great potential for future development, and being an integrated part promotes financial reform and financial deepening. Meanwhile, despite the recent rapid expansion, Internet finance in China still has a long way to go with challenges ahead, such as how to develop a regulatory framework that supports healthy development of Internet finance with effective risk-management mechanisms.

References

Accenture. 2014. The Digital Disruption in Banking. *North America Consumer Digital Banking Survey*. Accenture Consulting.

Accenture. 2016. Banking on Value—Rewards, Robo-Advice and Relevance. *North America Consumer Digital Banking Survey*. Accenture Consulting.

Allen, F., J. Qian, and M. Qian. 2005. Law, Finance, and Economic Growth in China. *Journal of Financial Economics* 77 (1): 57–116.
Analysys. 2016. Report on Crowdfunding Market in China [Online]. Available from http://m.analysys.cn/report/detail/1000240.html. Accessed 10 Aug 2016.
Belleflamme, P., T. Lambert, and A. Schwienbacher. 2014. Crowdfunding: Tapping the Right Crowd. *Journal of Business Venturing* 29 (5): 585–609.
BI Intelligence. 2016. The Emerging Technologies and Firms Driving Change in Financial Services and How Legacy Players Can Navigate the Disruption. *The Fintech Ecosystem Report*. Business Insider's Premium Research Service.
Boao Review Internet Finance Research Institute. 2016. *Report on Internet Finance 2016—Internetization of traditional finances*. Beijing: China Economic Publishing House.
Bodie, Z., and R. Merton. 2000. *Finance*. New Jersey: Prentice Hall.
Capgemini. 2017. *World FinTech Report*. Capgemini Consulting Technology Outsourcing.
Casu, B., C. Girardone, and P. Molyneux. 2006. *Introduction to Banking*. London: FT/Prentice Hall.
CASS. 2016. Credit Rating and Analysis Report of Internet Lending Platforms in China 2015–2016. Chinese Academy of Social Science.
CNNIC. 2016. The 38th Statistical Report of Development of Internet in China. China Internet Network Information Center.
Deloitte. 2015. Direct Banking—Exploration of Commercial Bank Transformation and Development Under Internet Finance Era.
Economides, N., and C. Himmelberg. 1995. Critical Mass and Network Evolution in Telecommunications. In *Toward a Competitive Telecommunications Industry: Selected Papers from the 1994 Telecommunications Policy Research Conference*, 47–63.
Erdenebileg, Z. 2016. Better Together: The Potential of Crowdfunding in China. *China Business Review*, The magazine of US–China Business Council (USCBC) [Online]. Available from https://www.chinabusiness-review.com/better-together-the-potential-of-crowdfunding-in-china/. Accessed 12 Aug 2016.
iResearch. 2014–2016. China Third-Party Payment Report. iResearch.
Liu, M.K. 2015. Internet Finance and Regulation in China (Main Report). Fung Global Institute Asian Perspectives Global issues.
McKinsey China. 2016. Disruption and Connection: Cracking the Myths of China Internet Finance Innovation. McKinsey Greater China FIG Practice.

McKinsey Global Institute. 2011. *Big Data: The Next Frontier for Innovation, Competition, and Productivity*. San Francisco: McKinsey Global Institute.

Mishkin, F. 1995. *The Economics of Money, Banking, and Financial Markets*. New York: Harper Collins.

Nath, R., P. Schrick, and M. Parzinger. 2001. Bankers' Perspectives on Internet banking. *E-service Journal* 1 (1): 21–36.

People's Bank of China. 2011–2016. General Report of Payment System in China.

P2Peye. 2015. Annual Report for P2P Online Lending: Co-existence of Chances and Risks [Online]. Available from http://www.p2peye.com/topic-nk2015.html. Accessed 15 Sep 2016.

PWC. 2017. *Redrawing the Lines: FinTech's Growing Influence on Financial Services*. Global FinTech Report.

Research in China. 2015. Third-Party Payment Industry Report 2015.

Rui, X.W., and H.L. Liu. 2014. *Internet Finance Development Report*. Beijing: China Social Sciences publishing house.

Varian, H.R. 2003. The Social Cost of Sharing. In *Proceedings of Workshop on Economics of P2P Systems*.

World Bank. 2013. *Crowdfunding's Potential for the Developing World, infoDev, Finance and Private Sector Development Department*. Washington, DC: World Bank.

Xie, P., and C.W. Zou. 2013. The Theory of Internet Finance. *China Economist* 8 (2), [online]. Available from: SSRN: http://ssrn.com/abstract=2235967. Accessed Apr 2017.

Xie, P., C. Zou, and H. Liu. 2016. The Fundamentals of Internet Finance and its Policy Implications in China. *China Economic Journal* 9 (3): 240–252.

Zheng, L. 2014. China's Internet Finance: Models, Impacts, Nature and Risks. *International Economic Review* 5: 103–118.

Zhou, M. 2014. The Features, the Flourishing Reasons and the Risk Countermeasures of E-finance. *Contemporary Economic Management* 36 (10): 69–72.

8

The Global Financial Crisis and China's Pawnbroking Industry

This chapter is largely based on a paper by Liming Zhou, Shujie Yao, Jinmin Wang, and Jinghua Ou published in the *Journal of Chinese Economics and Business Study* in (2016, 14(2), 151–164). We are grateful for all the authors and the journal to allow us to include this paper in this book as we believe that this provides a useful case study for the Chinese informal financial sector.

Preamble

In most countries, pawnbroking is an intermediate financial instrument to help private households or individuals meet their short-term and urgent consumption needs. In China, due to market imperfection and institutional discrimination against the small and medium-sized enterprises (SMEs) by commercial banks and other formal financial institutions, pawnbroking has been used as a supplementary financing source for SMEs and private entrepreneurs when they cannot get access to bank credits or other financial sources such as usury (underground money shops). This chapter uses first-hand survey data in 2009 in Zhejiang Province, China's pioneering region for pawn business, and secondary data for the whole country during 2004–2012, to analyze the special characteristics of the pawnbroking industry and explain why it has become a viable and useful financing instrument in China. It also

C. Jiang and S. Yao, *Chinese Banking Reform*, The Nottingham China Policy Institute Series, DOI 10.1007/978-3-319-63925-3_8

explains the puzzle of a serious setback and widespread losses in the industry during the global financial crisis in 2008. A corporate financing model of SMEs is developed to explain the substitution relationship between formal bank credits and pawnbroking. It suggests that the stimulus plan implemented by the central government of China during the global financial crisis reduced the borrowing cost and lowered the access barrier of bank credits to SMEs, leading to a temporary setback of an otherwise rapidly growing pawnbroking business in 2008 and 2009. However, as quantitative easing is gradually phased out after the global financial crisis, pawnbroking activities recover rapidly, implying that the industry will continue to play an important role in China's economic development given its current financial system which is still unfriendly to the SME sector.

This chapter is organized as follows. Section 8.1 introduces research background and provides an overview of pawnbroking activities in China in comparison with other countries. Section 8.2 introduces main features of the pawnbroking industry in China. Section 8.3 analyzes the role pawnbroking played in financing market in China. Section 8.4 analyzes the impact of monetary policy on the pawnbroking industry during the global financial crisis. Section 8.5 concludes and summarizes the main findings.

8.1 Research Background and Pawnbroking Industry in China

8.1.1 Research Background

China's economic reform, started in 1978, has aimed at transforming the traditional centrally planned system to a market-oriented one (Naughton 2007). The latest reform of the state-owned enterprises (SOEs) since 1997 has focused on shareholding reform. In the meantime, the private sector has started to play an increasingly important role in the national economy (Ma 2010). The number of SOEs has declined while that of the small- and medium-sized enterprises (SMEs) has increased rapidly (Gao and Banerji 2015). By the end of 2012, SMEs, including micro-sized enterprises, accounted for 99.7% of the number of enterprises and more than 80% of employment in the country (Xinhua Net 2013). However, the development of SMEs in China has faced and will continue to face many tough challenges and constraints, particularly in financing, as the country's financial industry is highly fragmented and inefficient with serious discrimination and biases against the SMEs (Zhang 2008; Dougherty et al. 2007; Duan et al. 2009).

Since SMEs in China have relatively limited access to bank credits than SOEs, many SMEs have no option but to actively seek alternative resources to overcome bank financing obstacles (Zhou 2009). Out of the large number of SMEs, only a few of them are able to gain access to enough capital to grow into mature enterprises and to achieve economies of scale (Fung et al. 2007). Although great changes have taken place in the financial system in the past decades, financial reform still lags behind that in the real industrial sectors. Unbalanced development and reform between the real economy and the financial industry can be best manifested by the mismatch between SMEs' contribution to economic growth and their share of borrowing from banks and other financial institutions in the country. The private sector was almost locked out of access to formal financial channels in the 1980s and 1990s (Tsai 2002; Vicziany and Zhang 2005) because banks preferred to lend money to SOEs rather than private SMEs, forcing the latter to raise capital from the informal, and often illegal, financial institutions (Allen et al. 2005).

The informal financial institutions include private lending, pawning, and usury based on underground activities (Newman et al. 2013). Informal financing typically consists of small and unsecured short-term loans to enterprises in the rural areas, agricultural contracts, households, and individuals (Meghana et al. 2010). Some empirical studies have shown that informal financing could facilitate firm growth more effectively than the formal banking sector in some developing countries (Meghana et al. 2010; Tsai 2004; Ruan and Zhang 2012). Pawn financing is one of the main informal financing sources in China.

Pawnbroking industry provides capital to mortgagees who deposit property as a pledge for getting financing from pawnshops. At present, the most common financing channels for SMEs include bank loans, finance leasing, pawn loans, and small loans. While finance leasing and bank loans usually meet the mid- and long-term financing needs of SMEs, pawn loans and small loans usually satisfy short-term financing needs.

It is important to understand the development of the pawnbroking industry in China and its role in supporting the development of SMEs in the post-reform era. This chapter develops a theoretical corporate financing model of SMEs to illustrate why pawnbroking is a viable financing source for SMEs and why the global financial crisis had a significantly negative impact on the industry. With a cross-country comparative analysis between China and other countries as well as the survey data in Zhejiang Province, east China, we aim to identify the main reasons for the puzzle of widespread losses in the Chinese pawnbroking industry during the global financial crisis. One main argument is that, due to the global financial crisis, the central government of China provided quantitative easing and relaxed its banking regulations to encourage more lending to the SME sector, hence reducing the need of SMEs to borrow money from pawnshops. However, as quantitative easing phased out, pawnbrokers in China continued to play an important role in financing SMEs due to market imperfection and inefficiency of the formal financial sector, which was still dominated by large state-owned banks and regional commercial banks owned by the local authorities (Fig. 8.1).

8.1.2 The History of Pawnbroking Industry and Pawn Rules in China

In the long history of Chinese civilization over many thousands of years, pawnbroking had always been one of the most important sources of civilian financing. China's pawnbroking industry began in the Northern and Southern Dynasty. The early pawnbroker was called Zhiku, a kind of pawnshop in the temple. At that time, the Buddhist temple ran pawn business through Zhiku to accumulate wealth, and

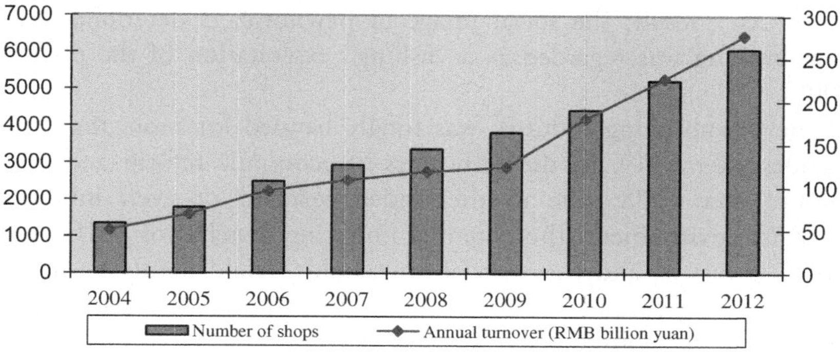

Fig. 8.1 The development of pawnbroking industry in China (2004–2012). *Source* Compilation based on the data from the Ministry of Commerce of China

also helped the poor. Therefore, the early temple pawnbroking appeared as a charity in the history. After the Tang Dynasty, a large number of private and official pawnshops were established to play an important role in civil financing. Pawnbroking as a traditional financial business reached its prosperous peak in Ming and Qing Dynasties. In the late Qing Dynasty and the early Republic of China, the regime changed frequently, and the government neglected the supervision and management of the pawnbroking industry. With the rise of the banking industry, the modern financial system was gradually established. As a traditional mode of financing, the pawnbroking industry gradually declined (Liu 1995; Li 2006). China's traditional pawnbroking industry mainly provided emergency funds for civilians (especially the poor). Its social image was neutral. However, since the end of the Qing Dynasty, affected by the war and the rapid development of the banking industry, pawnbroking failed to transform and adapt to meet the demands of rapid social changes. In the process of transformation from the traditional financial system to the modern financial system, lack of social responsibility and ineffective government regulation resulted in widespread dislocation of pawnbroking business in the country (Li 2006).

Under the situation of warlords and political devolution, the Chinese people lived in dire poverty, whereas pawnbrokers were still trying to raise interest rate and shortened the period of lending to extract the usury. As a result, the social image of pawnbrokers deteriorated and pawnbroking was regarded as a "fishing" exploitation of the poor (Li 2006).

The pawnbroking industry was totally banned for more than three decades after 1949. In the early days of economic reform and opening-up after 1978, due to the underdeveloped or even inhibitory financial environment, the potential financing demand of SMEs, individual industrial and commercial households, could hardly be met by the financial repression environment in China, leading to the restoration of the pawnbroking industry. As an important debut of the modern pawnbroking industry, Chengdu Hua Mao Pawnshop in Sichuan Province was established in December 1987 (Qu 2007). The implementation of the Pawn Management further promoted the development of pawnbroking industry in 2005.

The long-term trading habits in China's pawnbroking industry have gradually formed the inherent operation procedures (see Fig. 8.2). The pawnbroker provides credits to customers (clients), as a convection condition, customers shall provide their mortgaged property as a guarantee for the pawnbroker. Our survey shows that the amount of pawn-loan is usually only accounting for 40–70% value of the collateral. When the loan deadline approaches, the customer needs to repay the loan plus interest and commission to the pawnbroker.

If the repayment is full, the pawnshop will return the original collateral to the customer. If the customer defaults and cannot repay the loan within the agreed period, the pawnshop will have ownership of the collateral.

However, when the global financial crisis erupted in 2007, the pawnbroking industry in China suffered from a severe shock, although it resumed its fast development path after 2009. Although Fig. 8.1 shows that the size of pawn financing did not decrease significantly in 2008 and 2009—it even increased slightly—given the number of newly opened pawnshops was still rising and compared with the size of pawn financing in other years, the size in 2008–2009 implied an apparent setback. For example, in Hangzhou, the capital city of Zhejiang Province, 21 out of 47 pawnshops in our sample experienced losses

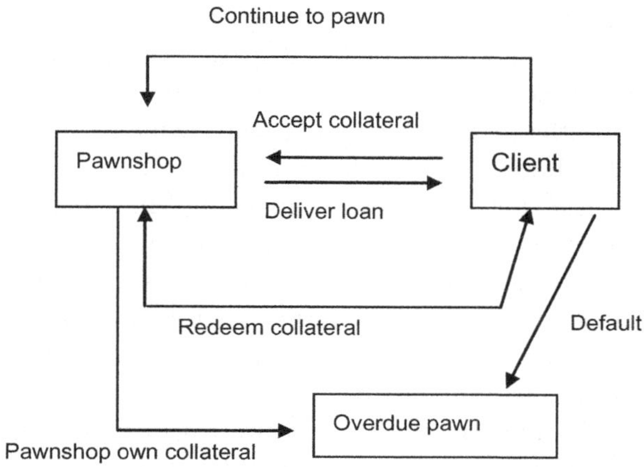

Fig. 8.2 Operational procedure of pawn loans in China

in those two years. In particular, six out of eight pawnshops that were newly established in 2008 suffered from losses. Hangzhou City Trade Bureau reported that nearly 90% of pawnshops in the city experienced a sharp decline in their profitability during 2008–2009 after a few years' fast expansion and growth before the global financial crisis (Hangzhou City Trade Bureau 2009). The pawnshops in Shanghai, Chongqing, Guangdong, Shanxi, Shandong, and Jiangsu had the same problem.

8.2 Main Features of the Pawnbroking Industry in China

As a useful and valuable supplement to formal financing, pawnbroking has its specific features such as small size, easy access, short term, and security (NPA 2015). Pawn financing and bank financing differ in collateral, interest rates, loan period, and the speed of lending. Banks only accept real estate as collateral, but pawnshops accept almost any valuable object as collateral including real estate, chattel, and rights pledge. The interest rate of bank loans is usually much lower than the pawn lending rate. Bank lending lays particular emphasis on long-term capital. However, the longest period of pawn lending is no more than 6 months. The majority of pawn loans are within one month. It usually takes a few months to approve a bank loan, while getting a pawn loan only needs a few hours or even a few minutes.

The difference between pawn financing and usury is as follows. Pawnbroking is a legal financing industry, which has relatively high entry barriers and needs to go through a strict examination and approval process. Usury has low entry barriers, but it is highly risky and usually prohibited by law. Pawnshops implement the legal interest rates. The usurious lending rate is far higher than the legal lending rates. For example, the underground usury rate reached more than 43% in Wenzhou City, Zhejiang Province in 2010 (Zhang et al. 2013).

The cost of pawn financing includes interests and comprehensive administration fees. According to the Act of Pawn Management in 2005, pawnshops can charge a lending rate that is not four times higher than the bank basic lending rate in the same period, and a comprehensive administration fee. The Act also stipulates that the monthly comprehensive rate of movable property pledge be no more than 0.42% of the loan, the monthly comprehensive rate of real estate mortgage no more than 0.27%, and the monthly comprehensive rate of property right pledge no more than 0.24%. The cost of pawn financing lies between bank loans and usurers. Therefore, the pawnbroking industry has not only become an important complement to the financial system in China, but also alleviated the high demand for usurers and illegal private banking by the self-employed and SMEs (Yan and Li 2016).

There are significant differences between the pawnbroking industry in China and other countries or regions. By October 2010, the registered capital of pawnshops in China reached RMB 58.4 billion (The Ministry of Commerce, 2011). In the first half of 2010, the total amount of pawn lending had cumulatively amounted to RMB 84.7 billion, of which, three-quarters, or about RMB 63.9 billion were issued to SMEs or commercial households. This lending critically alleviated the lack of formal bank loans to small businesses, and contributed to their economic growth (Lu 2010). For example, in Zhejiang Province, one of the most developed areas of pawnbroking activities in China, the total revenue of pawnbroking was RMB 22.25 billion in 2008, of which movables pledge accounted for 22.8%, property rights pledge for 28.5%, and real estate mortgage pledge for 48.7%. When it was broken down by borrowers, SMEs accounted for 47.4% and natural persons accounted for 52.6% (Department of Commerce, Zhejiang Provincial Government, 2009) Unlike other countries, the main businesses of pawnshops in China are in real estate mortgage and property rights pledges. In the first three quarters of 2009, business real estate mortgage was RMB 57.1 billion, accounting for 55.5% of all the business transactions, while the businesses of movables pledge and property rights pledge accounted for only 44.5% (The Special Industries, Department of Commerce 2010).

Pawning activities in China are distinctively different from those in other developed countries such as the United Kingdom and the United States. In China, pawning has been used as a useful supplement to the formal banking sector by SMEs, whereas in other countries, pawning is predominantly used by private individuals for small value pledges rather than by SMEs as an alternative financing source. According to the National Pawnbrokers Association (NPA), the UK pawnbroking market witnessed a rapid growth in the past decade, reaching £851 million in 2012. The average loan was between £150 and £200 (NPA 2015). The pawned objects included various types of gold and silver jewelry, vehicles, musical instruments, and various tools. About 80% of British pawners were low-income people, most of whom were women in their thirties. More than two-thirds of those families had school-aged children. They were low-paid workers with an annual income of less than £19,000, or recipients of social welfare (Xu 2005).

In China, low-income people do not go to pawnshops for financing for a number of reasons. First, historically "pawn" has a negative image in the Chinese society. Going to pawnshops is considered a disgrace. After the government banned pawnbroking in 1949, "pawn" was excluded from daily consumption and the financial system until 1978 when China started its reform program. Second, modern pawnbroking has restrictions on pawn objects. Low-value objects require storage space and incur relatively high costs. In addition, pawned money cannot be used for wholesale funding. Consequently, although modern pawnshops do not limit definitely the types of pawn objects, if the value of items is low, pawnshops will not accept them. Third, there are relatively few pawnshops, and the network is far and apart. As of December 2009, there were only about 4000 pawnshops in China. The density of pawnshops in China is far less than that in countries like the United States where pawnbroking has been well developed. Furthermore, most Chinese pawnshops are located in the cities and few in the countryside.

The situation of pawners and pawned objects in the United States is similar to that of the United Kingdome. The average pawn loan was around $100 (Goldin and Homonoff 2013). Many pawners had no checking accounts in 28 states of the United States. Only 12% of the US borrowers had borrowed from banks within a year. None of these borrowers had enough financial savings to overcome their short-term financial stress (Johnson 1998). Most pawners in the United States belonged to a group of people who were rejected by banks or other formal financial institutions before turning to pawnshops for help. This group of people consisted of those who were relatively low-income and poorly educated. Many of them were in a very bad personal financial situation (Caskey 1994). According to Caskey (1997), about 17% of American families did not have a current checking or savings account. In these families, 56% of them had an annual income of less than $10,000, and 24% of the household heads had 8 years of education or less. These people were usually denied access to any credits provided by the formal financial institutions. So in order to pay for their daily expenses, most of them turned to pawnshops for help. As a result, many pawned objects in the United States were common household tools, such as electric drills, grinding machines, lawn mowers, and washing machines. In addition, watches, musical instruments, vehicles, gold and silver jewelry were also common.

However, the average pawn size in China is substantially larger. According to our survey of 82 pawnbrokers in Zhejiang Province from July 2010 to June 2011, the average pawn size was RMB 138,300 (about USD $21,952) in 2009. As Table 8.1 indicates, the lowest average loan value of Hengfeng Pawnshop was RMB 15,000 (USD $2197) while the highest average loan value of Gongxin Pawnshop reached RMB 2 million (USD $292,912). Hengfeng Pawnshop, which opened in 1988, was mainly engaged in civilian products while Gongxin Pawnshop, which was founded in 2006, was mainly engaged in the real estate mortgage and property rights pledge.

Although the level of economic development in Sri-Lanka, India, the Philippines, and Indonesia is far lower than that in the United Kingdom or the United States, the types of pawners are similar, including merchants, shopkeepers, craftsmen, millers, blacksmiths, carpenters, or handicraftsmen. The pawned objects include gold and silver jewelry, common life equipment, and farming tools (Bouman and Houtman 1988). Pawners are mainly those with economic problems or those who are failing to maintain their daily consumption needs, both in developed and developing economies. The most common pawned objects in these countries or regions are gold, silver jewelry, and other kinds of household goods.

The preceding comparison of pawn sizes between China and other countries or regions shows that pawnbroking in these economies has the following common characteristics. First, the average pawn size is relatively small, usually ranging from USD $10–$700. Second, the income of most pawners is low and many of them lack credit records. Middle-class pawners during economic recession with high unemployment are forced to use pawnshops to finance their daily expenses. Third, it is convenient to get loans from pawnshops, and pawners can get small sums of money quickly. Fourth, pawn money is generally used to pay for daily household consumption. Therefore, the mainstream type of pawnbroking in countries other than China is "pawning for consumption." In contrast, the average pawn size in China is much higher than that in any other country or region discussed. Pawners are mainly owners of SMEs, individual businesses, or private investors. The pawn business is closely related to real estate mortgage and the property rights pledge. Pawners usually go to pawnshops to get loans for covering the funding gap in investment instead of paying for daily consumption.

8.3 Pawnbroking as an Important Financing Source of SMEs in China

Our survey data shows that most pawners were SMEs in Zhejiang Province, east China. Table 8.1 indicates the enterprises in litigation with Xiang Yi Rong Tong Co., Ltd during 2005–2010. It was the only listed company engaged in the pawn business in China. Xiang Yi De Qi and Yuan Tai were the two subsidiaries of the listed company. More than 80% of pawners in litigation were SMEs specialized in household textiles, water machines, printing and dyeing machines, aluminum foils, sheet materials, metal painting, precision sheet metals, metal tubes, cement, electrical equipment, cables, aquatic products, sewing machines, surveillance cameras, telecommunication equipment, and so on.

The following corporate financing model of SMEs is developed to explain why pawnbroking is a credible and important substitute for formal bank financing for SMEs in the Chinese context. The demand for capital by SMEs tends to be small, frequent, and short-term loans. Assume there is a labor-intensive SME that is in need of short-term financing. The production function has two main factors: labor and capital. Labor (L) is a fixed factor and capital (K) is a variable factor. The market is perfectly competitive, and market demand remains intact in the short term. The SME has only one investment project and produces only one product. The product price is given and exogenous. This is a simplistic model, but it allows us to explain why pawn financing has its advantage in supporting SMEs in China. The assumption of fixed labour is based on the short-term consideration that workers cannot be laid off immediately even when capital is in shortage.

In the short term, the financial demand of labor-intensive SMES is often urgent, and other factors of production are fixed. At this time, increasing capital investment can greatly improve output, and hence profit. If conditions permit, SMEs will continue to increase the variable input factor K to improve total output until the marginal production value is equal to the marginal cost of capital. Short-term loans coming from pawnbrokers are usually used as a supplement to the firm's working capital, and eventually will improve production. Thus, the variable

Table 8.1 SMEs in litigation with Xiang Yi Rong Tong Co. Ltd, Zhejiang Province, China during 2005–2010

Year	Brokers	Pawners	Product types	Values RMB million
2008	XiangYiDeQi	Senyang Textiles	Household textiles	2.6
2008	XiangYiDeQi	Kaka Appliance	Water machine	10.0
2010	XiangYiDeQi	ZJ P&D Machine	Printing/dyeing machine	1.0
2008	XiangYiDeQi	Longbiao Group	Aluminum foils	16.2
2008	XiangYiDeQi	Wenling Xinlong Panel	Sheet materials	16.2
2008	XiangYiDeQi	Xinlong Metal Company	Metal painting	16.2
2008	XiangYiDeQi	Xinshuijin Electronics Ltd	Crystal rods	16.2
2008	XiangYiDeQi	Baori Precision Sheet Metal	Precision sheet metals	20
2008	XiangYiDeQi	Ningbo Juncheng Metal Tube	Metal tubes	20
2008	XiangYiDeQi	Ningbo Hecheng Metal Tube	Metal tubes	20
2010	XiangYiDeQi	Panzhihua Dadi Cement	Cement	20
2010	XiangYiDeQi	Dadi Paper Group	Paper	10
2009	YuanTai	Hualun Group	Electrical equipment	10
2010	YuanTai	Fuyang Huanshan Cable	Cable	20
2009	YuanTai	Zhongqi Automobile Group	Car sales	6.5
2007	XiangYiDeQi	Zhoushan Weilongaquatic	Aquatic products	0.7
2009	YuanTai	Feiyue Group	Sewing machines	50
2009	XiangYiDeQi	Feiyue Group	Sewing machines	10
2008	YuanTai	Nanwang Group	Surveillance cameras	20
2006	XiangYiDeQi	Junzheng Applications	Other manufacturing	0.53
2007	YuanTai	Fuchunjiang Telecoms	Telecom equipment	7.96
2005	XiangYiDeQi	Changcheng Precision	Precision sheet metals	6

Sources Compiled by the authors according to the survey data factors of production will determine the level of final production when capital is urgently needed.

To simplify the analysis, it is assumed that the factor market is also perfectly competitive and the price of labor is fixed. The prices of capital borrowed from banks and pawnshops are respectively r_A (bank loan rate) and r_B (pawn comprehensive rate). In fact, in addition to the cost of capital, there are two main costs in financing. First, the SME needs time to wait for the approval of a loan. That is, there is a time difference between the application for a loan and when the money is received. Using t_i as the time of financing, γ as the waiting cost of time, so γ_{ti} is the total waiting cost of financing. Second, considering the differences of human resources endowment in SMEs, the possibility of obtaining a bank loan is uncertain, which creates extra cost to the SME. If the SME cannot borrow money from banks in the end, it is necessary to seek other lenders to keep its business afloat. So we assume that the cost coefficient, which is the uncertainty brought to the SME, is $\sigma_i, i = A, B$, where $\sigma_i \geq 1$, and the bigger σ_i is, the more uncertain obtaining a loan will be.

Based on the assumptions and notations given,we derive the following formula in Eq. (8.1) for the financing cost (C), using two alternative financing channels.

$$C_i = \sigma_i(r_i + \gamma t_i)K_i, i = A, B \tag{8.1}$$

Where the amount of financing for the SME consists of two parts: K_A is financing from banks and K_B is financing from pawnshops, both are homogeneous (perfect substitutes) and meet the total financing constraints $K_A + K_B \leq \overline{K}$, where $\overline{K}$ is the optimal (profit maximization) level of capital input required by the SME.

It is further assumed that labour input, the total amount of capital employed, prices of factors, and business incomes are all fixed for simplification. It follows that the optimal financing arrangement will only rely on the marginal costs of the two different financing modes. That is, the allocation of financing modes is at its optimal level when their marginal costs are equal as shown in Eq. (8.2).

$$\sigma_A(r_A + \gamma t_A) = \sigma_B(r_B + \gamma t_B) \tag{8.2}$$

In other words, for a given total amount of financing, if the SME chooses to finance from banks and pawnbrokers at the same time, the choice will not be the most efficient until the marginal costs of the two financing modes are equal. At this point, the total cost of financial cost in minimized.

Obviously, whether Eq. (8.2) is correctly specified will depend on a number of exogenous parameters. We suggest that it is a "blade condition." Normally it is hard to meet the conditions in equal levels exactly. In fact, once the above constraint condition is taken into account, the optimal planning solution is a corner solution. We can see exactly the specific forms of the solution in Fig. 8.3.

In Fig. 8.3, the vertical axis represents financing from banks and the horizontal axis represents financing from pawnshops. To the SME, there is no difference whether the capital comes from banks or from pawnshops; K_A and K_B are perfectly substitutable. Apparently the constraint line $K_A + K_B \leq \overline{K}$ should be a 45° line (dotted line). Given the constraint, the optimal financing decision of the SME is to choose the cost line based on the cost minimization principle. Point J in Fig. 8.3 corresponds to the optimal financing arrangement of the SME.

Based on the preceding, the slope of the cost line is $\theta = \frac{\sigma_A(r_A+\gamma t_A)}{\sigma_B(r_B+\gamma t_B)}$. The different slope represents the difference in the ratio of two marginal financing costs, which leads to a different choice of financing modes. Specifically, when $\theta < 1$, corresponding to sub-graph (a), the marginal cost of A (bank-financing) is less than B (pawn-financing), hence the SME chooses bank-financing only. When $\theta > 1$, corresponding to sub-graph (b), the marginal cost of B (pawn-financing) is less than A

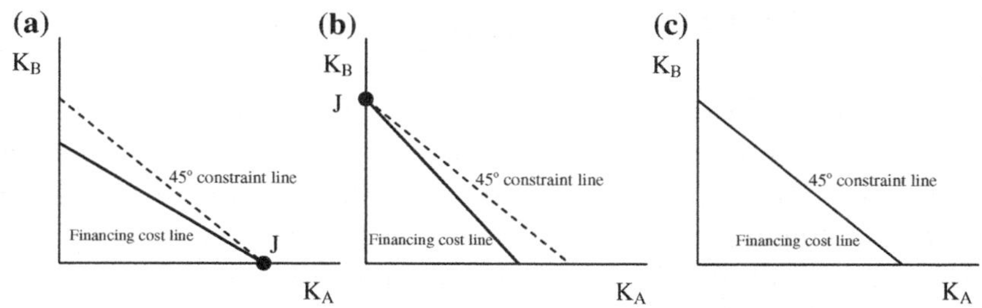

Fig. 8.3 Choice of financing modes. *Source* Compiled by the authors

(bank-financing), hence the SME chooses pawn-financing only. When $\theta = 1$, corresponding to sub-graph (c), the marginal costs of A and B are equal, there is no difference between the two modes, hence the SME can choose the two modes by an arbitrary proportion.

According to the model design, the corner solution is related to perfect substitution between the two financing sources and the assumption of the financing cost. The assumption of perfect substitution means that there is no difference between \$1 coming from a bank and \$1 coming from a pawnbroker. The linear assumption of financing cost means that the two financing modes depend on the same parameters and the marginal cost is unchanged. The two assumptions are a simplification to the unnecessary complexities of reality, and it removes the influencing factors, which do not affect the core conclusion. In this particular point, we are concerned about the relationship of balance and choice between bank loans and pawn financing. So, as an extreme performance, the corner solution illustrates concisely the key factors influencing the SME's financing decision.

One may argue, of course, that the assumption of a linear cost line may be naïve and simplistic. However, making an alternative assumption to accommodate a non-linear cost line, it still leads to a similar result indicating that borrowing decision from any financial source will depend on its relative cost of borrowing compared to an alternative choice. In that regard, the previous simple model has served our purpose well.

8.4 The Impact of the Global Financial Crisis on the Pawning Industry in China

After the global financial crisis broke out in the United States in 2007, the Chinese government decided to implement a RMB 4 trillion fiscal stimulus plan at the end of 2008, which lowered the financing cost and the lending threshold of bank loans for SMEs (Yang and Huizenga 2010). As a result, the borrowing cost of pawn financing became higher than that of bank loans. A large number of coastal Chinese SMEs, especially in Zhejiang Province, were mainly export-orientated before the crisis. Due to the weaker demand from the international market under the global financial crisis, some SMEs in our sample had to reduce (or even close) their productive activities, hence they needed less pawn loans to support their working capital. Consequently, there was a slowdown in pawnbroking activities in China during 2008–2009 after a steady growth in the previous years as shown in Fig. 8.1.

However, China was not the only country that implemented the fiscal stimulus plan to promote economic growth under the global financial crisis. The United States and the European Union launched a series of quantitative easing schemes to stimulate their sluggish economies. But why was only China's pawnbroking industry severely affected? The main explanation is that the pawnbroking industry in China has been driven more by the investment need of SMEs than the consumption need of individuals or households in other countries or regions.

In the United States and the European Union, the main funding of their fiscal stimulus plans went to investment projects. As a result, it did not have a direct impact on the consumption-oriented pawnbroking industry. In contrast, the fiscal stimulus plan in China had a powerful and negative impact on pawnbroking activities, which were used as a supplement to the formal financial system to provide services for SMEs. Under the fiscal stimulus plan, as banks lowered their lending threshold and accelerated the approval process, the costs of bank financing were greatly reduced. In the meantime, the financing costs through pawning remained more or less unchanged. Consequently, SMEs were tempted to shift their borrowings from pawnshops to banks.

The change in borrowing behavior caused by the stimulus plan can also be explained by the theoretical model outlined in the previous section. Since banks had boosted their lending speed under the fiscal stimulus plan and lowered the lending threshold, the corresponding parameters, σ_A and t_A, would have declined, lowering the marginal cost of bank financing, that is, lowering the value of $\sigma_A(r_A + \gamma t_A)$. Given other conditions unchanged, financing from banks became more attractive to SMEs. As reflected in Fig. 8.3, SMEs faced a declined slope of financing cost line and their choice was more likely to be tilted toward Fig. 8.3(a). The situation of the corner solution SMEs chose to finance from banks was more likely to take place. Once more SMEs gave up borrowing from pawnshops and turned to bank lending, the losses of pawnbroking were inevitable.

Many pawnbrokers also took positive measures. For example, they attracted clients by reducing their own lending costs. A pawnbroker who reduced its lending cost was trying to reduce σ_B, r_B, and t_B to boost the attractiveness of pawn financing. However, the difference between pawn lending and bank lending is that the former does not need much cost on favor and social interaction, so σ_B has little space to be reduced. Pawnbroking can only reduce r_B and t_B to attract clients. Our survey data show that from the financial crisis to the end of 2010, many pawnshops canceled their comprehensive fees and only collected the interest of pawn money. Since the pawning interest rate was strictly controlled by the People's Bank of China (PBOC), reducing the lending interest rate during the global financial crisis further compressed the profitability of pawnbrokers. In terms of boosting lending speed (reducing t_B), the transaction of a common pawn loan was already fast anyway, so the scope for making it faster was also limited. For example, the transactions such as real estate mortgages lasted for only 2 to 3 days. Therefore, the marginal cost of pawn lending $\sigma_B(r_B + \gamma t_B)$ was relatively stable because pawnshops had little leverage to reduce their costs to compete with banks when quantitative easing made bank lending easier and quicker than before.

There are other factors that may have exaggerated the losses of pawning activities in China during the global financial crisis. For example, the crisis made many export-oriented SMEs lose foreign orders, reducing their demand for pawning funds directly. In addition, there were extra costs brought about by governmental regulations on pawning activities. According to the Act of Pawn Management, a pawnbroker cannot automatically obtain a pledge whose value is more than RMB 30,000. When the client does not redeem it, the pawnbroker has to take legal action against the pawner or sell it through public auction. During the financial crisis, the number of disputes and litigations increased sharply. The costs of disposing large-loan-pledges were pushed up. Finally, the increasing uncertainty of pawning activities governed by the regulations amplified by σ_B and t_B further reduced the attraction of pawning to SMEs.

It needs to be pointed that the negative impact of the world financial crisis on China's pawnbroking industry lasted for less than two years during 2008–2009. As the stimulus plan was gradually phased out after 2010, the demand for pawn financing started to rise sharply (Fig. 8.1), reflecting its important role as a useful supplement to bank credits for SMEs, which were constantly discriminated against by the formal financial institutions in China.

The pawnbroking industry demonstrated a clear ascendant trend along with the implementation of tight monetary policy by the PBOC after 2010. A fiscal stimulus plan under the global financial crisis led to the decline of pawning business since the relative cost of pawn financing became higher than bank lending. Confronted with the inflationary pressure, the PBOC had raised the interest rate five times sequentially by the end of July 2011. The reserve requirement ratio (RRR) reached a historic high of 21.5% after 12 consecutive rises. Owing to the tight monetary policy, the commercial banks in China reduced their lending, making it more difficult for SMEs to secure bank loans.

We surveyed some SMEs in Zhejiang Province, East China, in February 2011, and found that there were changes in their financing means during 2007–2010. The following two cases in the survey illustrate the preceding statement. Yong Kang XD Door Making Company and Long You YQ Cloth Art Firm, two small businesses with registered capital of RMB 500,000 were the clients of Yong Kang HF Pawnshop and Long You HJ Pawnshop, respectively. From 2007 to 2008, Yong Kang XD Door Making Company borrowed nine times from Yong Kang HF Pawnshop during 2007–2008. The amount of loans ranged from RMB 50,000 to RMB 300,000. The longest borrowing term was 2 months while the shortest was only 7 days. However, when the central government of China carried out the stimulus package of RMB 4 trillion during 2008–2009, the company only borrowed once from the pawnshop in March 2008 with an amount of RMB 100,000. The company borrowed twice from the pawnshop in 2010 with RMB 100,000 in July and RMB 150,000 in October. There was no pawn loan record from April 2009 to June 2010. But during the period, a one-year loan of RMB 500,000 was granted to the company by a local commercial bank under the guarantee of a large door-making industrial company in May 2009. It is the same case for Zhejiang Long You YQ Cloth Art Firm. From 2007 to 2008, the firm had five pawn loan records two times in 2007 and three times in 2008 with the amount ranging from RMB 70,000 to RMB 200,000. The longest borrowing term was 1 month while the shortest was 10 days. However, there was no pawn record from 2009 to September 2010. During the same period, a bank mortgage loan of RMB 300,000 was granted to the enterprise in March 2010. In October 2010, the firm borrowed RMB 120,000 from Long You HJ Pawnshop. Obviously, in the case of national monetary easing, SMEs owners prefer to borrow from banks rather than pawnshops. However, under the tight monetary policy, the lending rates of banks went up so that pawn financing regained its popularity.

Consequently, the pawnbroking industry expanded rapidly after the global financial crisis. It implies that pawnbroking has become an important component of the Chinese financial system. It is particularly beneficial for the financing of the SME sector in China.

8.5 Conclusion

Pawnbroking had a long history in China since ancient times. It was banned after the People's Republic of China was founded in 1949 for more than three decades. Since the economic reform and opening-up in 1978, pawning activities have been legalized and become a useful supplement to the formal financial system, providing valuable finance for millions of SMEs, which have been largely discriminated against by the banking and other formal financial institutions.

Pawning activities became prosperous and grew rapidly before the global financial crisis broke out in 2007. However, the industry suffered from a severe setback and many pawnshops incurred losses under the financial crisis. This phenomenon emerges as a puzzle that requires explanation. This chapter develops a theoretical model to explain this puzzle. Our key argument is that SMEs can choose to borrow from formal financial institutions or pawnshops. To minimize their borrowing cost, SMEs usually borrow up to a point where the marginal costs of borrowing from both sources are equalized. When the marginal cost of one source is less than that of the other, the optimal solution will be a corner point. Otherwise, the optimal solution is any mix of these two sources.

Before the global financial crisis, given that applying for bank loans was uncertain and time consuming, many SMEs tended to seek financial loans from pawnshops. During the financial crisis, banks lowered their lending rate due to the government's fiscal stimulus plan. As a result, more SMEs tended to borrow more from the banks and reduced their demand for pawn financing. This explains why the global financial crisis had a negative impact on the pawnbroking industry in China.

As the world economy gradually recovered from the financial crisis and China stopped its quantitative easing, pawn financing became popular again for SMEs in China. With the deepening financial reform in China, pawnbroking will continue to be a useful and beneficial supplement to the formal financial system, providing active and timely financial support to millions of SMEs, which have huge development potential but usually face severe financial constraints.

This chapter provides some first-hand survey data from Zhejiang Province to understand the development of the pawnbroking industry in China. The experience in Zhejiang implies that pawnbroking can provide a quick and efficient source of financing to solve SMEs financial problems when they face credit constraints. There are two important reasons for the fast development of pawnshops in Zhejiang Province. First, Zhejiang Province has been historically short of formal capital provided by the state-owned banks (Tsai 2002). Second, numerous SMEs have to resort to usury for their financial needs. However, usury is illegal and costly. Pawnbroking is legal and cheaper than underground money shops. The only limitation is that the value cap of each pawn is small, as regulated by the government. However, the advantages of pawning provide a valuable and efficient source of financing for the numerous micro-firms and SMEs that have been and will continue to be the backbone of the Chinese economy. The new government financial reforms will create an even more open and liberal market for the development of small banking institutions and pawnshops in China.

Since the 18th National Congress of the Chinese Communist Party in 2012, the central government of China has implemented a new set of policy instruments to deepen the financial reforms. For example, the small and medium-sized banks have been allowed to compete with the existing large state-owned commercial banks, particularly in the rural areas. These new small and medium-sized commercial banks mainly target the SME sector and thus reduce the difficulty and cost for SMEs to secure commercial bank loans. Competition from such new banks may have some negative impact on pawning activities. However, the relaxed regulations by the government may also imply that pawnbrokers will enjoy more autonomy and preferential policy to facilitate the development of the country's entire financial system. If this is the case, China will develop a far more comprehensive financial system than before and SMEs will be able to have access to more diversified financing channels including pawnshops in the future.

Appendix

Zhejiang Pawn Trade Association, Zhejiang University, Joint Investigation Questionnaire
(Thank you for your support to pawn-broking industry in Zhejiang province!)

Company Name: ________________ Tel: ___________________

1. The establishing date of your company: ______________, registered capital: ________, fund-provider: State-owned: ____%, collective : ____%, private: ____%.

2. Why do you want to set up a pawnshop? Was the approval going smoothly? Could you talk about it briefly? (Including the background of setting up your pawnshop)

____

____

3. How many employees when the company was set up? ________. Master's degree or higher : ____, bachelor degree: ____, associate college degree: ____, others: _____.
The age structure of the employees when the company was set up: under 20: _____, 20–30: _____, 30–40: _____, 40–50: _____, 40–50: _____, more than 60 years of age: _____.

4. How many employees now? _______. Master's degree or higher : ____, bachelor degree :____, associate college degree: ____, others: _____.
The age structure of the employees now: under 20: _____, 20–30: _____, 30–40: _____, 40–50: _____, 40–50: _____, more than 60 years of age: _____.

5. How long after setting up your company netted the first clients? _______. The pawn item was ( ) a. Jewelry b. Car c. House property d. Equipment e. Antique paintings. f _______

6. What kind of pawn business could be engaged in at the beginning of the company set up? ( )
a. Pledge of movables pawn business b. Property rights pledge business c. The real estate mortgage business

7. What kind of pawn items could be used at the beginning of the company set up? ( )
a. Gold and silver jewelry b. Calligraphy and paintings c. Watches d. Cars e. Antiques f. Equipment g. House property h. Land use right i. Property rights j. electronic products k.others
What kind of pawn items in recent years ( )?
a. Gold and silver jewelry b. Calligraphy and paintings c. Watches d. Cars e. Antiques

f. Equipment g. House property h. Land use right i. Property rights j. electronic products \ k. others

8. What's the composition of pawn business in your company?

a. Gold and silver jewelry b. Calligraphy and paintings c. Watches d. Cars e. Antiques f. Equipment g. House property h. Land use right i. Property rights j. electronic products k. others

9. When did your company carry out the property rights pawn business? ______________.

How much business that year? ___________. The proportion is _____%.

10. When did your company carry out the real estate pawn business? ______________. How much business that year? ___________. The proportion is _____%.

11. The loan period of Civilian goods pawn in your company is _______. What is the change in 2009? _________.

12. How many people in your company have work experience in banks? ( ) a. 1 b. 2 c. 3 d. more than 3.

13. Did your company have financing from banks in recent years?

Yes ( ), No ( ).

If the answer is yes, could you tell us what percentage of bank financing in registered capital ________%.

14. Do you have special the appraiser of civilian goods identification?

Yes ( ), No ( ).

15. How long does it usually take to deal with a common civilian goods pawn business? ( )

a. 10 minutes b.15 minutes c.20 minutes d.25 minutes e. 30 minutes f. 40 minutes g. about 1 hour h. more than 1 hour

16. How long does it usually take to deal with a real estate business or the property right business? ( ) a. 1 day b. 2 days c. 3 days d. 4 days e. about a week

17. Could you tell us whether the pawn rate is negotiable, or say, different customers may have different pawn rates? ( ) a. Yes b. No

18. If your company have some benefits to the customers, mainly considered ( )

a. the customer has a good pawn item, the risk is controllable b. the customer has good personality traits c. the customer is regular customer d. the customer is potential to be a good customers e. never profit-sharing to customer

19. Do you have any special provisions for SMEs financing? Is there any change of pawn rates in the past two years? ( )

a. Yes, the pawn rate is preferential b. Yes, the procedure is simplified c. Yes, there is a longer loan period d. Yes, there is a number of preferential measures e. Never

20. The total amount pawn business is ______. What's the proportion of business structure in 2008 and 2009?

2008: The total amount pawn business _______. 1. pledge of movables _____%; 2. pledge of property rights ______%; 3. mortgage on real estate ______%.

2009: The total amount pawn business _______. 1. pledge of movables _____%; 2. pledge of property rights ______%; 3. mortgage on real estate ______%.

21. what percentage of individual clients and enterprise clients in real estate mortgage in the recent two years? Individual: ______%, enterprises: ______%.

22. How long a large loan period will take (more than RMB 500,000) ? ( )

a. half month b. one month c. one and a half month d. two months e. three months f. four months g. five months h. six months i. __________

23. What percentage of default rate of civilian goods pawn in 2008? ( )

a. less than 5% b. 5–10% c. 10–15% d. 15–20% e. 20–25% f. 25–30% g. 30–35% h. 40% i. 45% j. 50% k. 55% L. more than 60%

24. What percentage of default rate of large loan in 2008? ( )

a. less than 5% b. 5–10% c. 10–15% d. 15–20% e. 20–25% f. 25–30% g. 30–35% h. 40% i. 45% j. 50% k. 55% L. more than 60%

25. What percentage of default rate of civilian goods pawn in 2009? ( )

a. less than 5% b. 5–10% c. 10–15% d. 15–20% e. 20–25% f. 25–30% g. 30–35% h. 40% i. 45% j. 50% k. 55% L. more than 60%

26. What percentage of default rate of large loan in 2009? ( )

a. less than 5% b. 5–10% c. 10–15% d. 15–20% e. 20–25% f. 25–30% g. 30–35% h. 40% i. 45% j. 50% k. 55% L. more than 60%

27. What percentage of comprehensive default rate of all the pawn business in 2008/2009? 2008: ________. 2009: __________.

a. less than 5% b. 5–10% c. 10–15% d. 15–20% e. 20–25% f. 25–30% g. 30–35% h. 40% i. 45% j. 50% k. 55% L. more than 60%

28. In the pawn business over the last two years, from the transaction quantitatively, SMEs

financing accounted for _____%, natural persons accounted for ______%;

In the pawn business over the last two years, from the business turnover, SMEs financing accounted for _____%, natural persons accounted for ______%.

29. The proportion of regular customers is about ( ).

a. less than 5% b. 5–10% c. 10–15% d. 15–20% e. 20–25% f. 25–30% g. 30–35% h. 40% i. 45% j. 50% k. 55% L. more than 60%

30. What is the average amount of each loan last year? ____________.

31. In the past two years, the real estate pawn business accounted for the total amount of pawn business is about ( ). a.10% b. 10–20% c. 20–30% d. 30–40% e. 40–50% f. 50–60% g. 60–70% h. more than 70%

32. Is there any loss or a decline in business for your company in the past two years? Could you tell us the proportion of decline (setback) in business? ( ) a. less than 5% b. 5–10% c.10–20% d. 20–30% e. 30–40% f. 40–50% g. 50–60% h. more than 60%

33. Is there any customer loss (they had originally been intended to get pawn loans, but in the end turned to bank lending) in the past two years? Could you tell us why?

____

34. Does the company have affiliated enterprise which belongs to the downstream industry, such as the auction enterprise? ( ) a. Yes b. No

35. Have the company dealt with rights pledge pawn business in the past two years? ( )

a. a lot of b. a few c. never

36. Have the company dealt with the stock pledge pawn business in the past two years? ( )

a. a lot of b. a few c. never

37. Do you think if it' s necessary for pawnshop to add retail and consignment business?

( ) a. Yes, it 's necessary b. It is not necessary

38. The percentage of handling cost of default items account for its value in the past two years is about ______%. a. 5% b. 10% c. 15% d. 20% e. 25% f. more than 30%

39. The profit margin of handling cost of default items in the past two years is about ______%. a. -10% b. -5% c. 0 (break even) d. 5% e. 10% f. 15% g. 20% h. 25% i. 30% j. 35% k. more than 40%

40. What's your opinion on the changes of administrative department?

____

____

41. What do you think of what operations can improve the efficiency of pawn-broking industry?

____

____

42. What do you think are the main reason affect pawn business?

____

____

43. What do you think are the problems exist in the process of pawn business now?

____

____

44. What's your opinion on the prospects of pawn-broking industry?

____

____

45. What enterprises do you think has played a leading role in the development of the pawn-broking industry in Zhejiang province?

____

____

46. In your opinion, the problems in pawn-broking for government should solve, in order, are

____

Thank you again for your support to pawn-broking industry in Zhejiang province!

Zhejiang Pawn Trade Association, Zhejiang University

References

Allen, F., J. Qian, and M. Qian. 2005. China's Financial System: Past, Present, and Future. https://www2.bc.edu/~qianju/China-finsystem-book-072105-ALL.pdf.

Ayyagari M., A. Demirgüç-Kunt, and V. Maksimovic. 2010. Formal Versus Informal Finance: Evidence from China. *Review of Financial Studies* 23(8): 3048–3097.

Bouman, F.J.A., and R. Houtman. 1988. Pawnbroking as an Instrument of Rural Banking in the Third World. *Economic Development and Cultural Change* 37 (1): 69–89.

Caskey, J.P. 1994. *Fringe Banking: Check-Cashing Outlets, Pawnshops and the Poor*. New York: Russell Sage Foundation.

Caskey, J.P. 1997. *Lower Income Americans, Higher Cost Financial Services*. Madison, WI: Filene Research Institute.

Dougherty, S., R. Herd, and P. He. 2007. Has a Private Sector Emerged in China's Industry? Evidence from a Quarter of a Million Chinese Firms. *China Economic Review* 18: 309–334.

Duan, H.D., X.J. Han, and H.B. Yang. 2009. An Analysis of Causes for SMEs Financing Difficulty. *International Journal of Business and Management* 4 (6): 73–75.

Fung, H.G., Q.F. Liu, and J. Yau. 2007. Financing Alternatives for Chinese Small and Medium Enterprises: The Case for a Small and Medium Enterprise Stock Market. *China & World Economy* 15 (1): 26–42.

Hangzhou Trade Bureau. 2009. *Analysis of Pawnbroking Business in the First Half of 2009*. Zhejiang Province: Archived Data of Hangzhou Trade Bureau.

Gao, Q., and S. Banerji. 2015. The Growth Appraisal System for Chinese SMEs. *Journal of Chinese Economic and Business Studies* 13 (2): 175–193.

Goldin, J., and T. Homonoff. 2013 Consumer Borrowing After Payday Loan Bans. https://scholar.princeton.edu/sites/default/files/Goldin_Homonoff_11_5_2013_0.pdf.

Johnson, R.W. 1998. *Pawnbroking in the U.S.A.: Profile of Consumers*. Washington, DC: Georgetown University, Senior Research Associate Credit Research Center.

Li, S. 2006. *Pawnshops: The Unique Fast Mode of Financing*. Beijing: Xue Yuan Press.

Liu, Q. 1995. *The History Of China's Pawn-broking System (in Chinese)*. Shanghai: Shanghai Ancient Books Press.

Lu, Z. 2010. Ministry of Commerce, Pawnbroking Industry Development Planning will be made in Twelfth Five-Year Period. *China Securities Journal* (中国证券报), October 27.

Ma, S. 2010. *Shareholding System Reform in China: Privatizing by Grouping for Stones*. London: Edward Elgar Publishing Limited.

National Pawnbrokers Association (NPA). 2015. Pawnbroking: A Successful and Established Profession. http://www.thenpa.com/pdf/NPA-Brochure-WEB.pdf.

Naughton, B. 2007. *The Chinese Economy: Transitions and Growth*. Cambridge: The MIT Press.

Newman, A., D. Borgia, and Z. Deng. 2013. How do SMEs with Single and Multiple Owners Finance their Operations Differently? Empirical Evidence from China. *Thunderbird International Business Review* 55 (5): 531–544.

Qu, Y. 2007. *The History of China's Pawn-broking (in Chinese)*. Shenyang: Shenyang Press.

Ruan, J., and X. Zhang. 2012. Credit Constraints, Clustering, and Profitability Among Chinese Firms. *Strategic Change* 21 (3): 159–178.

The Special Industries. 2010. Department of Commerce, Beijing.

Tsai, K.S. 2002. *Back-Alley Banking: Private Entrepreneurs in China*. Ithaca: Cornell University Press.

Tsai, K. 2004. Imperfect Substitutes: The Local Political Economy of Informal Finance and Microfinance in Rural China and India. *World Development* 32 (9): 1487–1507.

Vicziany, M., and G. Zhang. 2005. Entrepreneurship and Technology in the Growth of Private Enterprise in Western China: The Tongwei Group. *UNESCO International Centre for Engineering Education (UICEE)*, Bangkok.

Xinhua Net. 2013. China Spends Big to Support SME's Innovation, http://news.xinhuanet.com/english/china/2013-10/25/c_132831353.htm.

Xu, Q.J. 2005. British Pawnbroking Industry Research Report, Archived Data of Commercial Section, Embassy of the People's Republic of China in the United Kingdom of Great Britain and Northern Ireland.

Yang, L., and C. Huizenga. 2010. China's Economy in the Global Economic Crisis: Impact and Policy Responses. In *The Financial and Economic Crisis of 2008–2009 and Developing Countries*, ed. Sebastian Dullien, Detlef J. Kotte, Alejandro Márquez, and Jan Priewe. New York and Geneva: United Nations.

Yan, Q., and J. Li. 2016. *Regulating China's Shadow Banks*. Abingdon: Routledge.

Zhang, G.B. 2008. The Choice of Formal or Informal Finance: Evidence from Chengdu. *China, China Economic Review* 19: 659–678.

Zhang, X.C., Z. Xu, and D. Qin. 2013. Informal Lending Rates and the Way Out of the Private Capital in Wenzhou. *Journal of Financial Research* 3: 1–14.

Zhou, W.B. 2009. Bank Financing in China's Private Sector: The Payoffs of Political Capital. *World Development* 37 (4): 787–799.

9

Conclusions and Policy Implications

Preamble

This book presents a series of our studies on various aspects of the Chinese banking industry over the last 15 years. It starts from the economic and banking sector reform, which matches China's long-term ambition to build a modern financial services industry. When we initially started our research on the Chinese banking industry, we encountered two important international events. The first was China's accession to the World Trade Organization (WTO) in 2001, forcing the authorities to gradually open up for international competition and inward foreign direct investment into the otherwise tightly controlled domestic financial market; and the second was the world financial crisis triggered by the US subprime crisis in 2007.

In the first major event, the Chinese banking industry was still overwhelmingly dominated by the four big Chinese commercial banks, which were also on the verge of insolvency due to the large and ever-mounting levels of nonperforming loans (NPLs). The Chinese government used foreign exchange reserves as well as huge cash subsidies to strip off the NPLs from these gigantic state-owned banks. The cost to the taxpayers was high, equivalent to 20% of China's GDP in 2004.

C. Jiang and S. Yao, *Chinese Banking Reform*, The Nottingham China Policy Institute Series, DOI 10.1007/978-3-319-63925-3_9

However, the reform was rewarding in the sense that China avoided a systematic financial crisis like that experienced by many major industrialized economies in 2007. In contrast to the sharp downturn of economic performance and the debt crisis in the EU member states in the aftermath of the world financial crisis, China was able to expand its economy at an almost two-digit level up to 2012. China's extraordinary economic performance should have in part been due to the radical banking reform carried out in the late 1990s through the first few years into the twenty-first century.

However, the huge bailout and subsidies to the state-owned banks have not fundamentally resolved the long-term problems of moral hazard, principal-agent and soft-budget constraints. To resolve these problems, the Chinese government has not followed the western model of total privatization of all the state banks. Rather, it has followed a gradual and pragmatic approach as it has done in the real economic sector. China's approach includes: (1) using share-holding as a way to improve the government structure and efficiency, and (2) allowing diversified ownership in the market so that state-owned banks are subject to peer pressure from foreign invested banks, city commercial banks, joint-stock banks, and more recently, small-scale rural banks as well as private banks. Currently, the four big state-owned commercial banks have a market share of about 39%, down from its peak level of 58% attained 15 years ago. On the surface, it appears that ICBC, BOC, CCBC and ABC are still the most profitable banks in China and in the world. In terms of stock market values, four of the world's top 10 banks are Chinese state-owned banks.

In recent years, a new phenomenon has emerged to the surprise of everyone in the banking industry. This is the rapid expansion of internet banking, and the rising activities of shadow banking in China. The emergence of shadow banking and internet finance has posed serious challenges to the dominant position of traditional banking, which is dominated by the state sector.

Therefore, before we conclude this book, we have to predict what will happen to the Chinese banking industry in 10 or 20 years' time. Is the current banking institution able to maintain its structure and operation mode? How may further banking reforms affect the state-owned banks and other financial institutions? How is internet finance going to affect investors, consumers and the traditional banking sector? In recent years, the Chinese government has been trying to make their currency (renminbi or RMB) more internationalized with the hope that it will become a major world currency to compete with the US dollar and the Euro. How realistic is this goal? What challenges and constraints will China face to make this happen? How may RMB internationalization affect the way that the extant banking industry operates in China and in the rest of the world? What kinds of policies will the government adopt to deepen financial reform and maintain a steady rate of economic growth in the aftermath of the world financial crisis? Our research and analysis in this book may have answered some of these questions, but the empirical results have not given us a clear direction of where to go. This chapter will answer some of these questions based on our research and observations on the most recent developments in the Chinese banking industry.

In the rest of this chapter, we will make some conclusions as to how we may assess the success or lessons of the banking reform in China. We will then present the opportunities and challenges faced by the Chinese monetary authority. Finally, we will suggest some policy recommendations for further policy reforms.

9.1 Current State of the Chinese Banking System

Before economic reform, China was a strictly centrally planned economy. In the real economic sectors, production, employment, sales and prices were all controlled by the state. As a result, commercial banking was unnecessary and strictly forbidden. This historical condition is today relatively unknown to the policy and academic circles, but any study on the Chinese banking industry should bear this in mind.

It would be difficult to imagine that a modern economy can be run without a well-functioning commercial banking and financial industry. However, only 40 years ago, China's only bank was the central bank, or the People's Bank of China (PBOC), which worked along with the State Planning Committee (SPC) and the Ministry of Finance (MOF) to manage the national economy. PBOC was basically the issuer of RMB and acted as an accountant for both the SPC and MOF.

The interest rate was close to zero and fixed, deposits were taken largely from state-owned enterprises, and there were no real lending activities taking place. The PBOC was simply a fund allocator, following the instructions given by the MOF who, in turn, had to be dictated by the SPC. In other words, investment projects were determined by the SPC, and the MOF decided the amount of investment for each project after a comprehensive review of all the projects proposed. Once the amount of investments was decided, the PBOC just allocated requested funds to the approved projects.

Economic reform changed all of this traditional way of finance and banking. Not only was the state sector reformed so that prices, outputs and sales were all gradually subject to market forces and could no longer be entirely controlled by state planners. Commercial interests become more and more important and enterprises, state- or non-state-owned, need commercial banking for their investment and production activities.

The initial banking reform was to separate the role of a central bank from the role of commercial banking from within the PBOC. The four big state-owned banks, ICBC, BOC, CCBC and ABC were respectively restored to take over the commercial banking activities with each focusing on a special sector. For example, ICBC was primarily responsible for urban and industrial development, CCBC was responsible for large construction projects, BOC was responsible for dealing with the external sector and ABC was responsible for rural and agricultural development.

The division of business between the four big state-owned commercial banks did not move away entirely from the centrally planned system as they were created to automatically have market monopoly with state-regional government influence right from their inception. As a result, despite a huge improvement from the pre-reform era, the banking industry in China was highly inefficient as the survival of the banks was guaranteed by the unusually high interest rate spread between the lending and deposit rates. The interest rate spread of more than 3 percentage points lasted for decades until recently when market reform started to narrow the gap.

Inefficiency in the state banking sector has its historical root, however, it also arises from the inertia of state-ownership and lack of competition from the private and foreign sectors. In addition, the moral hazard problem prevailed as state-owned banks and their regional branches were subject to central and local government intervention, particularly when central and local state-owned enterprises were under financial stress. Banks were often asked or coerced to lend to loss-making firms without a clear idea of when these firms might become profitable and be able to pay back loans.

The mixture of social/policy needs with commercial needs for profits were two conflicting objectives for state-owned commercial banks. Once these conflicting needs were confused by political interference, it was impossible to objectively assess the real performance of the banks.

By the end of the 1990s, the problem of NPLs became so serious for all of China's large state-owned banks, which controlled more than 60% of the country's financial assets, that the whole banking industry was technically insolvent. By a western standard, none of the Chinese state-owned commercial banks could survive for any competition.

However, the Chinese government was able to pump billions of RMB to strip off the NPLs from these banks. Four state-owned asset management companies were specifically set up to handle the NPLs for each of the four big state-owned banks. By 2006, after more than eight years of cleaning and recapitalization, the four big banks became miraculously healthy and they were able to be listed on the stock exchanges. In the following decade, these banks became some of the most profitable enterprises in China and the world. China's four big banks also enter the top-10 list of the global banking industry in terms of market capital.

In retrospect, there are pros and cons for the efforts to reform the big commercial banks in China. The cost of reform was unusually high for China, particularly the high interest rate spread ensured by the central bank, and the write-off of the large NPLs, which accounted for more than 40% of the total loans in the late 1990s. The benefits are also obvious. Given the history of China as a centrally planned economy and the lack of bank development, China has been able to transform the state-banking sector, which is now quite competitive in the international market.

Apart from the reform of the state banking institutions, China has rigorously developed the joint stock banks, city commercial banks, rural credit corporations and urban credit unions. In addition, after China's accession to the WTO, there are hundreds of foreign banks or foreign bank subsidiaries opening their business throughout the country.

The latest statistics show that China has now more than 4000 banks or business-related financial institutions. The amount of assets also increased exponentially in the last two decades, amounting to two times that of the country's GDP.

9.2 Economic Rationale of Banking Reforms and Bank Efficiency in China

After nearly four decades of economic reform, China has become the second largest economy in the world. In 2016, China's GDP accounted for 15% of the global total GDP, which was equivalent to 60% of the United States' and more than twice of Japan's and almost four times of the United Kingdom's. However, the reforms in the banking industry have not matched that of the real economy.

For example, the small and medium-sized enterprises account for more than 90% of China's new employment, but assume less than one-third of the total bank loans. Large banks have interest in lending to the large enterprises, particularly the state sector. In the last few years, about 60% of bank loans were channeled to the housing market, accelerating urban house price rises across the country.

There are a number of problems associated with bank reform. Firstly, the financial market is still dominated by a few large banks, which have little incentive to provide services to the rural and private economies, particularly the small and medium-sized firms. Secondly, the state has too many restrictions in the informal financial markets that are targeting the rural and private sectors as well as the SMEs. There have been numerous reports in Zhejiang and other prosperous provinces that private individuals use "mass finance" (pooling money from wealthy individuals and lending it to SMEs at a much higher interest rate than the maximum rate allowed by the monetary authority) to make abnormal profit. This illegal financing channel is attractive to SMEs as they are unable to obtain formal credits from the legal financial institutions. Although "mass finance" can facilitate the production and expansion of SMEs when they are denied for formal credits, it is considered illegal and the persons involved could be subject to imprisonment or death sentences. The case of Wu Ying in Zhejiang province was a highly controversial one as she was initially sentenced to death by a regional court. However, there was a popular revolt in the media where most commentators denounced the local court for granting such a severe penalty on Wu. After the second hearing by the Supreme Court in Beijing, Wu was re-sentenced to life-time imprisonment. But this re-sentence is still considered to be unfair for the young lady. As a result, Wu's case still remains controversial.

Thirdly, the state-owned commercial banks are still considered to be not as efficient as the joint stock banks for three reasons. The first reason is a moral hazard issue where state banks cannot be truly commercialized as they are still subject to frequent interference by the central and local governments. Moral hazard also arises from the fact that more than 80% of the state-owned banks' revenues depends on the wide spread between the deposit and lending rates. Why the monetary authority allows this wide spread of interest rates is because the central authority fears that the state-owned banks are "too big to fail." If they fail, it could render the entire economy into serious depression and the entire country will be subject to a disastrous financial crisis.

The second reason is the principal-agent problem exiting within the state banking institutions. On the one hand, the senior managers of these banks are appointed by the central and regional governments. On the other hand, the senior managers, once appointed, will have their own interest. Today, a senior government official will earn a normal civil servant's salary. Tomorrow, once appointed as a senior bank manager, he or she will earn a few times more than the normal civil servant wages.

Despite this huge earning differential, bank managers may not feel happy about their lifted salary, as they are comparing their earnings with private entrepreneurs or their foreign peers who could get more than a few hundred times a Chinese civil servant wages. The authority (principal) faces a real dilemma in reforming the management of state-owned banks. The authority expects bank managers to perform as well as any private bank manager but still wants to cap their payment so as not to be too excessive using civil servants' salary as a benchmark. Bank managers (agents) are unlikely to perform as well as private bank managers as they feel they are underpaid compared to foreign peers in the same industry and private firm owners who manage a firm of similar size at home.

The third reason is soft-budget constraint. In Chap. 2 of this book, we have provided the details of how the four big state-owned banks were bailed out by the central government in the late 1990s and the early 2000s. Without the massive bail-out programme, these banks would have been insolvent. After further reform in the last decade, these banks have been listed on the stock exchanges. In theory, they should have been subject to a hard budget, as it would be unreasonable for the central government to bail them out again in the future. Indeed, we have seen the significant improvement in their performance in all aspects, including the growth in assets, profits and scale of operation. However, the better performance of these banks coincided with a booming Chinese economy due to the WTO entry before the world financial crisis and the four trillion RMB stimulus package implemented by the central government after the crisis. In the most recent years, particularly since 2012, when China entered a period of "new normal," economic growth has slowed down to a single-digit level and the growth of domestic investment has declined from more than 20% per year to less than 10% per year. The slowdown in economic and investment growth has become a serious challenge to the banking sector, especially the state-owned banks for their ability to generate a high-profit growth as they did in the previous decade. In fact, the growth rate of profits has slowed down substantially and NPLs started to creep up again.

Currently, the reason the banks are still able to maintain a relatively high level of profit is two-fold: (1) the spread between deposit and lending rates is still high, maintaining a high level of interest rate incomes for the banks; and (2) banks are lending to a rapidly expanding and profitable housing market.

These seemingly advantageous conditions for the Chinese banks, however, may not be sustainable. For one, the monetary authority has opened up the interest rate market so that banks are able to adjust their deposit and lending rates. This implies that state-owned banks are now subject to serious competition from the non-state banking sector. For another, the housing market in China cannot be expanding forever. In many large cities, house prices have become unusually high and no one would predict that the housing bubble may burst at some point. In the last few years, more than 60% of bank loans have been directed towards housing mortgages. Once the housing bubble really bursts, what will happen to the Chinese banking industry? At best, the banking industry will not be able to make so much profit, and at worst, the Chinese government may be forced to bail the banks out as it did in the late 1990s.

Obviously, the state-owned banks are either unaware of any possible credit crunch or in hope of another big bailout once they were to suffer from another bad NPL problem.

From the authority's viewpoint, none of the aforementioned problems will be tolerated and it would do everything possible to avoid any major trouble arising from the banking sector in general and the big state-owned banks in particular. This certainly requires further major reform to the banking system. For example, to minimize or even fundamentally resolve the moral hazard problem, the state has tried to reduce its direct intervention in the daily operation of the state-owned banks and further diversify the ownership structure, subjecting the state banks to more market pressure and closer scrutiny by non-state stakeholders. Ownership diversification not only allows private investors in China but also foreign investors and foreign banks to take up a significant proportion of shares of the listed Chinese state-owned banks. Our empirical analysis in this book indicates that both IPOs (banks listed in the stock exchanges) and foreign participation have significantly improved the performances of the listed Chinese banks, state-owned or non-state-owned. This implies that further banking reform may still be guided to deepen the reform in the ownership structure of the state-owned banks.

Although the most senior managers are still appointed by the central and regional authorities, these managers are subject to non-pay assessment criteria as political and moral standards are implicitly imposed on their behavior. Bank managers have a strong desire for promotion when they are in a relatively early stage of career development. The political desire for promotion can enter manager's utility functions. As a result, even when their salaries are not comparable to their foreign peers and private entrepreneurs at home, they still have a clear motivation to perform well as big banks have gradually lost their absolute monopolistic position in terms of deposit- and profit-making capability. The higher authority has to balance the "political incentives" with "pecuniary incentives" when senior bank managers are appointed, evaluated and promoted. In addition to market pressure, competition and peer pressure, the higher authority has been effectively searching for a comprehensive solution to improve corporate governance and resolve the principal-agent problem under the precondition that the state would hold onto the lion's share of the state-owned banks' market capitalization.

Another reform to resolve the moral hazard problem is the liberalization of interest rates. Although the deposit and lending rates are no longer fixed, the central bank (PBOC) still issues the guided upper and lower limits for China's large commercial banks. The relatively inflexible interest rate bindings are in part responsible for the mismatch of supply of and demand for formal bank credits by the SME sector. As the lending rates to the SMEs are capped, large banks do not have as much incentive as smaller banks in lending to SMEs and private individuals, which bear relatively higher risks for repayment and higher cost per unit of lending compared to large firms. Consequently, further interest rate liberalization may relax the restrictions on interest rate capping as well as allow more rural private and joint stock banks to serve the rural communities and urban SMEs, leading to more market competition.

Technological progress in the internet has enabled the emergence of internet banking and other related financial services, providing more and more financial products to meet the financial needs of private individuals and SMEs. China's new micro-finance giant, Ants Financial Services, which is closely associated with one of the country's internet giants, Alibaba, has extended its relatively cheap and efficient financial services to tens of thousands of SMEs and private individuals. Alipay and WeChat Pay have also imposed significant challenges on the traditional banking system in terms of pay settlement. This is a new and rapidly expanding business that is fundamentally changing the lifestyle of all the Chinese people.

China UnionPay, the country's dominant card-payment processor, has officially launched a mobile payment service called UnionPass in cooperation with more than 40 of the country's banks, including CCBC, ABC and BOC. Using a smartphone app to scan a merchant's QR code, bank customers can pay at the shop counter by using Alipay or WeChat Pay. UnionPass will also be used in some foreign countries, including Singapore, Thailand and South Korea.

The emergence of Alipay, WeChat Pay and now UnionPay has been driven by innovation and technological progress in the internet sphere. China appears to be a front-runner for this kind of fast, secure and convenient service, as within a few years, on-the-counter pay by Alipay and WeChat Pay has become so popular that even elderly women buying vegetables in open markets are using this method of payment.

The challenge to the traditional banking sector, particularly the state-owned banks, has arisen not only from the pressing needs to avoid the moral hazard problem but also from technological progress and the rapid and unstoppable emergence of new financial services modes such as internet banking and mobile payment.

To avoid a systematic financial crisis induced by bank's lending to the real estate sector, many local authorities have imposed quantitative restrictions on the number of houses and the number of mortgages each household can buy in one city. In addition, the central and local banks are also requested to charge a much higher interest rate and demand a much higher deposit for households buying two or more houses. The Beijing Municipal Government just announced that even first-time buyers have to pay 10% more than the basic interest rate. This is by far the strictest restriction imposed on house buyers in Beijing and China.

Further reform in the banking and housing market is also warranted to prevent any major financial market failure in China. A balanced development between cities in terms of healthcare, education and other public services is needed for the second- and third-tier cities and fourth-tier towns to reduce the population pressure on the first tier and other megacities in China. Land supply should become more rational, accounting to the population need and planning. Government taxation and fees related to housing development should also provide scope to accommodate rural migrants and the urban poor so that the current one-sided housing development exclusively focusing on the urban rich can become more balanced; so that both the rich and poor can find a better way to cohabit in the urban areas without driving house prices much higher.

Government regulations are not just for the well-established banking institutions, they should also be implemented to monitor the emerging institutions that tend to incur more financial and security risks for the countries and consumers. For example, the recent peer-to-peer (P2P) scandals have revealed that internet finance and shadow banking without a well-articulated regulatory mechanism can harm consumers enormously.

9.3 The Effects of Institutional Changes on Bank Efficiency

China's banking reform strategy follows that of the real sector reform. In the real economic sectors, state-owned enterprises still play a pivotal role in the national economy. In the 1990s, a large proportion of state-owned enterprises were loss-making and many state firms should have been closed had their performance been assessed by the criteria of a free-market system.

China has not followed a reform trajectory based on a western style of market economy. Rather, it follows the belief that a socialist market economy with Chinese characters should be a different model that fits the Chinese real society and history.

If loss-making, state-owned enterprises were all forced to close down, then the government would have to bear a huge social cost in the sense that state employees may become a formidable force of social instability.

Bearing this in mind, China has adopted a gradual and pragmatic strategy for economic reforms, particularly when it comes to reforming the state industries. On the one hand, state-owned enterprises (SOEs) experiment with all kinds of market-oriented reforms to improve their performance. In the 1980s and early 1990s, the bonus system, director-responsibility system, taxation/profit delivery system and price system were all subject to major reform to fundamentally transform the centrally planned economy into a dynamic and market-oriented economy.

Throughout the reform process, however, China never gave up state ownership. Rather, the central authority believes that state-ownership is a pre-condition and solid foundation for a Chinese social market system. As a result, whatever reform method is implemented, the central authority would not allow the key enterprises to be totally privatized and the state would never give up the control over the appointment of senior managers.

The desire to maintain state ownership may conflict with the need to improve the efficiency and profit-making capability of state-owned firms. To resolve this problem, SOEs have been subject to different kinds of reform themselves and the government encourages the non-state firms to create competition with SOEs to make them behave according to market forces.

By the end of the 1990s, however, the costs to the state became somewhat unbearable as a result of soft budgets to protect SOEs, dragging down the state-owned banks, which were asked to lend relentlessly to the loss-making SOEs. The reform in the late 1990s was critical in two respects. One was to make sure that the state would no longer have to bear huge costs for protecting the SOEs from bankruptcy. The other was to make sure that state-owned banks should clearly separate their policy lending from commercial activities so that a better corporate governance structure could be implemented within the state-owned banks to avoid a systematic financial crisis.

On the other hand, in the real economic sectors, small and medium-sized SOEs were either completely privatized or merged with other firms. The large SOEs were reorganized and put under the administration of the State Administration of State Assets (SASA). The number of SOEs controlled by the SASA was 159 initially, compared to tens of thousands before the radical reforms. These large enterprises either enjoy a certain degree of natural monopoly or they have superior capital, know-how and human resources that the private sector cannot easily compete with them in a particular market segment or industry.

The reform successfully freed the central government from frequently bailing out failing state-owned firms. In addition, after the reorganization, the remaining and gigantic SOEs put under the administration of SASA started to perform unusually well, making huge profits and expanding their business exponentially at home and abroad. Despite all kinds of criticism, the large SOEs have been a formidable force in driving the rapid economic expansion in China in the first decade of the twenty-first century. Although further reform in SOEs is still required to maintain their comparative advantages and to face the tough challenges imposed by the emerging private economy, the radical reform carried out in the late 1990s can be considered to be a great success in the sense that China does not need to totally abandon state ownership while making the large SOEs perform much better for the country's long-term economic ambition.

China has emerged to become a big player in the world market in the following areas: bridge and tunnel construction, nuclear power, high-speed rail, new materials and renewable energies. All these areas could become the backbone of economic development in the world in the new century. The development and successful expansion of these industries have been due to large Chinese SOEs and the development of a modern banking sector.

Since 2014, under the leadership of Xi Jinping, China has launched the "One Belt, One Road" initiative (BRI) to promote bilateral and multilateral cooperation between China and more than 60 countries along the Silk Road Economic Belt and the Maritime Silk Road. This initiative is not just for foreign trade, it is also for investment and people-to-people exchanges. Investments along the Belt and Road countries could be risky, financially and politically, but they may create long-term benefits for China for its ambition to become a developed nation toward the middle of this century.

China initiated the creation of the Asian Infrastructure Investment Bank (AIIB), the Silk Road Fund and the New Development Bank for the BRIC countries. The total investment into these banks and fund amounts to some $200 billion dollars. Some critics believe these projects may cause China to lose money on a big scale, but supporters believe that China's generous investments for these projects will not only benefit other countries but that the biggest beneficiary will be China itself for two reasons. Firstly, China is able to bear the risk right from the beginning; any big losses through the AIIB, Silk Road Fund or the New Development Bank will be controllable by the Chinese central authority. Secondly, the investments made by China in other countries will promote Chinese trade, products, human capital, and above all, they will create a large and stable foreign market for Chinese goods and services.

However, the success of BRI will not just depend on China's ability to bear risk, but it will also depend on China's state-owned banks and enterprises to penetrate their business into foreign soils.

Domestic reform for the SOEs has provided the necessary conditions for China's strategy to go big and global for two reasons. One is that the small number of SOEs are large and powerful and many of them have become highly competitive in both the domestic and foreign markets. The other is that China has created and developed a comprehensive private economy that is growing more rapidly than the state economy and some of the private firms have become a formidable force in their respective areas. For example, in the internet sector, Alibaba, Tencent and Baidu are now some of the largest internet firms in the world, and Huawei has become a formidable force in the global telecommunications industry.

The experiences of real sector reform have more or less been duplicated in the banking industry. The Chinese government has also used all kinds of reform methods to improve the performance of the state-owned banks. In addition, the non-state banking institutions, particularly the joint stock banks and city commercial banks are created to compete directly with the large state-owned banks. After the WTO accession, foreign banks have also been allowed to operate in China and buy a certain proportion of shares of the listed Chinese commercial banks.

In other words, the central authority has not abandoned state ownership, but it has also promoted ownership diversification and multi-ownership competition to create a comprehensive, competitive and efficient banking sector.

The reform so far has been successful as the big banks have maintained good balance sheets, keeping the level of NPLs relatively low and maintaining a relatively high level of profitability. Market competition, the emergence of new forms of financial services, and China's desire to go big and global will certainly impose more challenges and threats to the big state-owned banks and other commercial banks in China.

9.4 Findings with Respect to Research Methodology

This book uses different qualitative and quantitative research methodologies to study the banking sector reforms and assess the reform outcomes. In Chap. 2, we review the reform process and discuss the evolution of the Chinese modern banking industry from a mono-bank system before economic reform to that comprising about 4000 banking institutions.

Bank reform went through different stages of changes and each stage involved different policy actions. In the early stage, the institutional reform was just to separate the commercial banking activities from PBOC to four large state-owned commercial banks. The second stage involved the creation of three policy banks, more than a dozen joint stock banks and more than 100 city commercial banks. The purpose was to create a more competitive environment and to meet the rising demand for financial services due to rapid economic expansion and diversification. The third stage was to open up the Chinese financial market for foreign involvement and competition after China's accession to the WTO. The latest reform was to allow state and non-state banks to be listed in the stock markets, introducing a free-market style of corporate governments for the banking institutions.

Our empirical research presented in chapters focus on the efficiency analysis with respect to all kinds of reforms. We use both the SFA and DEA approaches to study the efficiency levels of China's commercial banks. Bank profitability, cost and loans are used as different dependent variables to measure firm performance. Intermediate inputs and human resources costs are used as key explanatory variables. We also use ownership, equity/asset ratio, foreign participation, IPOs and the time lengths of foreign participation and IPOs as key variables to measure the efficiency differentials between different types of banks.

In general, our empirical results indicate that state ownership is relatively less efficient compared to other kinds of ownership. Foreign participation and IPOs all helped Chinese banks, including state-owned banks, to improve performance.

In conclusion, we indicate that non-state ownership, ownership diversification and foreign participation are all useful reforms that have enhanced the overall bank efficiency in China. In addition, the gradual reform process for state-owned banks has produced good and expected results.

Improved bank performance is supported by the empirical results presented in Chap. 5, which uses five different measures to estimate the levels of banking completion in China over the period 1995–2015.

The main finding of this chapter is that comprehensive and radical banking reforms from 2000 had improved the level of banking competition in the Chinese banking industry. The degree of competition accelerated from 2012 after the monetary authority started to liberalize the interest rate market, suggesting a positive and rising impact of banking reforms on competition.

The problems of moral hazard, principal-agent and soft budget constraints have been gradually mitigated as banking reform deepens over time, but these problems have not been fundamentally resolved. The world financial crisis has witnessed the bad failures of many large western banks, indicating that private ownership may not be the only and ultimate solution to the problems encountered by the Chinese state-owned banks. This, to some extent, has justified the state's desire to maintain majority shares in China's largest state-owned commercial banks.

China's bank reform has used the programmatic approach with a certain degree of political and social doctrines that could not be broken. Put more simply, the Chinese government so far has not allowed total privatization of the large SOEs and the large state-owned banks.

Economic reform is not a pure economic and efficiency issue, it needs to take into account China's social and political reality.

The central government strongly believes that keeping a significant proportion of state ownership in the real economy and banking sector is an important condition to maintain social and political stability in China with its own characteristic socialist market economy.

From an economic point of view, state monopoly and private monopoly are different. In the key industrial and banking sectors, if monopoly power were entirely controlled by private entrepreneurs, consumers and the society would suffer more unreasonably. However, if the monopoly power is put in the state hands, as it has been, the state will have power to regulate prices charged to consumers more effectively and abnormal profit could be delivered to the state and benefit the whole society.

In the economic literature, privatization is most regarded as the only way to improve performance and profitability of state-owned enterprises and banks. But why is privatization better than state ownership? And can the central authority use the incentive mechanism inherent within a private firm to a state-owned firm so that the latter can improve performance without changing its ownership?

We believe these are the long-lasting questions that the Chinese government has been trying to find clear answers for. Through presenting the theoretical and empirical analysis on the Chinese banking industry, this book shows the empirical results to testify whether the Chinese government has been successful in finding these answers.

In the real sector, the reforms in the late 1990s could be described as "grasping the large and letting the small go" reforms. In other words, small and medium-sized enterprises that did not enjoy much monopolistic power and were less important for the national economic security were allowed to be privatized or merged with the large SOEs. The remaining large SOEs were also subject to various institutional reforms to improve their performance, including the last reform of going global and going public.

In the banking sector, the reform mirrored the real sector reform. The large state-owned banks have been largely state owned despite a certain degree of ownership diversification through IPOs and foreign participation. In parallel, smaller banks without a dominant state ownership have been encouraged to be created and expanded. The latest statistics suggest that the share of total banking assets accounted for by the large state-owned banks has declined to less than 40% from its peak level of more than 60%.

The pragmatic reform in both the real sector and the banking sector has achieved remarkable outcomes in the following respects. Firstly, the reform has brought about a sustainable and high-growth path for the Chinese economy. Secondly, the level of profit and profitability in the SOE and state-owned bank sectors has risen over time, implying that they are no longer a financial burden to the central government; instead, they have contributed significantly and vitally to the central budget.

However, the reform in the Chinese banking industry still has a long way to go. The key challenge is the fragmentation in the banking industry, which is large and comprehensive, but does not serve all the needs in different sectors of the economy. The private sector, especially the SME sector, has long been overlooked by the formal financial system. The newly emerged internet financial sector has not been well regulated and as a result cannot play its maximum role to serve the society. The problems in the state-owned banking sector have not been completely resolved, particularly in corporate governance and its social behavior toward SMEs and the housing market.

9.5 Policy Implications, Remaining Problems and Possible Solutions

Both the Chinese real economic and financial sectors are facing huge challenges for their transformation. In the real economic sector, China aims to change from a "low and medium range" manufacturer to a "medium and high range" manufacturer. This means the traditional mode of manufacturing, which relies on massive labor and capital inputs to produce low-valued manufacturing goods for exports, has to be replaced by high-end manufacturing dependent on technological upgrading and innovations. New production areas will be developed, such as high-speed rail, automation, robotics, nuclear power, solar power, wind power, new materials, jumbo jets, new energy automobiles, and so on. The development of all these new products and industries requires huge investments and may bear significant risks.

The banking sector reform should also encourage the financial services industry to meet the needs of the real economic sector instead of focusing on short-term profitability, particularly on excessive lending to the real estate sector. The traditional banking industry should also use new technology, particularly internet banking and mobile payment, to improve their efficiency and retain customers. In recent years, the profitability of the traditional banking industry has weakened due to a slower economic growth and intensive competition from the newly emerged internet banking business. Big commercial banks have started to lay off workers for the first time in recent history. In a sense, this is to improve productivity, but it also implies that competition has become more intense as more and more banks are chasing the same business. In addition, many commercial banks are now trying to attract depositors through offering a much higher interest rate than the official guided rate as the central bank has been promoting the liberalization of the interest rate market.

From the policy viewpoint, the government should deepen the reform of the interest rate market, allowing more flexibility and autonomy for individual banks to pay and charge interest rates to depositors and borrowers. The central authority should focus more on the macro-economic balances and the growth of money supply.

The central authority also has an important duty to maintain a stable exchange rate for RMB. After the RMB was included in the International Monetary Fund's (IMF) basket of special drawing rights (SDR) along with the US dollar, the Euro, the Japanese Yen and the British pound in October 2016, the Chinese currency has depreciated against the US dollar by more than 13%. Although measured against other major currencies, the Chinese RMB is still strong; the market sentiment about the strength of RMB is largely based on its exchange rate with the US dollar.

From 2005 to 2014, the RMB exchange rate with the United States rose monotonically for almost a decade, with an effective appreciation of more than 30%. As a result, most investors had been used to a strengthening RMB. All of a sudden, however, the RMB exchange rate against the US dollar started to fluctuate in both directions in 2014 and entered an 18-month period of depreciation. During this period, the Chinese foreign exchange reserves were depleted by more than one trillion US dollars. As the trade surplus in 2015 and 2016 amounted to more than one trillion US dollars, it implied that China had lost the equivalent of more than two trillion US dollars in two years. The loss of foreign exchange reserves, trade surplus and other capital from China was huge, primarily due to the need to stop a continuing depreciation of RMB against the US dollar, and due to the unexpected money outflows in the forms of outward direct investments and money laundering.

The total amount of outward foreign direct investment during 2015–2016 was about 300 billion US dollars. This implies that China must have lost 1.7 trillion US dollars, either to support the currency and/or due to capital flight as a consequence of RMB further depreciation. Part of the capital flight could also have been due to some wealthy Chinese quietly and illegally moving their money abroad through the official and illegal channels.

In the first three months of 2017, China's outward foreign direct investment plummeted by more than 70%. This spectacular drop in outward investment could be an overcorrection to stop illegal capital flight to safeguard the stability of the RMB exchange rate against the US dollar, which, in turn, is to restore market confidence by investors, domestic and foreign, and consumers.

Unlike the consumers in the matured industrialized economies, Chinese consumers are not used to massive volatilities of prices and foreign exchange rates due to a relatively short period of market reform. Consequently, if the exchange rate is believed to move in one direction, consumers and investors will speculate and take action to exuberate in avoiding losses or in making short-term gains. Because the population is large, if everyone does the same, the situation could become uncontrollable. For example, the Chinese authority allows each individual to exchange for 50,000 US dollars each year. The exchange liberalization is designed to help the people who are in need of foreign currencies. However, once the depreciation or appreciation of RMB against the US dollar is moving in one direction, many individuals will use their "rights" to change for foreign currencies not because of need, but because of speculation to make a quick profit or to avoid losses.

Policy-makers should be aware that China has not reached a mature industrialized nation status and the extent of speculation is huge so that any policy instrument and market liberalization should take this market phycology into consideration. Banking reforms should also take this into account, including a comprehensive monitoring system to distinguish real outward investment from pure capital flight.

The short action in 2017 is to stop the loopholes of capital flight, but it has inevitably made real outward investment more difficult and could harm China's long-term interest of globalization. In addition, capital account liberalization should also be gradual and the RMB internationalization should also need time and wisdom along with China's rising importance in the world economy.

The current supply-sided reform articulated by the central government aims to: cut down overproduction capacity of some traditional industries such as coal, cement and steel; cut down inventory, including housing stock, so resources are released for the newly emerging sectors; and reduce leverage so that a systematic financial crisis can be avoided.

Banking reform is relevant for cutting down leverage. The informal financial sector, particularly the shadow banking sector, is an important supplement to the formal banking sector. However, the rapid and uncontrolled expansion of shadow banking could also become a time bomb, as many formal banking institutions are using shadow banking to avoid regulatory controls. The amount of shadow loans and risks are difficult to measure and monitor, this could lead to excessive leverage, particularly in the real estate sector. The housing sector accounts for only 6% of the country's GDP, but it absorbed up to 60% of bank lending in recent months. How to balance the demand and supply of leadings without hurting the real economy and without incurring an uncontrollable financial crisis is a priority area of policy in the supply-side reform today in China.

Index

C. Jiang and S. Yao, *Chinese Banking Reform*, The Nottingham China Policy Institute Series, DOI 10.1007/978-3-319-63925-3

The manufacturer's authorised representative in the EU is Springer Nature Customer Service Centre GmbH, Europaplatz 3, 69115 Heidelberg, Germany. If you have any concerns regarding our products, please contact ProductSafety@springernature.com

Printed and bound by CPI Group (UK) Ltd, Croydon, CR0 4YY

30/09/2026

02225565-0012